EXPANDING READING COMPREHENSION IN GRADES 3–6

Also Available

Assessment for Reading Instruction, Fourth Edition
Katherine A. Dougherty Stahl, Kevin Flanigan,
and Michael C. McKenna

Developing Reading Comprehension:
Effective Instruction for All Students in PreK–2
Katherine A. Dougherty Stahl and Georgia Earnest García

Reading Assessment in an RTI Framework
Katherine A. Dougherty Stahl and Michael C. McKenna

EXPANDING READING COMPREHENSION in Grades 3–6

Effective Instruction for All Students

Katherine A. Dougherty Stahl
Georgia Earnest García

THE GUILFORD PRESS
New York   London

Printed in the United States of America

This book is printed on acid-free paper.

Last digit is print number: 9   8   7   6   5   4   3   2   1

Library of Congress Cataloging-in-Publication Data

Names: Stahl, Katherine A. Dougherty, author. | García, Georgia Earnest,
   author.
Title: Expanding reading comprehension in grades 3-6 : effective
   instruction for all students / Katherine A. Dougherty Stahl, Georgia
   Earnest García.
Description: New York : The Guilford Press, 2022. | Includes
   bibliographical references and index.
Identifiers: LCCN 2021057120 | ISBN 9781462549351 (paperback) |
   ISBN 9781462549368 (hardcover)
Subjects: LCSH: Reading comprehension—Study and teaching (Elementary)
Classification: LCC LB1573 .S824 2022 | DDC 372.47—dc23/eng/20220106
LC record available at *https://lccn.loc.gov/2021057120*

About the Authors

Katherine A. Dougherty Stahl, EdD, is a literacy consultant and author who focuses on translating literacy research into practice. Formerly, she was Clinical Professor of Literacy at New York University (NYU), where she taught graduate courses and served as Director of both the Literacy Program and the NYU Literacy Clinic. Before entering academia, Dr. Stahl taught in public elementary and middle school classrooms for over 25 years. She is the coauthor or coeditor of several books, and her articles have appeared in the leading journals of research and practice. Dr. Stahl specializes in reading acquisition, comprehension instruction, reading intervention, and literacy assessment. Currently, she partners with educators as a consultant to support their efforts to improve reading achievement, especially for students with reading difficulties.

Georgia Earnest García, PhD, is Professor Emerita in the Department of Curriculum and Instruction at the University of Illinois at Urbana–Champaign. She served on the RAND Reading Study Group on Skillful Reading and the National Literacy Panel on Language-Minority Children and Youth. Dr. García is coauthor or coeditor of several books and has published in leading academic and practitioner journals. Before acquiring her PhD, she was a bilingual/ESL/EFL and English language arts teacher at the elementary, middle school, high school, and community college levels. Although retired, she continues to collaborate with teachers and schools and conduct research on the literacy development, instruction, and assessment of students from diverse cultural and linguistic backgrounds, with a specific focus on bilingual students. Dr. García was inducted into the Reading Hall of Fame in 2019.

Preface

In 2015, we published the book *Developing Reading Comprehension: Effective Instruction for All Students in PreK–2* as part of The Guilford Press series "The Essential Library of PreK–2 Literacy" (Sharon Walpole and Michael C. McKenna, series editors). At that time, we received several queries about whether we had plans for a book that addressed reading comprehension instruction in the intermediate grades. University literacy faculty requested a book that had a consistent philosophy and format for reading comprehension instruction across the elementary grades that they could share with their students. Similarly, elementary school faculty and administrators were looking for a text set to address comprehension instruction cohesively across the primary and intermediate grade levels. We created the current book to meet these needs. It can be used in isolation or in tandem with the earlier text.

Developing students' reading comprehension calls for deliberate attention to helping students transition from listening comprehension to juggling decoding, meaning-making, and self-monitoring during reading comprehension. In the intermediate grades, students need to move toward independence in their employment of comprehension strategies, purposeful use of texts, and critical analyses of complex texts. Students expand their comprehension as they cope with the increased volume of reading and writing that builds knowledge within disciplinary content areas.

Our goal in this book is to describe the instruction that intermediate students need to locate and recall, integrate and interpret, critique and evaluate, as well as use and apply information from a wide range of texts with increasing independence (Pearson et al., 2020). In keeping with the science of reading, we describe research-validated instructional practices that teachers can implement in third through sixth grade. Although we recognize that some sixth graders may be in departmentalized middle school settings, the majority of our examples emphasize the elementary setting. If you teach sixth graders in the middle school, we encourage you to adapt our recommendations to fit your setting.

A dominant focus of this book is teaching intermediate students how to use literacy skills and strategies for learning and communicating knowledge across the content disciplines. The newest research indicates that when integrating literacy and disciplinary instruction mindfully, the learning of both is enhanced, not compromised (Pearson et al., 2020). We address many of the findings from the over 200 publications on comprehension studies that the U.S. Institute of Education Sciences (IES) Reading for Understanding (RfU) research initiative funded from 2011 to 2016. A summary of these studies is available in Pearson et al. (2020) for those of you who would like more details on the most recent science of reading comprehension instruction.

We structured this book similarly to *Developing Reading Comprehension*. Each chapter begins with guiding questions, and most chapters open with a practice-based vignette related to the topic. Additionally, each instructional chapter includes considerations for emergent bilingual students. Please note that we use the term *emergent bilingual* to refer to children who use one language at home but who are acquiring English at school. When citing research, we use the terminology that the cited authors used in their article (e.g., *English learners*).

Our current comprehension model is based on the same instructional components portrayed in *Developing Reading Comprehension*. However, our new visual model also reflects the role of systemic and sociocultural factors involved in reading comprehension (Figure 1.1, p. 10). The reader plays an active role and is at the center of the comprehension process. The middle circle includes the instructional components that all students need to achieve to arrive at their highest potential when interacting with texts. We thoroughly address each instructional component in a complete chapter. The outer circle addresses the classroom context. Contextual factors include the content of instruction, the texts, and how teachers scaffold instruction to meet the needs of diverse learners while gradually releasing responsibility to them. The outer square addresses ecological and systemic factors that influence classroom instruction (e.g., policies, trends, district mandates, school climate). Finally, sociocultural influences overlay what happens at each level.

Since our model of comprehension is consistent in both books, many of our chapter topics are parallel to the topics addressed in the earlier text: unifying theory, research, and practice; considerations for diverse populations; strategy instruction; dialogic learning; writing to express and expand comprehension; and the assessment of reading comprehension. Although most of the topics are the same, the developmental learning needs of intermediate students are different from those of young children, so we rely on research that informs instruction in grades 3–6. Unique chapters emphasize knowledge building, the range of texts available to older readers, and academic vocabulary instruction. Describing the instructional interventions for students in the intermediate grades with reading comprehension difficulties was beyond the scope of this text. Flanagan and Hayes (in press) address the topic comprehensively, including the relationship between decoding, fluency, and comprehension in the intermediate grades.

This book begins with a look at the influences that have changed the definition of comprehension and how learner expectations have changed over time. We explain how several theoretical models contribute to our understanding of comprehension. Then we look at recent research findings that inform what we consider essential elements in an all-inclusive model of comprehension.

Chapter 2 addresses what recent research has to say about culturally responsive literacy instruction and effective reading comprehension instruction for diverse learners. We provide information about the effective comprehension instruction of students in high-poverty schools, emergent bilingual students, marginalized dialect speakers, and other students from diverse cultural and linguistic backgrounds.

In Chapter 3, we explore the relationship between knowledge and comprehension. Although there are common cognitive comprehension strategies that are essential for understanding all texts, there are also unique attributes and challenges associated with texts within each discipline. We review research that investigated protocols that integrated literacy instruction with science and social studies content. Based on this research, we share integrated instructional principles that enhance achievement in both literacy and content areas.

Intermediate students encounter a variety of texts throughout an academic year. In Chapter 4, we discuss factors that teachers should consider in making text selections for their students. This discussion includes recent research findings on matching intermediate students' reading abilities and suitable texts. Finally, we provide explicit suggestions for scaffolding students as they read a wide assortment of texts across the curricula.

Chapters 5, 6, 7, and 8 address the middle circle of our comprehension curriculum model, the key instructional components. These chapters dig deeply into academic vocabulary development, comprehension strategy instruction, dialogic learning (powerful classroom discussions), and disciplinary writing. Schools that emphasize the science of reading will find the clear connections between research and practice in these chapters reassuring. Teachers will appreciate the realistic classroom examples and text boxes that clearly outline the recommended procedures. In all the instructional chapters, we include a section on how to teach emergent bilingual students.

Although we recommend that assessment should always precede instruction, we address assessment in our closing chapter as the last word. As comprehension is an unconstrained skill, no single test can tell you what your students are capable of comprehending. Different assessments provide you with pieces of information regarding what your students understood about a particular text in a particular setting. Chapter 9 provides descriptions of multiple types of comprehension data that you can collect to gauge different dimensions of your students' reading comprehension. Additionally, we suggest ways to group and work with students whose performance on multiple measures indicates that they need supplementary intervention to strengthen their reading comprehension.

We hope this guidebook will help you support your students' ongoing development in reading comprehension and knowledge building. We have tried to remain faithful to the research while translating it to fit the realities of most classrooms. Additionally, we have tried to balance succinctness with enough elaboration that will enable you to successfully meet the differing needs of *all* students regardless of economic background, ethnicity, first language/dialect, and current reading level. We welcome your feedback and questions as you implement the practices we recommend.

Contents

EXPANDING READING COMPREHENSION IN GRADES 3–6

CHAPTER ONE

Unifying Theory, Research, and Practice

GUIDING QUESTIONS

- How do we define comprehension?
- How well does the Simple View of Reading explain reading comprehension across the developmental continuum?
- How do theoretical models of reading contribute to our understanding of comprehension?
- Based on the most recent research, what essential elements must receive attention in the creation of an all-inclusive comprehension curriculum for students in the intermediate grades?

How do you define comprehension? How would your mother define reading comprehension? Most people base their perception of comprehension on their school experiences. As teachers, our definition of comprehension is likely to be influenced by the decade in which we attended our most recent teacher training on reading comprehension. Our understanding of what comprehension is and how best to tackle it in classrooms has changed across the decades as research has expanded and we learn more. In any scientific process, our understanding increases over time as the ongoing accumulation of knowledge provides new information and insights.

In this chapter, we will address how and why our conception of comprehension has changed over time. We will share some of the historical influences that have shaped our definition of comprehension and resulting classroom practices. Then we will describe a few theories that explain factors that influence readers' comprehension of what they are reading. Finally, we will establish some principles that summarize how the theories and research will inform the recommendations that we make throughout this book.

THE EVOLUTION OF COMPREHENSION'S DEFINITION
AND ITS INFLUENCE ON INSTRUCTION

Durkin's (1978) pivotal classroom observation study revealed that many teachers used postreading questions as their primary way to address reading comprehension. In that era, teachers and tests required children to respond to mostly literal questions as evidence of understanding explicitly stated information in the text. However, both teachers and researchers knew less about explicitly teaching students to engage in strategies that contribute to understanding.

In 1976, the U.S. Department of Education funded the Center for the Study of Reading to address the large number of children failing to read successfully. During this era, researchers produced a large body of work that focused on comprehension and vocabulary instruction, including the seminal work that supported explicit strategy instruction and related protocols for teaching comprehension strategies. Cognitive science dominated comprehension research in the late 1970s through the 1980s. We learned the importance of employing *declarative* (what it is), *procedural* (how to do it), and *conditional* (when and why) knowledge when teaching students to use cognitive strategies. Cognitive strategies emphasized during this time period included prediction, visualization, text structures, summarization, ideational prominence (main idea), monitoring, and inference generation (Paris et al., 1983). Pearson and Gallagher (1983) published their ubiquitous model of the *gradual release of responsibility* that described the teacher's shift of instructional responsibility to the students during comprehension instruction. The body of work from this era defined comprehension and influenced instruction throughout the late 1980s and early 1990s.

The National Reading Panel (NRP, 2000) completed a clearly defined, systematic study of the five pillars of reading: phonological awareness, phonics, fluency, vocabulary, and comprehension. Although the panel's report recognized that phonological awareness, phonics, fluency, and vocabulary played a role in comprehension, they did not discuss the reciprocity of the pillars. The NRP defined comprehension as *the act of understanding and interpreting the text's message.* The majority of the comprehension research studies reviewed by the NRP focused on comprehension instruction in the intermediate grades.

In 2002, the RAND Reading Study Group (RRSG) reported its findings on what research and instruction were needed to improve reading comprehension achievement in the United States. They defined *comprehension* as the "process of simultaneously extracting and constructing meaning through interaction and involvement with written language" (RRSG, 2002, p. 11). Their report included a heuristic that centered on the interactions between the reader, the text, and the literacy activities within a sociocultural context that influences and is influenced by those interactions. This model represented an agreed-upon shift in the field from viewing the reader as a recipient of the author's ideas to viewing the reader as an active co-constructor of the text's meaning.

Policies have also influenced our definition of comprehension. The introduction and implementation of the Common Core State Standards for English Language Arts (CCSS) or similar state modifications shaped the perception of comprehension in many ways (National Governors Association Center for Best Practices & Council of Chief State School Officers [NGA & CCSSO], 2010). First, CCSS prioritized comprehension standards in the primary grades that called for teachers to spend instructional time on and give attention to high-level comprehension of complex texts with young children. Additionally, the CCSS focused on integrating reading, writing, and speaking with various multidisciplinary texts. (See Appendix A.)

The introduction of the Next Generation Science Standards (NGSS; Next Generation Science Standards Lead States, 2013) and the C3 Framework for Social Studies Standards (C3SSS; National Council for the Social Studies [NCSS], 2013) forced teachers to instruct elementary students to address the challenges encountered when reading to learn something unknown. The disciplines of literacy, science, social studies, and math each have their own Discourse and criteria for building knowledge and communication of that knowledge (see Chapter 3). Elementary teachers had to think about comprehension from a disciplinary expert's perspective. Disciplinary experts in secondary education began learning the nuances of the reading comprehension and writing demands unique to their discipline. An educator's definition of comprehension is never in stasis.

CURRENT INFLUENCES

From 2011 to 2016, the U.S. Institute of Education Sciences (IES) funded the Reading for Understanding (RfU) research initiative. IES selected six research teams to examine the process of comprehension, identify the targets for effective comprehension interventions, and develop and test interventions intended to improve reading comprehension for prekindergarten (PreK) through grade 12. "The ultimate goal defined in the [IES] call was to redress the disappointing performance of students in the United States on national assessments of reading" (Pearson et al., 2020, p. 12). IES also funded a committee of independent scholars and representatives from each research team to synthesize the outcomes of over 200 studies conducted by the five university research teams and the Educational Testing Service (see Pearson et al., 2020). The synthesis committee divided the studies' contributions into three categories: (1) nature and development of comprehension, (2) assessment, and (3) curriculum and instruction.

These studies confirmed that developmental differences influence variability in contributions to comprehension. However, over time comprehension monitoring and inferencing consistently make the most significant cognitive contributions to reading comprehension. Both word and world knowledge support readers' abilities to monitor and infer. In addition to declarative, procedural, and conditional knowledge, the committee concluded that reading comprehension instruction must incorporate disciplinary knowledge and epistemic knowledge (how knowledge is generated and evaluated within a discipline). From the earliest grades through high school, *learning to read* and *reading to learn* have a complementary relationship and must coexist. In their concluding comments, Pearson and colleagues (2020) determined that this extensive body of research provided a glimpse at an alternative culture of comprehension in which "the job of comprehension is not complete until one uses the resulting understanding to do something—tell a story, explain a situation, argue with an author or a classmate or maybe even plan to change the world" (p. 286). The next generation of curricula and assessments will likely incorporate the findings from this research and the updated comprehension construct.

THE SIMPLE VIEW OF READING

The Simple View of Reading (SVR) is a theory that has been widely applied in research and practice since its development (Gough & Tunmer, 1986; Hoover & Gough, 1990). The developers of the CCSS and related curricula materials used it to guide their work (NGA & CCSSO, 2010). Several of the RfU research teams used the SVR to underpin their studies while directly investigating the nuances of the theory's components. The SVR states that Decoding/Word Recognition × Language Comprehension = Reading Comprehension. In a recent paper discussing this theory, Hoover and Tunmer (2018) defined *decoding* as the automatic recognition of written words "to efficiently gain access to the appropriate word meanings contained in the internal mental lexicon," *language comprehension* as "the ability to extract and construct literal and inferred meaning from linguistic discourse represented in speech," and *reading comprehension* as the ability "to extract and construct literal and inferred meaning from linguistic discourse represented in print" (p. 304).

The RfU studies validated the SVR application in the lower grades, with cautions for basing curricula or assessments on it. Lonigan and Burgess (2017) determined that reading comprehension is not measurable separately from decoding until grade 3 or until readers achieve a decoding threshold.

However, the RfU studies and several other studies have found many limitations in applying the SVR beyond early reading. When studies require readers to engage with more complex tasks and texts, the simple theory fails to explain the process (e.g., Paris & Hamilton, 2009; Snow, 2018). When we look at how the definition and expectations for reading comprehension have changed over time, it is easy to see that both today's definition of reading comprehension and the construct of reading comprehension are more complex than the expectations were in the 1980s. In the intermediate grades and beyond, comprehension is no longer simple. The SVR does not account for the strategic processing, critical evaluation, or application that are requisite aspects of reading comprehension (Pearson et al., 2020; Snow, 2018; Stahl et al., 2020). In light of the failings of the SVR to account for the complexities of reading in the intermediate grades and beyond, we will rely more on other theories that account for the multidimensional aspects of comprehension at this stage of development.

READING DEVELOPMENT

Chall's Stages of Reading

Chall's (1996) model of overall reading development includes six stages, each of which emphasizes a different aspect of the reading process (see Table 1.1). However, it is noteworthy that Chall's detailed descriptions of each stage demonstrate that she never intended for each stage to have a singular focus. For example, during the confirmation and fluency stage, instruction should also address a continuation of systematic word recognition competencies, conceptual vocabulary development, and comprehension instruction. Additionally, at all stages of development, we want students to interact with compelling texts with appropriate levels of support.

Other researchers recommended that the boundaries between stages should be viewed more as overlapping, fluid waves than as rigid boundaries. Significantly, the idea that "learning to read" and "reading to learn" occur in different grade levels is no longer applicable. The RfU research studies confirmed that our youngest students could and should be learning from texts as they learn how to read. Additionally, older students also have new things they must learn about reading disciplinary texts, which contain unique grammatical structures, organizational characteristics, and text features.

Constrained Skills Theory

Unlike Chall's model that looks at readers' typical reading characteristics throughout their schooling and beyond, Paris (2005) looked at the interactions of skill sets as they develop over time and their impact on the reading process. In his constrained skills theory, Paris proposed a continuum of skills ranging from high to low levels of constraint, as shown in Table 1.2. Highly constrained skills include concepts of print, letter knowledge, and phonics because they each include a limited set of items that can be taught to mastery. Additionally, there is only a short span of time when there is a range of age-level performance on a specific constrained skill. For example, children in PreK and kindergarten will vary in the number of letters they can name. However, by the end of first grade, all children typically know all the

TABLE 1.1. Jeanne Chall's Model of the Stages of Reading Development

Stage	Name	What child is learning	Typical activities	Materials
Stage 0: Birth to grade 1	Emergent literacy	Functions of written language, alphabet, phonemic awareness	Story reading, "pseudoreading," alphabet activities, rhyming, nursery rhymes, invented spelling	Books (including predictable stories), letters, writing materials, *Sesame Street*
Stage 1: Beginning grade 1	Decoding	Letter–sound correspondences	Teacher-directed reading instruction, phonics instruction	Preprimers and primers, phonics materials, writing materials, trade books
Stage 2: End of grade 1 to end of grade 3	Confirmation and fluency	Automatic word recognition, use of context	Reading narratives, generally about known topics	Basal readers, trade books, workbooks
Stage 3: Grades 4–8	Learning the new (single viewpoint)	How to learn from text, vocabulary knowledge, strategies	Reading and studying content-area materials, use of encyclopedias, strategy instruction	Basal readers, novels, encyclopedias, textbooks in content areas
Stage 4: High school and early college	Multiple viewpoints	Reconciling different views	Critical reading, discourse synthesis, report writing	Texts containing multiple views, encyclopedias and other reference materials, magazines and journals, nonfiction books, etc.
Stage 5: Late college and graduate school	A worldview	Developing a well-rounded view of the world	Learning what not to read as well as what to read	Professional materials

Note. From Stahl et al. (2020). Copyright © 2020 The Guilford Press. Reprinted by permission.

letter names. There also is interdependence between constrained skills such as the ability to learn letters and phonics. Lastly, mastery of constrained skills can be demonstrated uniformly by those who have acquired the skill.

Phonological awareness and fluency are moderately constrained. The duration of development spans multiple years for each skill. After a plateau of expertise, there may still be variation in a reader's fluency that is responsive to the purpose of reading or text content. Individual differences in highly and moderately constrained skills only exist for a short period, and they tend to be codependent. For example, phonological awareness skills and phonics skills tend to develop linearly and in tandem. These abilities are codependent. However, these constrained abilities have little to do with wider curricular and subject-area knowledge. Knowledge of the world does not contribute to a child's ability to learn the vowel–consonant (VC) phonogram pattern, nor does reading ability or spelling VC words contribute to their expertise in any outside areas.

TABLE 1.2. Dimensions of Constrained or Unconstrained Skills

	Constrained	Unconstrained
Scope	Constrained or set number of items to be learned (e.g., alphabet)	Unlimited
Importance	Small set of central important features need to be learned (e.g., word boundaries; period at the end of a sentence)	Not local and varies by context and text (e.g., strategies should be used flexibly)
Range of influence	One skill or skill set is narrowly tied to the knowledge of other skills for a short period of time (e.g., reading and spelling the vowel-consonant pattern)	Knowledge in one area has a wide influence on other competencies (e.g., knowledge of the word *democracy* influences knowledge building and communication)
Mastery	Skill is mastered within a relatively short developmental period (e.g., writing one's first name; phonics skills)	Competency is acquired incrementally across a lifetime (e.g., world knowledge developed over time influences one's understanding of text)
Universality	Once mastered there is little variance among individuals (e.g., letter-sound relationships)	Competence varies within and across individuals dependent upon context and texts (e.g., individual life experiences influence one's understanding of text)
Codependence	Linear development makes one skill depend on another (e.g., spelling depends on the ability to segment words)	When a threshold of mastery is achieved in one skill, codependency and correlations are minimized (e.g., fluency's influence on understanding diminishes once a threshold has been achieved)

Comprehension and vocabulary development are unconstrained and multidimensional skills. Unlike constrained skills, comprehension and vocabulary develop incrementally over a person's lifetime and there are no unitary indicators of mastery. There are always more word meanings to learn and a range of challenging texts to explore. It is more difficult to teach and test unconstrained skills, such as comprehension and vocabulary, compared to constrained skills because of the variation in factors that affect individuals' development of unconstrained skills: the sociocultural milieu in which individuals are raised and live, the instructional contexts, individual student differences, and the texts they read. Additionally, the world knowledge that readers acquire influences their ease of reading, their abilities to make inferences, and their interest in reading. Reciprocally, variations in reading quantity influence knowledge building and vocabulary development.

The differences in constrained and unconstrained skills have implications for curriculum development, instruction, and assessment. Most importantly, although individuals need phonics and fluency to read texts, comprehension and vocabulary must also be a priority in PreK–grade 2 (see Stahl & García, 2015). The language and experiential opportunities that occur in the earliest years of children's lives contribute to their ability to understand texts and communicate those understandings to others. Today we know that comprehension instruction is more effective when it is combined with authentic knowledge building about the human condition or the world around us (Pearson et al., 2020). Due to the multifaceted nature of unconstrained skills, our instruction and assessment must incorporate opportunities for children to demonstrate their comprehension development by speaking, writing, and completing activities in response to many kinds of reading materials, including new technologies.

The Role of Pulse Points in Reading Comprehension

Reading comprehension is never all or nothing. Each reader's quantitative and qualitative comprehension of a text varies by individual. Even as "expert" readers, we can all think of a reading task that challenged us. What made the task challenging for you cognitively or affectively? What strategies or coping techniques did you use? Was your difficulty related to understanding the text or communicating your understanding? How did your understanding differ from someone else's reading experience? Why? There are two critical takeaways from this exercise. First, despite the level of difficulty, you were likely to have understood something from what you read. Additionally, gauging your success depended on achieving some purpose, usually resulting in some form of response. This is the nature of comprehension for our students and for us.

The foundational early reading skills of phonics and fluency are necessary but not sufficient for reading comprehension as we move into the intermediate grades and beyond. We support the position of Paris (2005) and others (Paris & Hamilton, 2009; Pearson et al., 2020; Snow, 2018) that as readers achieve a decoding or fluency threshold, and texts and tasks become more complex and varied, the role of constrained skills diminishes. Due to the traits that define constrained skills, they can only be used to predict overall reading achievement for a short window of time. This premise contradicts the SVR. While reading comprehension is dependent on a threshold of competency in automatic word recognition, once a reader meets a fluency threshold, contextual, text, and individual factors contribute more to understanding (O'Connor et al., 2002; Wang et al., 2019). Contextual factors include things such as the level of instructional support and response format required. Text factors include text density, genre, organizational structure, and text features. Individual factors beyond fluency include prior knowledge, vocabulary, interest, engagement, self-regulation, and working memory (Perfetti & Adlof, 2012).

This concept of contributing pressure points is essential as we consider curricula and pedagogical choices in our classrooms. Both of us have visited classrooms that placed extreme limitations on children's school reading experiences. Children are often only exposed to texts within a narrow reading level identified by an unrehearsed read of a random book from a benchmark test kit or a computer-based test.

While we respect the diagnostic process used to estimate a child's reading level, teachers need to consider the role of pressure points that influence children's reading comprehension development (O'Connor et al., 2002; Brown et al., 2018).

The complexity of reading comprehension and the interaction of multiple pressure points mean that comprehension instruction must provide children with sustained explicit instruction in the application of reading strategies with many texts that vary in difficulty, genre, and medium. The integration of knowledge building while developing comprehension is integral given the role of knowledge in the monitoring and inference generation process. Teaching related vocabulary during the instructional units promotes vocabulary development, comprehension, and the construction of networks of knowledge. Finally, a single assessment cannot capture all the nuances of comprehension. Readers need to have opportunities to express their comprehension through various means, which include but are not limited to oral responses, written responses, collaborative work, and products or projects.

ESSENTIAL ELEMENTS

In our book on the development of comprehension in the early grades (Stahl & García, 2015), we created a model that incorporated the essential elements in an all-inclusive comprehension curriculum for young children. We have modified that model somewhat to incorporate an outer layer of external factors that are likely to influence the inner circles that represent the classroom factors (see Figure 1.1).

Sociocultural Influences

Although not drawn on top of the figure (to avoid graphic confusion), the sociocultural influences serve as a filter that overlays all school interactions, those within the classroom and outside the classroom. In the most extreme case, we can consider the sociocultural impact of the COVID-19 pandemic. Small conversation groups and group projects were difficult to undertake while still maintaining safe social-distancing regulations. Additionally, food scarcity anxiety, economic transitions, and health concerns made it difficult for many children to focus on schoolwork when families dealt with life and death matters.

Systemic Elements

The outer square elements impact the effectiveness of classroom comprehension instruction positively or negatively. The new field of improvement science (Bryk et al., 2015; LeMahieu et al., 2017) is a problem-solving approach that involves community networks (CN) of experts from various backgrounds working together to solve problems of practice. These CN investigations not only look at classroom

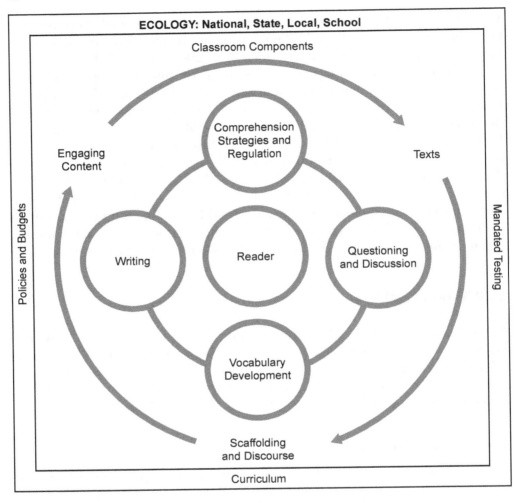

FIGURE 1.1. Model of an all-inclusive comprehension curriculum. *Note.* Sociocultural dynamics influence all aspects portrayed in this figure. Adapted from Stahl and García (2015). Copyright © 2015 The Guilford Press. Adapted by permission.

data but also incorporate the influence of systemic factors on school improvement efforts. Our model's outer box includes factors that live outside the classroom, yet they influence the decisions and forces at work in the inner classroom circles.

Government policies at the federal and state levels have a strong influence on school protocols and procedures. The No Child Left Behind Act (2001) required every public school to disaggregate annual literacy test data. This policy forced many "successful" schools to recognize that while most of their students performed above average, there were subsets of children (e.g., children in low socioeconomic groups, special education students, or emerging bilingual/multilingual students) whose needs were not being met.

Annual state English language arts tests are designed to demonstrate that schools are meeting their promise to their constituency by ensuring that their students are making the expected yearly achievement progress in the agreed-upon state standards. However, classrooms often lose months of high-quality instructional time preparing for the tests in rote ways with worksheets. In an improvement science analysis, the CN would collect data on these lost hours. The CN might also compare the ways that instruction differed across schools throughout the year.

Finally, each district and each school has a unique ecology. As with any ecology, that means that there is an interdependence within elements and that interaction among these elements impacts the individual elements and results in the creation of a unique environment. Teachers who have taught at multiple schools can attest to these differences and their influence on classrooms. Ecological differences influence budget allocations, professional development, teacher decision-making independence, and curricular decisions. Therefore, even if a standard curriculum is selected, the teachers often implement the instruction differently from district to district, school to school, and classroom to classroom in a single school.

Classroom Context Elements

In the outermost circle, we consider elements that serve as the contextual frame for all comprehension activities. We present a brief overview here and cover each element more deeply in its own chapter.

Content and Texts

Historically, rich content has taken a backseat to isolated literacy skills in the intermediate grades. Most longstanding publishers of basal reading programs built units around a single thematic topic, such as persistence or courage. However, these themes often served as catchalls for texts and learning targets that were only loosely related. There was no systematic attempt to build either a body of related knowledge or enough sustained practice in specific comprehension targets to help students gain control over comprehension strategies (Dewitz et al., 2009; Piloneata, 2010).

Since the CCSS (NGA & CCSSO, 2010), several core reading programs have made efforts to construct units of study that include connections between reading and writing skills. These units are often related to common grade-level disciplinary topics. For example, the third-grade Expeditionary Learning curriculum includes the units Adaptations and the Wide World of Frogs, A Study of Peter Pan, and Wolves: Fact and Fiction. Despite the efforts to balance informational and narrative text reading and narrative, informational, and argumentative writing, the units were constructed with a humanities lens. For example, the frog and wolf units' final assessments call for the students to compose narratives about each topic. At the conclusion of the Peter Pan unit, the children engage in "opinion writing about a new character." Literacy skills trump disciplinary knowledge building in these units.

Rather than building units that provide a range of reading materials designed to help students acquire disciplinary knowledge, these publishers created a balance of informational and narrative texts on a given topic with loose learning goals related to the science topics, not disciplinary learning standards. Publishers and teachers often fear that teaching knowledge during the literacy block will compromise the students' acquisition of grade-level literacy standards (Connor et al., 2017; Williams et al., 2009). Disciplinary experts worry that integrated units dilute or misrepresent content knowledge (see Chapter 3).

Calkins (2017) approaches the balance of narrative and informational text similarly in her popular reading and writing units of study. Her third-grade reading materials include four narrative units, two expository units, and a poetry unit (Calkins, 2015). Although the interactive teacher read-aloud involves the whole class, all the children read different texts. In this instructional model, the children's independent reading level and personal interests inform their text selection. Therefore, there is no connection to community knowledge building that comes from reading and collaborating. Additionally, there is little to no connection to state-mandated disciplinary standards. The informational writing lessons adhere more closely to literary ideals than teaching and providing practice in helping children use disciplinary standards for informational and argumentative writing.

Researchers recently confirmed that word and world knowledge are essential for comprehension (Pearson et al., 2020). Vocabulary development and word recognition facilitate each other. The collection of studies conducted as part of the RfU initiative indicated that reading comprehension should be integrated within content-area learning and exploration even before children can read independently (*www.ets.org/research/report/retooling-literacy/part2b*). By third grade, comprehension instruction should directly address strategic processing, thinking, and reasoning. Multicomponent instruction that focuses on multiple strategies rather than specific skills is most effective.

Additionally, the environment should be language rich and include discussion, debate, and collaborative activities. Discipline-specific writing that responds to text and communicates thinking should be an integral part of instructional units. The research results in third grade and beyond suggest that integrating reading and content instruction can boost learning in both areas rather than sacrificing either (Connor et al., 2017; Romance & Vitale, 1992, 2017). If we do not teach children how to learn from reading, we resort to reading to them, using PowerPoints, or teaching by telling (Pearson et al., 2020, p. 222). (See Chapter 3.)

Balancing the quantity of informational and narrative text should not be the driving force in text selection within a unit of study or across a year. That balance should be an effect of the curriculum. When units of study are constructed across the year to address essential learning in literary, science, and social studies content, the effect is a collection of texts that vary in genre, readability levels, text type, and media format.

The authentic, purposeful learning about meaningful topics in interactive, collaborative settings promotes student curiosity and engagement. This level of student interaction and agency yields motivation and increased engagement. The Educational Testing Service summary of the RfU curriculum recommendations calls for teachers to foster and monitor positive reading dispositions that go beyond the simplistic "joy of reading" (*www.ets.org/research/report/retooling-literacy/part2b*). In our experience, we observed children whose authentic classroom explorations led them to delight, fulfillment, and a yearning to dig more deeply into classroom topics. In this book, we hope that our recommendations might create that level of excitement for teachers and their students.

Scaffolding and Discourse

In the 1970s, most intermediate classrooms only allocated time for a brief prereading introduction to a story, time for students to silently read the story, followed by an IRE (initiate–response–evaluate) discussion format. Teachers explicitly taught skills such as identifying the main idea, and students practiced the skills in workbooks throughout the week. The following week the class moved to a different set of skills. Today we know that students need sustained practice using a range of materials and various activities to acquire the skills and strategies necessary to understand the text. Equally important, students need to learn how to express their comprehension verbally, in speech and writing. These competencies take a great deal of time compared to the efficiency of teaching constrained skills.

History has affirmed the effectiveness of using the gradual release of responsibility (GRR) to teach comprehension and writing processes (Pearson & Gallagher, 1983). Therefore, teachers need time to walk through the phases that shift the responsibility to the students. Explicit teaching should be direct and precise. However, the modeling often requires the examination and creation of multiple examples, particularly in writing. The more knowledgeable other must provide focused attention and feedback during guided practice, not just a walk-by. Suppose we shortchange these steps or neglect to move back and forth along the continuum during the learning process. In that case, we risk creating learners who cannot transfer the skills when they are asked to apply them independently in novel experiences. All classroom teachers have had the experience of scratching their heads and saying, "Why can't they do this? I taught it to them two weeks ago." Rushing through the GRR or skipping steps is one possible answer. Often reading programs do not allocate the time needed to teach processes thoroughly before moving on to a new target.

Language development contributes to both listening and reading comprehension in significant ways. Chapter 2 addresses the unique needs of our students from diverse backgrounds. Our classrooms need to accept, nurture, and expand multiple forms of discourse ranging from social to academic. Gee (1990) distinguishes between discourse (language in use) and Discourse (with a capital *D*). According to Gee, Discourse is a particular way of using language that reflects a way of thinking, feeling, and valuing. It identifies one as being an insider within a specific social network. The Discourse that we use in our spiritual community is probably different from the Discourse we use at our employment place. What is newly relevant for most children in the intermediate grades is the Discourse shifts required when engaging in their academic assignments. The Discourse for each disciplinary area is unique. The Discourse used when one reads, writes, discusses, or critiques literary text is not the same Discourse that one would employ with social studies or science texts (Goldman, Britt, et al., 2016; Stahl, 2014). By integrating disciplinary learning with literacy, we provide the opportunity for our students to use the Discourse of the academic community and build knowledge in authentic ways.

Instructional Elements

Comprehension Strategies and Regulation

In the intermediate grades, teaching cognitive comprehension strategies is among the top priorities. Any curriculum for grades 3–6 should include thorough instruction of the declarative, procedural, and conditional knowledge of purposeful predictions, utilization of relevant prior knowledge, visualization, text structure, ideational prominence (level of importance), summarization, questioning, inference generation, and monitoring. The RfU studies indicate that the ability to generate inferences and conduct self-monitoring makes the most substantive contribution to comprehension. Therefore, teachers should emphasize them across all grade levels.

Additionally, we know that although each strategy should be explicitly taught in isolation, they need to be applied as quickly as possible within routines that employ multiple strategies. Instructional programs, such as reciprocal teaching (Palincsar & Brown, 1984) or transactional strategy instruction (Pressley et al., 1992), can be helpful. However, the goal of strategy instruction is for readers to use strategies flexibly, as needed, to overcome meaning-making hurdles (see Chapter 6).

Questioning and Discussion

Classroom discussion plays a crucial role in comprehension instruction. The value of teacher-led discussions goes well beyond the goals of checking for understanding. Teachers often provide the bridge that moves the students' thinking to higher levels. Teachers also serve as powerful Discourse models for how we think and talk about texts associated with each discipline. Teaching students to ask the questions that literary critics, scientists, and historians ask paves the way for student-led conversations and knowledge building in each discipline. Classroom talk might also be more likely to take the form of book clubs, debate teams, video performances, and research teams than it has in the past. These formats encourage active learning, student agency, student engagement, and joy (see Chapter 7).

Vocabulary Development

Comprehension of any text is dependent on knowledge of the vocabulary in the text. Therefore, if teachers expect their students to understand the texts they will be reading, instructional provisions must be made to address their students' vocabulary needs. In the intermediate grades, students have always encountered increasing volumes of academic vocabulary due to the emphasis on reading to learn new content. One of the benefits of teaching comprehension within disciplinary units is that the hands-on experiences and networks of knowledge needed to understand academic vocabulary are built into the unit of study. Additionally, the students have sustained opportunities to hear and say the words during learning experiences, read the words in multiple texts, and use them in their writing. Multiple exposures, especially multimodal activities, create a greater likelihood of word learning for all students (Stahl & Fairbanks, 1986; Wright & Cervetti, 2016). (See Chapter 5.)

Writing

Like speaking, writing helps readers solidify and expand their understanding of what they have read, mainly when synthesizing information or putting together ideas from multiple sources. Equally important, writing is a way for students to communicate what they have comprehended. Whether sending a chat message to get assistance on the Verizon website, responding to a note from a teacher, or commenting on a blog, composing a written response to something that we read is part of the fabric of everyone's lives. In today's world, many opportunities to talk to service providers have been replaced with online written directives and prompts for us to respond in writing. While writing personal narratives can be therapeutic and expand one's awareness of the human experience, most of the writing that we do in our daily lives responds to what we have read, informs, or argues a position. Our students' literacy learning activities should prepare them for life's demands (see Chapter 8).

SELF-ASSESSMENT

Before reading this book, we encourage you to self-evaluate your current instructional practices by completing Form 1.1 (at the end of the chapter). This is an opportunity for you to consider how your current instructional practices align with the most recent research findings. Our form provides a means for you to identify your strengths, face your challenges, and pinpoint voids in your curriculum. This process can help you determine a few minor changes that you can make immediately to increase the effectiveness of your instruction. Other changes may require a long-term plan and more sustained, supportive professional development. According to Pearson et al. (2020), high-quality comprehension instruction requires time, patience, persistence, and ideally, a network of support. We urge you to work with your colleagues, school, and district to recruit support for this valuable endeavor.

FORM 1.1

Self-Assessment and Goal Setting

	No	To Some Extent	Yes	Rank Top 3 Goals
Comprehension instruction integrates literacy with disciplinary knowledge and vocabulary building.				
I use a wide variety of texts that are chosen deliberately to support instructional content and to stretch student thinking.				
I implement large-group and small-group discussions about text throughout the week.				
I provide explicit, sustained strategy instruction.				
I employ a systematic word study program that includes fluency, multisyllabic words, and morphology.				
I explicitly facilitate children's use of verbal and written expression to reflect their thinking about texts.				
Student participation in debates, argumentation, and/ or projects is included in each unit of instruction.				
My instruction with diverse learners is informed by research on these populations.				

Note. Adapted with permission from Stahl and García (2015).

CHAPTER TWO

Teaching Reading Comprehension to Students from Diverse Backgrounds

GUIDING QUESTIONS

- What do we need to know about the reading comprehension instruction of students in high-poverty schools?
- What are the developmental, performance, and instructional issues related to the reading comprehension of emergent bilingual students?
- What do we need to know about the reading comprehension performance and instruction of marginalized dialect speakers?
- What are the implications of the cultural findings reported by the National Academies of Sciences, Engineering, and Medicine (2018) for students from diverse backgrounds?
- What do educators need to know and do to implement culturally responsive literacy instruction?

If you noticed increased diversity in your classroom, school, and state population, you are not alone. According to *The Condition of Education* (Hussar et al., 2020), the percentage of minority students enrolled in public schools increased substantially over the last 20 years, with projections indicating an even greater increase in future years. Between 2000 and 2017, the percentage of Hispanic[1] students enrolled in public schools increased from 16 to 27%, while the percentage of Asian/Pacific Islanders increased from 4 to 6%. Between 2000 and 2017, the percentage

---

[1]*Hispanic* refers to people from Spanish-speaking countries. It is the term used by the U.S. federal government. *Latinx* includes people from Latin America, including those from non-Spanish-speaking countries, such as Brazil. Although many Latinx are Hispanic, they may reject this term because Hispanic includes people from Spain. Many Latinx do not identify with Spain because it was a colonial power that exploited much of Latin America.

of emergent bilingual students (students who speak a language other than English at home and who acquire English at school)[2] increased from 8.1 to 10.1%. In contrast, between 2000 and 2017, the percentage of White students enrolled in public schools decreased from 61 to 48%, while the percentage of African American students decreased from 16 to 15% (Hussar et al., 2020). The percentage of American Indian/Native Alaskan students in public schools stayed steady at 1%.

Minority students are disproportionately enrolled in high-poverty schools, compared to White students. In 2017, 45% of African American students and 45% of Latinx students attended high-poverty schools compared to 8% of White students (Hussar et al., 2020). Forty-one percent of American Indian students also attended high-poverty schools.

The negative impact of high-poverty schools on minority students' academic achievement can be seen in the reading comprehension test scores for students in high-poverty schools on the National Assessment of Educational Progress (NAEP)—the only national reading test in the United States. In 2019, the average NAEP reading score for fourth graders who attended high-poverty schools (206) was significantly lower than those of other fourth graders who attended higher-income schools (between 217 to 240) (Hussar et al., 2020).

TEACHING READING COMPREHENSION TO STUDENTS IN HIGH-POVERTY SCHOOLS

Generally, the type of reading instruction observed in high-poverty schools was not recommended for promoting students' reading comprehension (Kamil et al., 2008; Shanahan et al., 2010). In a study of eight high-poverty elementary schools, Taylor and her colleagues (2000, 2002) reported that they observed passive reading instruction in grades K–6; that is, students listened to their teachers read aloud and talk much more than they actually read, discussed, or wrote about what they read. In contrast, in the few classrooms in which grade 2–3 students had relatively high reading comprehension test scores, small-group instruction, teacher coaching rather than telling, and teacher's use of high-level questioning characterized the instruction (Taylor et al., 2000). Teachers' use of high-level questioning also characterized the reading instruction in the small number of grade 4–6 classrooms with high reading comprehension test scores (Taylor et al., 2002).

To improve the reading instruction of low-performing, low-income students in grades K–3, between 2002 and 2008, the federal government provided Reading First grants to states and school districts (Gamse et al., 2008; U.S. Department of

---

[2] Historically, the federal government has used a range of terms to refer to emergent bilingual students. Among others, these included *limited English proficient* (LEP), *limited English speaking* (LES), *English language learners* (ELLs), and *English learners* (ELs).

Education, Office of Elementary and Secondary Education, 2002). The primary goal of Reading First was for all children to read at grade level by the end of grade 3. Schools that received Reading First grants had to provide teachers with professional staff development, implement certain types of reading assessments, increase the amount of time spent on reading instruction to 90 minutes daily, employ approved reading materials (i.e., specific basal reading series), and provide instruction in the five areas deemed important by the NRP (National Institute of Child Health and Human Development, 2000): phonemic awareness, phonics, fluency, vocabulary, and comprehension.

Although the federal evaluation of Reading First concluded that students improved their decoding skills, they did not improve their reading comprehension performance, nor did they perform at grade level by the end of grade 3 (Gamse et al., 2008). Critics pointed out that teachers in Reading First spent too much time developing their students' decoding and fluency skills and not enough time developing their students' reading comprehension (Cummins, 2007; Teale et al., 2007). Cummins complained that students in Reading First did less reading and "inquiry-oriented learning" compared to higher-income students who were not in Reading First (p. 564).

Between 2002 and 2007, Georgia (coauthor of this book) and her colleagues investigated the reading comprehension instruction that occurred in grades 2–4 in high-poverty schools that predominantly served emergent bilingual Latinx students. They reported that the teachers employed whole-class, teacher-directed instruction because they were concerned that their students would not benefit from small-group instruction (García et al., 2006, 2021). After 7 months of professional staff development and teacher educator/teacher collaboration, most of the teachers moved from whole-class, teacher-directed instruction to student-led small-group instruction, which resulted in active student participation rather than passive student participation. By the end of the school year, second and fourth graders who participated in dialogic cognitive strategies instruction, compared to students who participated in a different instructional treatment or a treatment control group, had significantly improved their reading comprehension test performance. Chapter 6 explains how you can implement dialogic cognitive strategy instruction.

Based on the above findings and two federal What Works Clearinghouses, for grades K–3 (Shanahan et al., 2010) and grades 4–6 (Kamil et al., 2008), we recommend that teachers in high-poverty schools collaborate with administrators, teacher leaders, reading educators, reading researchers, and each other to change their instructional practices. We say collaborate because it is difficult for individual teachers to make instructional changes when the school culture emphasizes passive student practices. We specifically recommend that teachers in high-poverty schools instruct their students on how to monitor and use strategies to resolve comprehension problems and enhance their comprehension; ask their students high-level questions that get them to think deeply about and discuss the texts they are reading; select and have students read high-quality literature and informational texts; teach them how to use the text structures in the texts they read to guide their comprehension and learning; and arrange for them to meet in student-led heterogeneous (mixed reading level) small groups to implement strategies as they read and discuss texts. We recommend that you use student-led heterogeneous small groups so that your students learn not only from you, but also from each other.

The two clearinghouses also stated that there was strong research evidence for providing grade 3–6 students with explicit vocabulary instruction and explicit strategy instruction, and moderate evidence for providing them with high-level discussions of texts (Kamil et al., 2008; Shanahan et al., 2010). Chapter 5 addresses vocabulary development; Chapter 6 explains how you can implement dialogic cognitive strategy instruction; and Chapter 7 explains how you can implement high-level discussions of texts.

TEACHING READING COMPREHENSION TO EMERGENT BILINGUAL STUDENTS

The current term for students who know one language at home and who are in the process of acquiring English at school is *emergent bilingual students.* According to *The Condition of Education* (Hussar et al., 2020), the percentage of emergent bilingual students (henceforth referred to as bilingual students) in U.S. public schools increased from 8.1% in autumn 2000 to 10.1% in autumn 2017. It is important to note that although bilingual students in the United States come from a range of countries and language backgrounds, 75% of them are Spanish-speaking Latinx students.

Given that most bilingual students who participate in bilingual education or English-as-a-second-language (ESL) programs still are learning English, it should not be surprising to learn that the average reading comprehension test score for bilingual fourth graders on a national English reading test in the United States (NAEP) was much lower (191) in 2019 than that of their native-English-speaking peers (224) (Hussar et al., 2020). Researchers and experts in educational evaluation have pointed out that it is difficult to know when bilingual students' low performance on English reading tests is due to their limited English proficiency and language test bias issues or to their low English reading performance (American Educational Research Association, American Psychological Association, & National Council of Measurement, 1999, 2014; García & DeNicolo, 2016).

Other researchers have warned that we should not rely on bilingual students' scores on English reading tests to evaluate their performance in U.S. schools, but rather we should use their reading comprehension test performance in both their first (L1) or home language and English or second language (L2). In a study of bilingual students' biliteracy development (i.e., literacy development in two languages), Hopewell and Escamilla (2014) observed that normal progress for bilingual Latinx students who were learning to read simultaneously in two languages was to score at grade level in Spanish, their L1, but slightly lower or below grade level in English, their L2. Chapter 9 provides more information on how to assess the reading comprehension performance of bilingual students in their L1 and English.

The Advantages of Reading in the L1 or Home Language

Bilingual students who received literacy instruction in their L1 and English outperformed bilingual students who only received literacy instruction in English. Meta-analyses (quantitative review studies) conducted with Latinx students who were taught to read for 2–3 years in Spanish and English found that these students had higher scores on English reading comprehension tests compared to Latinx students who only were taught to read in English (Francis et al., 2006; Rolstad et al., 2005; Slavin & Cheung, 2005). One reason for these findings is that it is easier for bilingual students to learn to read in the language they know best, typically their L1, than to read in their L2.

When young bilingual students are taught to read first in English, a language many of them do not know well, they may not recognize or know the meanings of all the words that they can decode. As a result, they may not understand that a major purpose of reading is to comprehend. Researchers who studied bilingual students' English decoding and comprehension development reported that when bilingual students received explicit decoding instruction, they decoded as well as native-English speakers, but their comprehension of English texts was much lower (Lesaux & Geva, 2006). Alternatively, when young bilingual students received literacy instruction in their L1, then they typically recognized the meanings of the L1 words that they could decode, and understood that a major purpose of reading is to comprehend.

Similarly, when bilingual students with limited English proficiency are placed in all-English classrooms, they may not understand their teacher's English instruction. As a result, they fall behind in their academic learning until they acquire enough English to understand their teacher's instruction. An evaluation of bilingual Latinx students' academic performance showed that students enrolled in bilingual education programs, in which they received instruction in English and Spanish, outperformed those who were enrolled in all English or ESL programs on English reading tests (Rolstad et al., 2005).

Bilingual students who participated in long-term bilingual education programs, which last throughout elementary school (i.e., developmental or maintenance bilingual education programs or dual-language programs),[3] performed higher on English academic measures than those enrolled in transitional bilingual education

---

[3] In developmental or maintenance bilingual education programs, all the students in the classroom are speakers of the same minority language. Their teachers are fluent in the minority language and English, and depending on the grade level, provide certain percentages of instruction in each language. Students are in the program throughout elementary school, regardless of their oral English proficiency. In dual-language programs, half the students are native English speakers and half are speakers of the same minority language. They are taught together in the same classrooms throughout elementary school. The percentage of instruction in each language varies according to the type of dual-language program.

programs, in which students were moved into all English classrooms as soon as possible, usually before grade 4 (Collier & Thomas, 2017; Rolstad et al., 2005). The students in the long-term bilingual education programs continued to receive academic instruction in their L1 as they acquired English so they did not fall behind academically. These findings supported Cummins' (1981) contention that bilingual students needed 4–7 years of bilingual instruction to develop cognitive academic language proficiency in English. Cummins explained that when bilingual students were exited from bilingual education early (before grade 4), they might be able to communicate in English on the playground or in stores due to their command of social English, but that they did not have the academic language they needed to further their learning in all-English classrooms.

Cross-Linguistic Transfer

Cross-linguistic transfer is one reason why bilingual students who received literacy instruction in their L1 and English might have outperformed those who only received literacy instruction in English. Cross-linguistic transfer occurs when bilingual students use what they learned in one language to approach learning in the other language. Cummins (1981, 2000) hypothesized that once bilingual students developed a cognitive/literate base in one language, and were adequately exposed to and motivated to use another language, they should be able to use what they had learned in the one language while in the other language. As proof, several researchers reported that bilingual students' reading performance in their two languages was correlated (Genesee et al., 2006). Other researchers found that students could use fable knowledge acquired in one language to comprehend fables in another language without any additional instruction (Goldman et al., 1984). Georgia and her colleagues reported that successful bilingual Latinx readers in grades 4–7 used the same cognitive strategies when reading in both languages (García & Godina, 2017; Jiménez et al., 1995, 1996).

Unique Bilingual Practices or Translanguaging

In the past, when bilingual individuals used two languages to communicate—such as code mixing, code switching, and translating—these practices often were viewed as deficit because they were different from the practices that monolingual (single language) individuals used (Heller, 1999). Code mixing is when bilingual individuals include words from both languages in a single sentence, as illustrated in the following example (the code-mixed words are in *italics*): "I want to eat *carne y ensalada* because *tengo mucho hambre*" ("I want to eat *meat and salad* because *I am very hungry*"). Code switching refers to switching between two languages at sentence boundaries. For example, the following illustrates code switching): "Let's go watch a movie. Estoy muy cansado de todo el trabajo que tengo que hacer" ("Let's go watch a movie. I'm really tired of all the work I have to do").

New theory related to bilingualism (see O. García & Wei, 2014; Wei, 2018) has resulted in a positive view of bilingual practices, which now are called *translanguaging* (O. García, 2009). Translanguaging practices are unique ways that bilingual individuals communicate compared to monolingual individuals, who are limited to using one language for communication. When bilingual individuals translanguage, they are thought to use all their linguistic resources, not separate languages, to communicate orally and in writing.

A number of researchers showed how bilingual students' employment of translanguaging practices enhanced their reading comprehension and writing performance (García et al., 2020; Jimenez et al., 2015; Lee & García, 2021; Velasco & O. García, 2014). For example, Georgia and her colleague conducted think-aloud research with bilingual Latinx fourth graders that revealed how the students employed translanguaging while reading (García & Godina, 2017). The students' use of translanguaging helped them to resolve comprehension problems that they might not have resolved otherwise. For example, Marisa (a strong Spanish reader, but below-grade-level English reader) engaged in code mixing (indicated by *italics*) and translating (indicated by <u>underlining</u>) to figure out the use of English words in an English passage on Venus, as illustrated below:

> TEXT: Those clouds are a special part of the planet's blanket of air, its atmosphere.
>
> MARISA: <u>Las nubes eran una parte especial del planeta,</u> cobija, *blanket*, *cobija* <u>de aire,</u> *de atmosphere.* [The clouds are a special part of the planet's, blanket, *blanket, blanket* of air, of *atmosphere.*] (García & Godina, 2017, p. 290)

Given the positive benefits of translanguaging, we recommend that you allow your bilingual students to use it, as well as their L1, when discussing how they are comprehending texts in English, and when writing responses to the English texts they read.

The Benefits of Cognates

A specific translanguaging practice that could benefit bilingual Latinx students' English reading comprehension is accessing cognates. Cognates are words in ancestrally related languages (e.g., Spanish and English, Italian and English, French and English, German and English, Greek and English) that are similar in form and meaning. Table 2.1 shows some of the cognates in English and Spanish that are useful to students when reading in either language, along with websites that list English–Spanish cognates.

Although some strong readers in Spanish and English automatically use cognates to figure out unknown vocabulary while reading in English and/or Spanish (Jiménez et al., 1995, 1996; García & Godina, 2017), most third- through sixth-grade bilingual students do not (García et al., 2020). In a study with fourth-, fifth-,

TABLE 2.1. Examples of English–Spanish Cognates and Online Cognate Resources

English cognates	Spanish cognates
adaptation	*adaptación*
benefit	*beneficio*
characteristic	*característico*
civilization	*civilización*
distance	*distancia*
geography	*geografía*
important	*importante*
invisible	*invisible*
lamp	*lámpara*
mystery	*misterio*
numerous	*numeroso*
product	*producto*

Online cognate resources

- 1001 Spanish words you already know: A guide to English–Spanish cognates—*www.realfastspanish.com/vocabulary/spanish-cognates*
- English Spanish cognates—*www.esdict.com/English-Spanish-Cognates.html#.X3T89pNKjBI*
- Erichsen, G. (2020). Cognates are words that have similar origins—*www.thoughtco.com/cognate-in-spanish-3078353*

and sixth-grade bilingual Latinx students, Georgia and her colleagues discovered that the students did not know how to use Spanish–English cognates while reading (Nagy et al., 1993). After giving the students a cognate definition and practice in using cognates, the fifth and sixth graders used cognates to some extent while reading, but the fourth graders still had difficulties. To give you an idea of how many Spanish–English cognates there are in English texts, in Figure 2.1, we underlined the cognates in a short excerpt from a book written for students in third through seventh grades. There are 17 cognates in the 37-word passage.

An advantage that benefits Spanish speakers while reading in English is that cognates are high-frequency words in Spanish, and low-frequency words in English (Lubliner & Hiebert, 2011). When Spanish speakers know the meanings of Spanish cognates, and how to use them, then they should be able to figure out the

---

Albert made several <u>important</u> <u>decisions</u> <u>during</u> those hikes. He <u>decided</u> <u>to</u> <u>study</u> <u>physics</u> <u>in</u> <u>college</u>. <u>Physics</u> <u>is</u> the <u>science</u> of <u>objects</u>, their <u>energy</u>, and the way they <u>move</u>. After that he wanted to become a <u>physics</u> <u>professor</u>.

FIGURE 2.1. Underlined cognates in a 37-word excerpt from an English text (Braillie, 2002, p. 27).

meanings of unknown English words. This advantage should be especially useful when Spanish–English bilingual students read science texts in English because these texts include high numbers of Spanish–English cognates (Bravo et al., 2007). In Chapter 5 (on vocabulary instruction), we include information on *how* to teach cognates to bilingual students in grades 3–6 so that they use them while reading in English.

Second-Language Issues

Emergent bilingual students often comprehend oral and written English better than they can speak or write in English. For example, due to phonological differences in their home language and English, bilingual students may know what English words mean but be unable to say the words correctly. In the following example, Marta, a fourth grader who was a strong reader in both English and Spanish, knew what the word *significant* meant but could not say it accurately:

> MARTA: The atmosphere of Venus has another *sci, science, sickness, sig nificant.* I know that word but I can't say it. I can't pronounce it. (García & Godina, 2017, p. 288)

Similarly, bilingual students may reveal increased comprehension of an English text when they are allowed to use their L1 to explain it. In the following example, a fourth grader with limited oral English proficiency used Spanish to discuss an English text. She showed that she not only understood the English text, but also was able to express novelty about the new information she had learned:

> TEXT: Although the whale's ears are only two tiny holes in the skin, they can hear underwater sounds from as far away as 1,000 miles.
>
> RESEARCHER: ¿Por qué te sorprendió? [Why were you surprised?]
>
> MONICA: Porque no pensaba que las ballenas podían oír de lejos con los oídos chiquitos. [Because I didn't think that whales could hear so far way with such small ears.] (García & Godina, 2017, p. 293)

If you do not know the students' L1, then we recommend that you ask a bilingual student or adult with proficiency in the students' L1 and English to explain their use of the L1 and/or translanguaging to you. A fourth-grade teacher (who did not know Spanish) with whom Georgia worked, explained that when she allowed her bilingual Latinx students to use Spanish and translanguage when discussing English texts, then the students talked much more. When she did not allow it, they were silent. Asking a student in the group with English proficiency to explain what the students were talking about resolved her inability to understand them (García et al., 2006).

Making English Instruction Comprehensible

If you are using English to teach emergent bilingual students how to read, comprehend, and write English texts, it is important to use ESL techniques. We recommend that you use ESL techniques regardless of where you are teaching—in a bilingual classroom, in an ESL classroom, or in an all-English classroom. In the text box below and the section that follows, we present principles that you can follow when teaching emergent bilingual students in English. There also are several instructional programs that you can use, such as the Sheltered Instruction Observation Protocol (SIOP; Echevarría et al., 2016; TESOL Trainers, 2016) and Specially Designed Academic Instruction in English (SDAIE; Harcourt Brace, 2000; Sidek, n.d.), which are beyond the scope of this book.

When you read an English book aloud or employ oral English to teach emergent bilingual students, you should use multiple modalities (seeing, speaking, writing, reading, touching, etc.). For example, you should accompany your speech and teacher read-aloud in English with gestures; physically act out what you read or said; point to illustrations; draw or show photos; illustrate key vocabulary with artifacts or objects, and use hands-on activities. A resource that you can use to show photos of English words and disciplinary vocabulary is TextProject. You can access it at *http://textproject.org/teachers/vocabulary-instruction/textproject-word-pictures*. Also, we recommend that you integrate reading, writing, listening, and speaking not only in your English presentation of material, but also in your students' responses to it.

You need to give your students frequent opportunities to show what they understand or comprehend. Here, you need to make sure that they actively demonstrate their knowledge or comprehension by reading, writing, listening, and speaking, and through other modalities (e.g., hands-on activities, drawings, drama, or physical

Principles for Making English Instruction Comprehensible

- In your English presentations and student responses, integrate reading, writing, listening, and speaking.

- Accompany your English speech, instruction, and teacher read-alouds with gestures; drawings, illustrations, or photos; realia; physical action; hands-on activities; and modeling.

- Assign your students to work in small groups so that they can figure out your instruction by using all their linguistic resources (English, L1, and translanguaging).

- For beginning emergent bilingual students, slow down your speech, clearly enunciate, use known or pretaught vocabulary, and check frequently for student understanding.

activity). A website created by a multistate assessment consortium (WiDA, 2020) not only provides teachers with information on how to instruct emergent bilingual students at different English proficiency levels, but also shows the types of responses that you can expect from students at the various English proficiency levels.

Unfortunately, just relying on a few modalities may not be enough for bilingual students to understand you. When Georgia worked with middle school teachers (grades 6–8), she noticed that the social studies teachers often showed 30- to 40-minute videos, which the bilingual students did not comprehend. Although videos involve two modalities—visual and audio—when bilingual students do not have the necessary English proficiency, background knowledge, or English vocabulary, it will be difficult for them to comprehend videos in English. You can make English videos more comprehensible when you provide specific purposes or questions for students to address while watching the videos; interrupt the videos at key points to check on students' understanding; and provide time for students to work in pairs or small groups to discuss what they saw in the videos. If the students can read in English, turning on the captions at the bottom of the videos may help.

When you work with beginning emergent bilingual students, we advise you to slow down your speech, clearly enunciate your words, limit your vocabulary, and check to see if your students understand what you are saying. In addition, you cannot assume that beginning emergent bilingual students will understand all the instructional practices common in U.S. classrooms. If you want your students to work in pairs or small groups, we advise you to post step-by-step instructions, bring some students to the front of the room, model the instructions with the students, and explain to the class what you want them to do by pointing to the step-by-step instructions.

Themed, Integrated Disciplinary Instruction

One way to make sure that bilingual students have the appropriate background knowledge, English vocabulary, and disciplinary knowledge to understand what is being taught in English, is to provide them with themed, integrated disciplinary instruction. For example, if bilingual students receive L1, ESL, and/or all-English instruction, it is useful if the teachers collaborate so that a new topic or theme first is introduced in the L1, the language the student knows best. Next, the ESL teacher needs to make sure that she helps the bilingual students to access in English the background knowledge already developed in their L1, and provide them with the necessary vocabulary, syntactic, and disciplinary knowledge to learn about the topic in the all-English setting. Lastly, the teacher in the all-English setting should expand on the student's knowledge about the topic through comprehensible input and hands-on experiences.

Even when a bilingual student is not taught in all three settings, providing themed or integrated instruction on the same topic across English language arts and other disciplines (i.e., mathematics, science, and/or social studies) is helpful. The themed instruction usually results in increased development of bilingual students' background knowledge because it is built in more than one instructional context. In addition, students' conceptual vocabulary in English benefits because students are repeatedly exposed to the same vocabulary and given multiple opportunities to read, write, speak, and use the vocabulary in different contexts. For more information on how to implement integrated disciplinary instruction, see Chapter 3.

READING COMPREHENSION ISSUES
RELATED TO SPEAKERS OF MARGINALIZED DIALECTS

Linguists claim that no one in the United States speaks a national, standard, or approved form of English because an official language never has been declared (Adger et al., 2007). Also, all English speakers in the United States speak a version of English, that is, an English dialect (Lindfors, 1987). Most importantly, dialects are not deviant forms of language, but structured, rule-governed versions of language.

Nonetheless, there are English dialects in U.S. society that are more respected than other dialects. Respected English dialects typically are spoken by middle- and upper-class Americans and appear in textbooks and the national media. They are called standardized versions of English or *Standard English* (the term that we use in this section). It is important to acknowledge that speakers of Standard English are born into households and communities where Standard English is spoken. It is not a foreign language that they had to formally learn, although schooling strives to improve their use of it.

Marginalized or less-respected dialects of English in the United States include African American Vernacular English (AAVE), Caribbean English Creole, Hawaiian Creole English (Smith, 2016), and Appalachian dialects, among others. Just like speakers of Standard English, speakers of marginalized dialects are born into households and communities where marginalized dialects of English are spoken.

Linguists and reading researchers determined that speaking a marginalized dialect does not result in cognitive problems related to the reading comprehension of texts in Standard English (Adger et al., 2007). However, there are affective issues that adversely affect the reading performance of speakers of marginalized dialects.

Changing Society's Negative Views of Marginalized Dialects

Smith (2016) pointed out that one solution for improving the negative view of marginalized dialects in U.S. society and schools would be for the country to embrace a policy of translingualism. She explained that such a policy would recognize and validate the multiple languages and dialects employed in the United States to communicate and create meaning. Such a policy would mean that everyone in U.S. schools would acquire additional languages and dialects as part of becoming an educated global citizen.

Other researchers recommended that teachers, student teachers, and middle school and high school students be instructed on language variation in the United States from a sociolinguistic perspective (Godley et al., 2006). They noted that when teachers and students recognized how they varied in their own personal language use when speaking and writing, they increased their acceptance of marginalized dialects.

We recommend that the above approaches be implemented at the same time that action be taken to improve the reading comprehension instruction of marginalized dialect speakers in the United States. In our discussion below, we focus on speakers of the most prominent marginalized dialect in the United States: AAVE.

Improving the Reading Instruction of AAVE Speakers

A transcript at the beginning of a *Reading Teacher* article (Wheeler et al., 2012) showed one of the authors, Rachel Wheeler, using Standard English to read aloud a Cajun version of "The Night Before Christmas" (Trosclair, 2000). As Wheeler and her authors pointed out, her translation of the Cajun text into Standard English indicated that she had comprehended it. They emphasized that when students employ marginalized dialects to orally read texts written in Standard English, they demonstrate that they actually comprehended what they read. Accordingly, their dialect usage should not be viewed as decoding errors.

As an illustration of the adverse effects that can occur when teachers consider dialect substitutions to be decoding errors, Wheeler et al. (2012) reported what happened when a teacher misinterpreted a third grader's use of AAVE as decoding errors when reading aloud. He was placed in a much lower reading group than his comprehension indicated, and instead of receiving instruction to facilitate his comprehension, he received phonics instruction, which he already had mastered.

Although oral reading assessment manuals advise teachers not to count dialect features as reading errors, Wheeler et al. (2012) noted that the manuals do not provide specific information about the characteristics of AAVE and other dialects. Therefore, if you have AAVE speakers in your class and school, we recommend that you learn about the rules that govern its use and become knowledgeable about comparative examples of AAVE and Standard English (Rickford, 1999; Smitherman, 1999; Wheeler & Swords, 2006, 2010). In Table 2.2, we present several rule-governed examples of AAVE and Standard English along with websites with more examples.

It is important to remember that language is a key part of all students' identity construction. Therefore, we strongly advise you not to correct your students' use

TABLE 2.2. A Comparison between AAVE and Standard English

	AAVE	Standard English
Phonological differences	*da, dis, dey, dat* *nuffin* *bruvah*[a]	*the, this, they, that* *nothing* *brother*
Grammatical differences	*I was gon' do it.* *Johnny don't got his. . . .* *She mad.* *Don't nobody like him.* *I ain't gone yet.* *He a teacher.*	*I was going to do it.* *Johnny doesn't have his. . . .* *She is mad.* *Nobody likes him.* *I haven't gone yet.* *He is a teacher.*
Grammatical structure with unique meaning (underlined)[b]	*She be workin'.* *Sometimes they be playin' games.*	*She always is working.* *She is usually working.* *Sometimes they are playing games.*
Websites	*https://sites.google.com/site/blackenglishhistory/what-is-black-english/features-of-aave* *www.languagejones.com/blog-1/2014/6/8/what-is-aave* *http://ethesisarchive.library.tu.ac.th/thesis/2017/TU_2017_5921040456_8816_6945.pdf*	

Note. [a]All the phonological examples listed here, except for "*da,*" are from *https://sites.google.com/site/blackenglishhistory/what-is-black-english/features-of-aave.*
[b]This is a grammatical structure not used in Standard English.

of AAVE when they read or talk. However, we are not saying that you should not help them to acquire Standard English. Several scholars recommend that you teach AAVE speakers when it is appropriate to use AAVE and when it is appropriate to use Standard English (Perry & Delpit, 1988; Wheeler et al., 2012). For example, Hill and Fink (2013) suggested that you use mentor texts to show when African American authors utilize AAVE in their texts and when they do not. Wheeler and her colleagues recommended that you introduce students to the different uses of AAVE and Standard English by first talking about formal and informal clothes and the settings in which each type of clothing is appropriate, then move to greetings in AAVE and in Standard English.

Wheeler and her colleagues (2012) suggested that, after introducing students to the settings in which different types of language are appropriate, you employ contrastive analysis (i.e., the systematic comparison of two languages) to show and teach the specific differences between AAVE and Standard English. A public television documentary, *Do You Speak American?* (Public Broadcasting Service, 2005), shows a video clip of a fifth-grade teacher in Los Angeles directing a Jeopardy game in which the students in his class demonstrate their knowledge of AAVE and how to translate it into English. Lastly, Wheeler et al. advised that teachers teach AAVE speakers how to become bidialectal by instructing them on how to code-switch or use each dialect for various purposes.

THE RELATIONSHIP BETWEEN CULTURAL DIVERSITY AND READING COMPREHENSION

According to a report from the National Academies of Sciences, Engineering, and Medicine (2018), researchers who investigated the nature of learning made important discoveries about influences on learning, particularly sociocultural factors and the structure of learning environments, which have strong implications for the instruction and assessment of reading comprehension in the United States. Members of the National Academies concluded that all learners grow and learn in culturally defined ways in cultural contexts. Most importantly, the report stated that learning does not happen in the same way for all people because cultural influences are influential from the beginning of life. Effective instruction depends on understanding the complex interplay among learners' prior knowledge, experiences, motivations, interests, and language and cognitive skills; educators' own experiences and cultural influences; and the cultural, social, cognitive, and emotional characteristics of the learning environment.

The National Academies' (2018) conclusions have major implications for the reading comprehension instruction of all students, but especially for the groups of culturally diverse students we discussed in this section—those who attend high-poverty schools, bilingual students, and students who speak marginalized dialects. As past research revealed, they are likely to approach and interpret the texts and curricula employed in most schools in significant ways that differ from the middle-class and upper-class native-English speaking students for which the texts and curricula were developed.

Georgia conducted research that showed how 51 Spanish-speaking Latinx fifth and sixth graders performed on English reading test passages compared to 53 native-English-speaking White classmates (1991). Few of the Latinx students had been in bilingual or ESL classrooms, and the Latinx and White students had been taught together in the same classrooms for the past 2 years, so Georgia assumed their background and vocabulary knowledge would be similar. However, the two groups of students significantly differed in their prior knowledge of the test topics and test vocabulary, with the Latinx students knowing much less than their English-speaking classmates. The differences were so great, that Georgia wondered how engaged the Latinx students and their teachers had been in their schooling.

Other researchers revealed the various ways that diverse communities in the United States taught their children and used language to communicate that were at odds with the middle- and upper-class practices expected in U.S. schools. For instance, Heath (1982) reported that African American elementary-age children in the Carolinas were not accustomed to answering questions for which their teachers already knew the answers (e.g., "Where is the setting in the story?"; "What did the main character do?") or questions that asked them to analyze the features of an event (e.g., "How was the county fair?"), yet these were the types of questions that their teachers employed in their reading instruction. Instead, the African American children were accustomed to questions that were high on Bloom et al.'s (1956) question taxonomy, but that their teachers did not use, such as, story-starter questions and analogy questions ("What's that like?")

Au and Jordan (1981) observed that Native Hawaiian children were used to working together in small groups to accomplish tasks; they did not rely on adults to explain what they should do. The Hawaiian children's desire to work together was in conflict with their teachers' custom of calling on individual students to answer questions about what they had read. When the teachers accepted the Hawaiian students' use of *text-talk*—overlapping speech in which several children added to each other's answers, then the Hawaiian students increased their level of participation in school (Au, 1980).

More recently, DeNicolo and her colleagues (2017) reported that many bilingual and immigrant students did not feel a strong sense of belonging to their school communities, which influenced their identity construction as school learners. This lack of belonging and identity often occurred when the students' home languages were not valued in school and when their unique talents and skills were not incorporated into their school instruction.

To offset the lack of belonging and identity issues that many minority students feel, several researchers called for schools and teachers to implement linguistically and culturally responsive instruction (DeNicolo et al., 2017; Ladson-Billings, 1995). Turner and Mitchell (2019) defined "culturally relevant pedagogy" as rooted in "caring socioemotional relationships that facilitate culturally diverse students' construction of new academic knowledge and the acquisition of literacy skills and practices while at the same time sustaining their cultural identities and worldviews" (p. 231). They also recommended a critical pedagogical component; that is, they encouraged teachers to specifically focus on getting marginalized students to identify, discuss, and address how larger society marginalized them, and how they were going to counter such marginalization.

To illustrate how culturally responsive literacy instruction can be implemented as a coherent program, we share a current example that focuses on Native Hawaiian students in Hawaii. According to Keehne and her colleagues (2018), when the Hawaiian monarchy was overthrown in 1893, Native Hawaiians no longer could educate their children in Hawaiian because speaking the Hawaiian language was forbidden. Since then, Native Hawaiian students generally have performed poorly on English literacy assessments.

The culturally responsive program consists of five components and has been implemented in a network of 17 Hawaiian charter schools. The first two components include reestablishing the role of the Hawaiian language and/or Native Hawaiian practices and customs in Native Hawaiian students' schooling and establishing and continuing connections with the Hawaiian community. For example, when the school day starts, "students chant in Hawaiian" to indicate that they are ready to learn, "asking permission to enter their classrooms" (Keehne et al., 2018, p. 12). All the schools support the Hawaiian language even when they do not choose to teach in it, realize the values of "'ohana (the extended family)," and view the schools as a way to sustain the larger Hawaiian community (Keehne et al., 2018, p. 14).

The third and fourth components focus on literacy instruction and authentic assessment. An aim of literacy instruction is to build "student ownership and literacy proficiency" in terms of students' contributing to their families and the larger Hawaiian community (Keehne et al., 2018, p. 17). Keehne et al. pointed out that an ideal graduate of the Hawaiian schools "should understand their cultural identity . . . and advocate for their communities" (p. 19). The assessment should evaluate how well students value the "Hawaiian language and culture" and demonstrate "ownership, higher level thinking, and community 'service'" (p. 21). A major accomplishment was getting the state of Hawaii to include evaluations of the students' Hawaiian literacy performance as part of the state's achievement scores.

The fifth and last component is "instructional content and context" (Keehne et al., 2018, p. 25), which focuses on developing English and Hawaiian literacies and student knowledge of the historical traditions of the specific Hawaiian schools that students attended. Two instructional aims are to highlight the past resistance of Native Hawaiians to colonialism and to "recognize the need for continued resistance to rebuild the Hawaiian nation and achieve social justice for Native Hawaiians" (p. 29).

To develop a culturally responsive literacy program similar to the one in Hawaii, you need to know the history of the community's educational efforts and attain a considerable amount of insider cultural information. It also is helpful if you know the community's language(s). Turner and Mitchell (2019) recommended that school personnel "learn about their students' cultural histories, practices, and literacies rather than trying to implement essentialized [e.g., stereotypical] static definitions of culture (p. 231). We agree with their warning. Two ways that school administrators and teachers can do this is to make home visits, in which their goal is to get to know the families of their students, and community visits, in which they attend local events and celebrations. Another way to infuse home and community literacy practices into classrooms is to invite family and community members to share hobbies, skills, talents, and uses of literacy with their students (Bezdicek & García, 2012; González et al., 2005; Hernández, 2000).

CONCLUSION

The reading instruction provided to students in high-poverty schools in the United States has not met the federal recommendations for improving students' reading comprehension. Teachers in high-poverty schools should emphasize active instruction, such as coaching, high-level questions, dialogic strategy instruction, and small-group instruction.

Bilingual Latinx students who received literacy instruction in Spanish and English outperformed those who only received literacy instruction in English. To improve the English reading performance of bilingual students, schools need to give them sufficient instruction in their L1 as well as instruction in English. In addition, they should be given the opportunity to employ unique bilingual practices, such as translanguaging, including cross-linguistic transfer, and when appropriate, cognates. Teachers also need to use ESL techniques to make their English instruction comprehensible.

To improve the reading performance of students who speak a marginalized dialect, society needs to reduce its negative views of dialects and help speakers of marginalized dialects attain Standard English through contrastive analysis. When teachers count students' dialect use as an error when students read aloud, adverse instructional consequences often occur. Therefore, teachers who work with dialect speakers should learn the differences between the dialect and Standard English.

New findings from the National Academies highlighted the important role that culture plays in how humans think and learn, with implications for the reading comprehension instruction and performance of diverse groups. Two issues that schools need to deal with are minority students' lack of sense of belonging and identity construction as school learners. Culturally responsive literacy instruction, in which educators include information from their students' families and communities in their literacy practices and curricula, can help provide students with a sense of belonging and improve their identities as school learners.

CHAPTER THREE

Integrating Comprehension, Thinking, and Knowledge Building

GUIDING QUESTIONS

- What function does knowledge play in comprehension?
- What are the unique attributes of each discipline and their relationship to reading comprehension?
- What are the perspectives on the integration of disciplinary knowledge building and reading comprehension instruction?
- What does the research say about specific protocols and programs that integrate reading comprehension instruction with disciplinary knowledge building in the intermediate grades?
- What are research-based principles to consider when transitioning to an integration of literacy and disciplinary knowledge building in the intermediate grades?
- What considerations are needed for emergent bilingual students when integrating comprehension, thinking, and knowledge building?

SETTING THE STAGE

While waiting to begin their grade-level team meeting, two fourth-grade teachers at Mercury Elementary School discuss their recent instructional experiences with the shared reading text, *Number the Stars* (Lowry, 1989). Ms. King reports, "It is a short book, but it has been slow going for my students. I have to stop frequently to explain the historical context that is both unfamiliar and incomprehensible to my students."

Mr. Beckum says, "We are having the same challenges. The book is beautifully written and has important themes. However, I wonder how much of this classic book's message is getting through to my kids when I have to spend time switching back and forth to a map of Europe and essential historical information. Probably 80% of my students have never left their neighborhood except for our school field trips or to visit relatives in another borough."

"I am torn because the message in this book is valuable, and it is a New-bery Award winner. The characters are the same age as our students. Neverthe-less, as 9-year-olds, my kids don't have the prior knowledge or life experiences to make the most of this book. If anything, my ongoing explanations of the historical background make the reading experience tedious for all of us. I feel like I am ruining the book and any chance for my students to ever appreciate it due to the current mismatch," complains Ms. King.

THE CONTRIBUTION OF KNOWLEDGE TO COMPREHENSION

The Mercury Elementary School teachers' experience is shared by many teach-ers working with a district-mandated English language arts (ELA) curriculum or in settings that rely on teacher favorites as their canon. Teachers use the texts as vehicles to support their students' acquisition of particular ELA standards. In order for readers to understand any text, they need to bring relevant prior knowledge to the reading experience (Kintsch, 1988). Prior knowledge is as essential for read-ing informational texts as it is as for reading narrative texts such as *Number the Stars* (Lowry, 1989). In most ELA classrooms, we see teachers supporting children in their efforts to activate the prior knowledge required to understand the shared text. However, children come to classrooms with wide variations in both range and depth of experiences and information. At Mercury Elementary, as in many schools in the United States, students are expected to read and understand texts that are disconnected from their preexisting knowledge or any knowledge that is systemati-cally built into their classroom curriculum. This disconnection puts the burden on teachers to add this content to their curriculum haphazardly, if at all. This demand adds weight to a literacy block that is already stretched thin. As stated by Ms. King, this weight tends to extend the length of lessons and units to the point of student disengagement, thus ruining the book and losing the learning focus.

The Function of Knowledge in Reading Comprehension

Over the years, researchers consistently demonstrated the vital role that knowledge contributes to comprehension (Kintsch, 1988; Recht & Leslie, 1988; S. A. Stahl & Jacobson, 1986; S. A. Stahl et al., 1989; Cervetti et al., 2016). A simple overview of Kintsch's (1988) construction–integration (CI) theory suggests that readers inte-grate text-based information with existing knowledge, prune unimportant or inac-curate information, fill in coherence gaps, and make inferences to arrive at what he calls a *situation model*. The ability to decode the text is necessary but insufficient to arrive at even a *surface* (verbatim) understanding of an academic text (Kintsch,

1998). A *basic* comprehension level requires that the reader apply individual word meanings, analyze complex sentences, and automatically retrieve relevant prior knowledge to arrive at a new mental representation or situation model.

Knowledge as a Comprehension Pressure Point

Kintsch's (1988) CI process also aligns with Perfetti and Adlof's (2012) concept of pressure points discussed in Chapter 1. Fundamental among these pressure points is the reader's prior knowledge. Baseball expertise has been used in many studies to investigate the influence of content knowledge on comprehension. Recht and Leslie (1988) had middle school students read a passage about baseball. Students with high baseball knowledge performed better on several different comprehension tasks than did students with low prior knowledge. Surprisingly, there was no benefit for high reading ability over high knowledge! Miller and Keenan (2009) also demonstrated that when poor readers possessed relevant prior knowledge, they recalled more information than peers who were more proficient readers. This finding has important implications for text selections for students. Students who perform poorly on benchmark text assessments may be disadvantaged by being restricted to low-level materials. When readers have some prior knowledge of a topic, they can read and understand at higher levels than indicated by a benchmark test.

Knowledge's Influence on Strategic Processes

Knowledge also influences a reader's ability to utilize cognitive strategies. Another baseball study demonstrated that poor readers familiar with baseball could better utilize the question-generating strategy with baseball texts than with nonbaseball texts (Gaultney, 1995).

The IES RfU studies indicated that students' ability to generate inferences and conduct self-monitoring made the most substantive contributions to their comprehension (Pearson et al., 2020). The above strategies rely heavily on the knowledge that the reader brings to the comprehension process (Kintsch, 1998). Readers with more background knowledge are more likely to connect sections of text to make text-based inferences and create cohesiveness within the text, particularly for texts that lack explicit cohesive connections. Additionally, knowledgeable readers can fill gaps in texts to make more distant or global inferences. Readers with knowledge about a topic are more likely to self-monitor their comprehension process than those without such knowledge.

Knowledge and Inhibitory Control

To comprehend speech or text, children need to inhibit knowledge that is not relevant to the oral or printed content. At a granular level, this would include irrelevant definitions of homophones in speech (*break/brake*), homographs in a text (*wind/wind*) or polysemous words (*run*). However, listeners and readers must also inhibit information that is not directly related to the content and that may distract from the central message or distort it. Listeners or readers with a richer vocabulary and more topical knowledge are more likely to inhibit incorrect information. For example, one of us (Kay) was listening to a child read a story about boys who ran a race around a track. However, when answering questions about the story, it became apparent to Kay that the child had applied the definition of *track* related to an *animal's footprint remaining in dirt,* not the definition for an athletic pathway.

Many children with limited prior knowledge will bring irrelevant information to the reading task, leading to confusion and misunderstanding. Children who are new to English may not have the English language skills to match the text with their bank of experiences. Additionally, children with attention difficulties may find retrieving and specifying the relevant prior knowledge to the passage they are reading challenging. Reading programs such as Guided Reading (Fountas & Pinnell, 2016) and Teachers College Units of Study (Calkins, 2015, 2017) limit children to reading texts at a particular level, and books vary by topic daily. As a result, these programs result in a disadvantage for many children because they do not build their knowledge and vocabulary within the proximal curriculum.

DISCIPLINARY KNOWLEDGE AND COMPREHENSION

The term *disciplinary literacy* has become more prevalent than *content literacy* in the last 15 years because our understanding of the differences in what counts as knowledge within literacy, science, social studies, and math has expanded. When we use the term *disciplinary literacy,* we recognize that each discipline has its own "*core constructs:* (a) epistemology (i.e., beliefs about how knowledge is built and communicated); (b) inquiry practices; (c) overarching concepts, themes, and framework; (d) forms of informational representation/types of texts; and (e) discourse and language structures" (Goldman, Britt, et al., 2016, p. 220). This ideology is very different from content literacy that focuses on teaching a set of facts and concepts. Disciplinary literacy encompasses each field's *epistemology,* or beliefs about how knowledge is built and communicated. These beliefs permeate the texts that learners read, write, and use to build their cognitive networks of knowledge.

Literary Knowledge

Literary texts teach us about humanity and the sociocultural influences of the world in which we live. Lived experience and linguistic craftsmanship intertwine to create the most powerful literary texts. Literary texts invite us to dialogue with others because multiple viewpoints will expand our comprehension of the themes, characters, and worldviews. Literary criticism evaluates how authors handle content, text structure, and linguistic craftsmanship to convey their message (see Table 3.1).

Delia Owens describes *Beloved* as the last great book that she read by saying that it "reached so deep that it tore my heart open with the roaming loneliness of *Beloved*" (Tamki, 2019). As readers, we often judge the quality of literature by the author's ability to help us understand others while opening the deepest part of our souls to remind us that we are not alone. As teachers of students in the intermediate grades, we want to convey these unique epistemological characteristics through questioning, discussion, and explicit examples during both the reading and writing processes.

Historical Knowledge

Historians try to understand historical events through the study of multiple primary and secondary documents. Historical and news sources are open to interpretation. However, unlike literary texts, historical documents often contain indisputable facts such as dates and major events for readers to consider. Both historians and readers of historical texts need to consider the source (author and media), context (time, place written), and level of corroboration for the information in the text (Wineburg, 1991). One example of how disciplinary literacy differs from content literacy is the shift from a focus on memorizing historical facts to becoming a participant in ongoing argumentation that contributes to the provisional interpretation of the past (Goldman, Britt, et al., 2016; Herrenkohl & Cornelius, 2013.) As teachers, we often ask our students to provide textual evidence for their responses to a question. What happens when they do not read multiple sources or critique the source, context, and corroboration for the evidence that they select? In that case, we violate the principles of historical knowledge building and, instead, we foster practices that lead to uninformed, flawed, and possibly dangerous conclusions.

TABLE 3.1. Disciplinary Criteria for Text Evidence

Literary (Rosenblatt, 1978)	Social studies (Wineberg, 1991)	Science (Duschl & Osborne, 2002; Herrenkohl & Cornelius, 2013)	Web resources (Beck, 1997; Coiro, 2003)
• Story grammar elements • Theme • Author point of view • Author craft • Universal human experience	• Context (time, place written) • Source (author and media) • Corroboration of information by other sources	• Precise language • Quality of data • Corroboration of information by other studies • Comprehensiveness of experimental sample • Visual evidence (tables, charts, diagrams, models)	• Accuracy • Author background • Objectivity • Recency • Comprehensive coverage of topic

Note. From Stahl (2014). Copyright © the International Literacy Association. Reprinted by permission.

The practice of asking students to identify evidence from a single piece of text contributes to some of the challenges associated with the saturation of information in the digital age. Today's iGens, those born between 1995 and 2012, are more likely to obtain information from short Internet blasts, memes, and tweets instead of primary sources or more comprehensive peer-reviewed sources (Twenge et al., 2019). Additionally, they tend to "pluck" the information they need to accomplish an isolated task rather than utilize their resources to contribute to an evolving network of knowledge (Alexander, 2018). During the 2020 election, US Americans across the political spectrum demonstrated a need for more education in critical reading skills concerning government and civic responsibility. As teachers, it is our responsibility to teach these essential disciplinary literacy skills.

Scientific Knowledge

The COVID-19 pandemic revealed the general public's lack of understanding regarding the scientific process. Many citizens lost confidence in federal health experts due to their frequently changing health advice rather than seeing the evolving protocol recommendations as part of a scientific process. As educators, we are responsible for teaching this process to our students as part of elementary science instructional routines (Next Generation Science Standards Lead States, 2013).

Science knowledge consists of learning about the physical world, life, Earth, space, and engineering. "Science inquiry builds scientific knowledge from developing coherent, logical explanations, models or arguments from evidence" (Goldman, Britt, et al., 2016, p. 232). Scientists develop theories or tentative explanations about their observations or the evidence collected. Scientists evaluate empirical data based on whether they meet the criteria for reliability (consistency of outcomes) and validity (tests measure what they intend to measure). As they learn more, they revise their theories.

Students need to become familiar with how scientists communicate the scientific process and outcomes. However, science discourse is quite different from most of the texts that we read daily. Grammatical structures, such as the use of a passive, objective voice; precise language; and dense, complex, and unfamiliar content make scientific texts among the most difficult to comprehend and compose.

In the elementary grades, administrators need to allocate resources and classroom time for the hands-on, concrete activities that demonstrate scientific concepts. In today's classrooms, videos also are a useful tool to support the development of students' scientific knowledge. Additionally, teachers need to invest the time needed to guide students' reading and writing of science-related texts. See Chapter 6 on how to use the gradual release of responsibility (Pearson & Gallagher, 1983) to guide students' comprehension of texts in science and Chapter 8 on how to write texts in science.

Epistemological Implications for the Intermediate Grades

As teachers, we should not expect students to automatically develop disciplinary literacy skills. During reading activities, we recommend that teachers point out the epistemological characteristics of texts. When students are writing scientific reports, teachers should model the appropriate text structure, the use of headings, precise language, and graphics before holding students accountable for writing a report independently. One of Kay's graduate students, Ms. Camellia, noticed that her fifth graders were describing every piece of data in separate sentences within the results section of their scientific experiment reports. Therefore, after their next experiment, Ms. Camellia provided a lesson on writing the results section of the report. She used her smartboard to model how to use precise language to describe the findings in a short summary statement and then displayed the facts and data in a table. She also made a class chart highlighting tips for writing each section of a research report. On this chart, she included specific words to exclude from the results section such as *suggests* or *because*. These features are unique to scientific writing. We need to call attention to them when we are reading scientific reports and model them before assigning students to write a scientific report.

In the intermediate grades, students begin to read a high volume of informational texts that include new, complex concepts. As we introduce these units to our students, we want to habituate the literacy behaviors that will serve them for a lifetime of learning. We all know that it is more difficult to break bad habits than to learn to do something the correct way from the start. Let's establish some early, basic disciplinary literacy skills before students leave elementary school to attend middle school.

INTEGRATING LITERACY AND DISCIPLINARY INSTRUCTION

In the past, curricula separated the instruction of literacy and content areas as distinctly unique sets of content items that students needed to learn. However, as our understanding of disciplinary literacy has increased, the boundaries have become less distinct. We know that readers need to meet a threshold of word recognition to achieve a basic level of comprehension (O'Connor et al., 2002; Wang et al., 2019). We also know that good readers use a common set of general cognitive strategies that supports reading comprehension in all disciplinary areas (Shanahan & Shanahan, 2008). These cognitive strategies include activating prior knowledge, making purposeful predictions, visualizing, summarizing, questioning, identifying and applying text structure, identifying the levels of importance, generating inferences, and monitoring comprehension (see Chapter 6). However, since the introduction of the CCSS, the NGSS (Next Generation Science Standards Lead States, 2013), and the C3SSS (NCSS, 2013), it has become increasingly important to teach elementary students how to read, write, and build knowledge in ways that reflect the practices of each discipline. In the last section, we addressed what it means to teach literary, social studies, and science standards in today's classrooms. However, if reading and communicating historical or scientific knowledge calls for understanding that community's procedural and Discourse nuances, how do we find time in the day to do it all?

Traditionally, each discipline wanted schools to preserve time to teach their discipline separately. Literacy experts and teachers were afraid that they would need to give up the essential time needed to teach basic skills or favorite literature if they integrated science or social studies into the too-short literacy block. Science and social studies experts often observed science and historical content becoming diluted and trivialized when taught in tandem with literacy. However, in most schools, reading is the "curriculum bully," crowding out science and social studies (Cervetti et al., 2006). Many elementary schools allocate 30–45 minutes in the afternoon to a rotating schedule of social studies or science. When schools have early closures, assemblies, or other disruptions, science and social studies are always the first to go. Many of Kay's university elementary education students report never seeing science or social studies being taught in their student teaching field placements. When they are taught, teachers often do not use the current standards for their grade level. Instead, they teach Native Americans in November and Black history in February. Other popular units include the solar system, plants, or biomes. Some grade levels spend a half year researching the city or the ocean. These half-year projects often involve decorating the room to look like a particular environment and creating engaging parent performances or displays. Expansive units like these crowd out the engineering or physical science units that often hold less appeal for elementary school teachers.

There is now strong evidence that when intentionally planned, the integration of science or social studies with literacy can yield positive results in each discipline, without compromising either field, and may increase learning more than when taught in isolation (Cervetti et al., 2012; Connor et al., 2017; Guthrie et al., 2004; Romance & Vitale, 1992). Romance and Vitale's (2017) longitudinal study of the Science IDEAS program, which integrated literacy and science, yielded statistically significant direct-achievement effects in grades 3–5 and transfer effects in grades 6–7 on standardized science and reading comprehension tests. In another experimental study that compared an integrated literacy and science approach with a business-as-usual control group in fourth grade, Cervetti and her colleagues reported that the integrated instructional group learned significantly more science concepts and more science vocabulary than the control group (Cervetti et al., 2012).

Connor et al. (2017) conducted a yearlong study of students' performance in the Content Area Literacy Instruction (CALI) program, which integrated social studies or science units with literacy for students in kindergarten through grade 4. CALI students performed better on standardized and researcher-constructed reading comprehension measures than a control group did, especially in grades 3 and 4. The students in CALI also increased their disciplinary content knowledge compared to the control group. Further, students' increased performance in science or social studies appeared to boost their performance in literacy, and vice versa, in a reciprocal manner. The CALI study provided *strong evidence* that instruction in science and social studies can be integrated with literacy instruction in elementary school without negatively impacting students' reading gains. In fact, there is growing evidence that integrating literacy instruction with disciplinary knowledge accelerates achievement in both, rather than compromising student achievement in either!

PROGRAMS THAT INTEGRATE LITERACY AND KNOWLEDGE BUILDING

Over time, several programs achieved success in integrating literacy, science, and/or social studies. Teachers often participated in these programs to help match the national, state, or district content standards with the proposed curriculum. Teacher involvement also ensured that the programs were managed within classroom constraints. As you review the programs below, we suggest that you read to extract the programs' common elements and how the planning teams manipulated the program features to accommodate the unique needs of each school. It is unlikely that you and your grade-level team will be able to adapt one of these programs, as is, for your setting. Most schools with whom we worked gradually transitioned to the model they selected, adding or revising a few units of study each year as they worked toward a master plan.

Science IDEAS

Science IDEAS (Romance & Vitale, 1992, 2017) initially was implemented in fourth-grade classrooms. Over the last 25 years, IDEAS has expanded to include all elementary grades. The model has remained relatively consistent in protocol and student outcomes over time. IDEAS classrooms combine their daily 90-minute literacy block and 30-minute science block to form an expanded 2-hour integrated instructional block. The knowledge-driven curriculum has been based on the district's science and literacy standards. In the original study (Romance & Vitale, 1992), teachers ensured a balance between the new science content and literacy objectives. Today's units are consistent with the NGSS (Next Generation Science Standards Lead States, 2013). The learning routine typically includes science concept introduction through hands-on activities and discussion; the reading of multiple sources that address processes and concepts; discussions in various configurations led by teachers and students; student writing in response to the activities and reading; and embedded assessments (see Table 3.2).

Results indicated that students in the Science IDEAS treatment made significantly greater reading comprehension and science achievement gains than did a business-as-usual group, who participated in traditional literacy and science

TABLE 3.2. Science IDEAS Model of Instruction

Element	Activities
Inquiry/scientific investigation	Hands-on activities, guided open-ended inquiry and discussions, concept verification, scientific proofs and practices
Reading comprehension/ strategy instruction	Explicit, general comprehension strategy instruction; reading multiple text sources; comprehension strategies specific to science
Propositional concept mapping	Unique and important facet of IDEAS; strategy for ongoing visual organization of science concepts and concept relationships
Journaling/writing	Use of gradual release of responsibility to teach students to record their thinking, understanding, and questions as a basis for developing and communicating scientific knowledge
Application activities/ projects	Research and a wide variety of activities in which students apply what they have learned
Prior knowledge/ cumulative review	Strategy development of prior knowledge retrieval and synthesis of knowledge development
Embedded assessments	Formative assessments are embedded within each unit of study

instructional blocks (Romance & Vitale, 1992, 2017). The students who participated in the IDEAS program also displayed a more positive attitude toward science and reading and greater self-confidence in science (Romance & Vitale, 1992). Despite early teacher reservations, teachers in the IDEAS program quickly overcame their misgivings as they saw the enthusiasm of their students and parents.

Concept-Oriented Reading Instruction

Concept-oriented reading instruction (CORI) has been implemented across the elementary and middle school grades with both science and social studies. Guthrie and his team designed CORI to determine how combining motivational techniques with cognitive strategy instruction would impact students' reading comprehension. Guthrie and Humenick (2004) found that utilizing rich content instruction fostered intrinsic motivation in students. *Intrinsic motivation* is the drive or a sense of purpose within the individual rather than originating from an external reward such as a prize. Prominent content goals seemed to contribute to students' close reading to obtain meaning, build knowledge, and understand deeply rather than merely acquiring superficial skills. Guthrie and Humenick also reported that using interesting texts, hands-on activities, collaborative work, and providing students with choices contributed to intrinsic student motivation.

Guthrie et al. (2004) tested CORI with third graders during two 6-week science units. Teachers conducted CORI during daily 90-minute periods. The integrated units employed disciplinary inquiry that featured hands-on activities;

various genres, formats, and levels of texts; student agency regarding reading material, inquiry topics within the unit topic, and work partners; and various opportunities for peer collaboration. Teachers provided explicit strategy instruction to support students' activation of prior knowledge, search for information, questioning, summarization, and use of text structures and organizational information.

CORI students outperformed strategy-only students and traditional-reading-instruction students in reading achievement, motivation, and strategy application on multiple measures, including researcher-designed and standardized assessments. However, the researchers did not conduct any measures of science achievement (Guthrie et al., 2004). Like Science IDEAS, there has been ongoing research on the effectiveness of CORI in other grade levels and with specific student populations. See more information, recent research, and examples of CORI units of study at *www.cori.umd.edu.*

Seeds of Science/Roots of Reading

Seeds of Science/Roots of Reading (SSRR) is an integrated literacy-science curriculum for grades 2–5. It is based on the theory that the development of knowledge and literacy are synergistic (Cervetti et al., 2006, 2007, 2012). The program focuses on in-depth scientific knowledge, academic vocabulary, and essential skills and strategies in literacy and science. A fundamental idea is that literacy instruction is most effective when contextualized within purposeful learning, not as an end to itself. SSRR assumes that knowledge and comprehension are reciprocal, vocabulary is conceptual, texts (read and written) play a dynamic role in the learning cycle, and literacy and science share a common set of cognitive strategies (Cervetti et al., 2006).

Fourth- and fifth-grade SSRR content units consist of four subunits (10 lessons each) to be taught during 45- to 60-minute daily sessions. SSRR utilizes a Do-it, Talk-it, Read-it, Write-it approach. Teachers explicitly teach students to build new knowledge, read, write, and discuss as scientists do. For example, explicit instruction, modeling, and guided practice in writing summaries and scientific explanations are included in the curriculum. Additionally, during Discourse Circles, students work collaboratively in small groups to analyze a claim or statement, collect evidence that supports and refutes the claim, and engage in a discussion to determine acceptance or rejection of the claim.

Research studies demonstrated that SSRR more effectively promoted science content knowledge, reading comprehension, academic vocabulary growth, and writing development than nonintegrated instruction in grades 2–5 (Cervetti et al., 2007, 2012). For example, Cervetti et al. (2007) found that second and third graders in SSRR performed better than students in business-as-usual literacy-only and science-only instruction. The same was true for fourth and fifth graders in SSRR compared to fourth and fifth graders who received instruction based on state-provided curriculum materials for the same content unit, time, and duration (Cervetti et al., 2012). Researchers also demonstrated that SSRR was effective with emergent bilingual students (Wang & Herman, 2006). For more information, see *https://seedsofsciencerootsofreading.wordpress.com*

Content-Area Literacy Instruction

We focused on the CALI program's design and positive research outcomes earlier in the chapter (Connor et al., 2017). This section will share the instructional elements of the CALI program in grades 2–5. The program integrated literacy and science units and literacy and social studies units at each grade level based on the Florida state standards. The researchers determined that 2–3 weeks was the ideal length of time for each unit of study. Unlike the other programs that we described, research team members, not classroom teachers, taught the lessons during the study. Instructors conducted the lessons four times a week, and taught each introductory *Connect* lesson during a 30-minute, whole-group session. Children worked in small homogeneous groups of five students or less during the *Clarify, Research,* and *Apply* components of the unit. These groupings were based on reading comprehension pretest scores. Instructors led each 15- to 20-minute, small-group session. Compared to the other programs, this program was more instructor-driven with less student agency regarding inquiry, text selection, or peer collaboration. See Table 3.3 for the details of each component in the instructional routine.

The researchers used qualitative and quantitative data from the preliminary design study plus teacher input to refine the CALI program so that it would be less difficult for classroom teachers to replicate. For example, they rewrote trade books to ensure that texts at different reading levels contained the same content

TABLE 3.3. CALI Routines

Process		Activities
Connect	Day 1; whole class	Students will connect the key unit concepts with local, personal life experiences to build enthusiasm, motivation, and interest.
Clarify	Next 3–4 contiguous days; small group	Teacher-supported reading of secondary sources about the topic; instruction on strategic reading and how to navigate the disciplinary demands; support Day 1 connections to build motivation
Research	Next 3–4 contiguous days; small group	Teach students how to read and use primary sources, including disciplinary evidence criteria Science: Conduct experiments/hands-on activities
Apply	Next 3–4 contiguous days; small group	Make connections, draw conclusions, communicate findings through writing, talking, media; reflect on findings

and conceptual vocabulary. They also recommended that teachers use comprehension pretest scores to group students in the homogeneous groups. Despite the above changes, the CALI lesson components are consistent with the processes and activities in the other integrated programs.

CONSIDERATIONS IN DEVELOPING AN INTEGRATED PROGRAM

In this section, we discuss how schools might approach either the purchase or development of an integrated program in grades 3–6. ELA standards address both literacy skills and literary content. There are several shared components among the programs that we reviewed (e.g., explicit comprehension strategy instruction, writing instruction). However, each study also had a few unique characteristics (e.g., attention to student agency, homogeneous grouping). Table 3.4 lists and describes the elements that a district or school should consider when creating or purchasing an integrated program. Although it is not possible for every unit to devote multiple lessons to each of these goals at every grade level, grade-level teams should move toward these goals over time. Incorporating these components into the program increases the likelihood of the cognitive reciprocity and efficiency that characterize the integration of science and/or social studies instruction with literacy instruction.

TABLE 3.4. Components of an Integrated Program

Component	Elements
Inquiry	Hands-on experiences or experiments, research
Content development	Experiences, reading, writing, and talking lead to the development of connected conceptual networks of knowledge shared by the classroom community
Vocabulary	Selection of 10–25 target conceptual and academic vocabulary words that are used multiple times throughout the unit
Reading	Multiples sources of information, primary and secondary sources, explicit cognitive strategy instruction using the GRR, attending to unique disciplinary reading demands such as visuals, tables, diagrams
Writing	Writing for multiple purposes related to the unit; explicit instruction using GRR of both general and disciplinary writing that is related to the unit
Epistemological awareness	Fostering practices of evidence gathering, evidence critique, writing and discussion practices that are unique to the discipline (e.g., participating in the unit like a historian or scientist)
Collaborative	Opportunities for students to work together to solve problems, discuss texts, create projects, and build knowledge
Agency	Some opportunities for students to choose texts, partnerships, and projects that serve the community knowledge-building mission related to the unit

Into Action

To our knowledge, there currently are not any commercial integrated programs that include literary, science, *and* social studies units. Each school that Kay worked with developed their own curriculum. Some schools purchased commercially produced units that included lesson plans and materials that publishers aligned with the NGSS (e.g., Rourke Educational Materials; *www.deltaeducation.com/foss/ next-generation*) or materials that were produced to meet the goals of the NGSS (e.g., *https://communitywaters.org*). We recommend that you approach this work patiently with a long-term plan. Most schools that Kay worked with made the transition over a 2- to 3-year period.

Scheduling Integrated Instruction

Schools need to decide on an integrated model option. Some schools prefer to commit to full integration (e.g., Science IDEAS, CORI, SSRR) that combines the literacy block and allocated science/social studies time to create a single extended 90- to 120-minute integrated time block.

The second option maintains separate existing time frames but plans for content unit consistency across the two time blocks. In the second option, schools use the traditional literacy block to do the reading and writing associated with the unit and a separate content-area time block to do the hands-on activities. Two schools that Kay worked with selected a teacher identified as the "content specialist" to teach the content block. The content specialist did all the hands-on activities, experiments, fieldwork, and some science units that did not fit into an integrated approach.

Kay taught in a school that used a parallel block scheduling model as a means of integrating literacy and content in grades 2–5 (see Figure 3.1). The school faculty decided to increase the classroom size from 20 to 25 students in order to utilize one member of each grade-level team as a content lab teacher and math interventionist (during the math period). Each grade-level team used this model to incorporate daily heterogeneous whole-class shared reading/writing, small-group homogeneous reading/writing, and in-depth content work centered on a single unit of disciplinary study. The classroom teacher provided all the reading and writing instruction related to the disciplinary unit. The content lab teacher conducted most of the hands-on activities and provided the experiences that took advantage of limited, expensive materials, including kits or technology. During literary-focused units, the content lab teacher either took the lead on unit-related research projects or taught science units that were difficult to integrate. Projects and presentations might be done in either setting or collaboratively. Although in this case, the content lab teacher did not have an advanced degree in any disciplinary content area, she quickly became a specialist in the grade-level content units and related resources. After the first year, her expertise and familiarity with available materials for each unit influenced

	Class 1	Class 2	Class 3	Class 4
7:50–8:00	Opening	Opening	Opening	Opening
8:00–8:45	Whole-Class Word Study	*8 Below-Level Students	*17 On-Level/ Above-Level Students	Whole-Class Shared Reading/ Writing
		17 On-Level/ Above-Level Students to Content Lab	8 Below-Level Students to Content Lab	
8:45–9:30	Whole-Class Shared Reading/ Writing	Whole-Class Word Study	*8 Below-Level Students	*17 On-Level/ Above-Level Students
			17 On-Level/ Above-Level Students to Content Lab	8 Below-Level Students to Content Lab
9:30–10:15	*17 On-Level/ Above-Level Students	Whole-Class Shared Reading/ Writing	Whole-Class Word Study	*8 Below-Level Students
	8 Below-Level Students to Content Lab			17 On-Level/ Above-Level Students to Content Lab
10:15–11:00	*8 Below-Level Students	*17 On-Level/ Above-Level Students	Whole-Class Shared Reading/ Writing	Whole-Class Word Study
	17 On-Level/ Above-Level Students to Content Lab	8 Below-Level Students to Content Lab		
11:00–11:45	Lunch (30 min.)	Lunch (30 min.)	Lunch (30 min.)	Lunch (30 min.)
11:45–12:30	Recess (30 min.) Class Miscellaneous (30 min.)	Recess (30 min.) Class Miscellaneous (30 min.)	Recess (30 min.) Class Miscellaneous (30 min.)	Recess (30 min.) Class Miscellaneous (30 min.)
12:30–1:15	Math	Math	Math	Math
1:15–2:00	Specials	Specials	Specials	Specials
2:00–2:20	Closure	Closure	Closure	Closure

FIGURE 3.1. Example of an integrated instruction schedule. Shading indicates heterogeneous- content class. *Small-group-differentiated integrated instruction with the homeroom teacher.

the classroom reading, writing, and projects. As years went on, the curriculum and learning periods become more homogenized.

The school ecology and resources will often dictate the scheduling decisions. However, it is likely that most schools will want to create a curriculum calendar that spends approximately 12 weeks each teaching literary, science, and social studies integrated units distributed across a 36-week academic year.

Building Integrated Units

The first step is to plan a calendar that incorporates the essential units dictated by the CCSS ELA standards, NGSS, and C3SSS, or the respective state standards. In our experience, grade-level planning teams at the school or district level do this work. Typically, teachers who previously taught related content in separate units, begin by combining literary and content-area units that fit together organically.

In a few schools where Kay worked as a consultant, grade-level teams began by creating a large calendar chart on butcher paper to display their current ELA and science/social studies units (see Figure 3.2). Another way to do it is on a shared Google document. However, the teachers with whom Kay worked were not fans of reading shared documents online to get the "big picture." After each grade level completed a chart, all charts were displayed in a meeting room and shared at vertical grade-level meetings. This landscape view of all the charts made it very easy to see connections and disconnections across grade levels. The teachers discovered that some content units, such as "plants," were being taught the same way in multiple grade levels.

At Lake View School (pseudonym), this process was undertaken shortly after the introduction of NGSS and C3SSS. Therefore, the aim was to use the new standards to create integrated units that met all the criteria for social studies, science, and literacy standards logically so that content was neither duplicated nor left out in a vertical curriculum. After comparing current units to units required by the new standards, the teachers created a new integrated unit calendar. They had to abandon some former literacy units. However, the richest literary content became part of a comprehensive literary unit with more cohesion and depth than their original units. They moved other isolated reading material within the appropriate science or social studies units.

Once the calendar was in place, the teachers planned the big ideas and objectives for each unit (see Form 3.1 at the end of the chapter). At this stage of the process, the teams began sharing their ongoing work on Google docs or another school sharing platform. Kay supported one school that began building its units during the spring and summer of 2017. During the 2017–2018 academic year, they taught units that they had developed. Many of these units were revisions and updates of units previously used in either ELA or science/social studies. The revisions were integrated and taught to achieve the new complexity of the C3SSS and NGSS. By

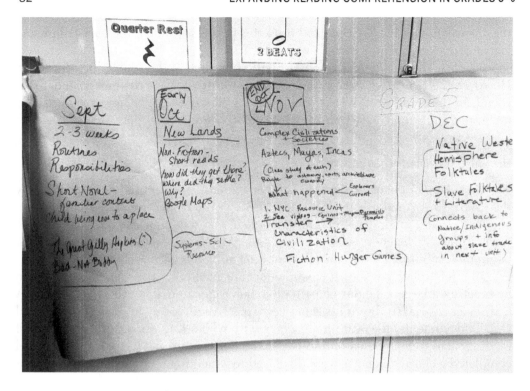

FIGURE 3.2. Example of a calendar chart for ELA and science/social studies units.

the 2018–2019 academic year, they had added newly required units and tweaked the 2017–2018 units based on observations and experiences they acquired while instructing their students. This time frame and process was somewhat similar across multiple schools that Kay supported.

CONSIDERATIONS FOR BILINGUAL STUDENTS

Providing themed instruction on the same topic across two fields (e.g., literacy and science or literacy and social studies) usually is helpful for current emergent bilingual students (those receiving bilingual or ESL instruction) and former emergent bilingual students (those exited from such instruction and now in the all-English classroom) because the increased amount of instructional time and the different contexts in which students are exposed to the same topic deepen all students' background knowledge. Also, integrated instruction often means that bilingual students are exposed to multiple uses of the same vocabulary, and provided with increased opportunities to hear, see, read, and write the same vocabulary, two characteristics of high-quality vocabulary instruction. However, bilingual students only accrue these benefits if they comprehend their teachers' English instruction. Therefore, if you are involved in integrated instruction that includes emergent bilingual students, please be sure to employ the bilingual and ESL instructional techniques described in Chapter 2.

An additional ESL technique that you can employ to make your integrated instruction comprehensible to bilingual students is from the SIOP (Echevarría et al., 2012, 2016). When fields like ELA and science or social studies are integrated, bilingual students often find it difficult to identify what they are supposed to learn, making it hard for them to focus their attention and monitor their learning. You can help offset these problems when you post in writing, orally read, and frequently review the specific learning objectives for each of the integrated fields by specifying the content to be learned, tasks to accomplish, and how students are to accomplish the tasks. For example, if you are integrating your study of science fiction in English language arts by reading a story about life in space and your study of the universe in science, you could post the following objectives:

English Language Arts
1. Decide on the parts of the story that are fiction (not true).
2. Write your answer in your response log.

Science
1. Complete the graphic organizer on how Venus and Earth are different.
2. Discuss with your partner why humans cannot breathe on Venus.

For information on how to write objectives for your integrated instruction, we refer you to the Center for Applied Linguistics websites (*https://cal.org/siop/about*; *www.tesoltrainers.com/siop-lesson-preparation.html*) or to one of the SIOP books (Echevarría et al., 2012, 2106). Classroom teachers who posted, stated, and reviewed lesson objectives for their classroom instruction, reported to Georgia that all their students benefited, not just their emergent bilingual students.

We also encourage you to provide bilingual education teachers, the school librarian, and ESL teachers who work with your emergent bilingual students with a list of the topics (in the summer or as early in the school year as possible) that you and your colleagues plan to cover during the school year. Because it is easier for emergent bilingual students to learn new information in the language they know best, it is helpful when you collaborate with the bilingual education teachers so that they present new conceptual information in students' L1 before the students encounter it in their integrated instruction. In addition, you can ask the school librarian to provide your bilingual students with L1 texts, abridged English texts, or easy texts in English that they can read independently on the topics that you cover in your integrated instruction. Lastly, we encourage you to ask the teachers in charge of ESL instruction (this could be the bilingual education teacher or ESL teacher) to present your emergent bilingual students with instruction on new English vocabulary items and syntactic/rhetorical structures for the topics that you plan to cover later in the school year. Although some bilingual education and ESL teachers may have set curricula that they have to cover, many of them will be interested in collaborating with you, especially if you give them advanced notice.

CONCLUSION

Knowledge plays a critical role in reading comprehension. Readers need to activate relevant prior knowledge before and during the reading process. During reading, readers need to prune irrelevant or inaccurate prior knowledge as they integrate what they know with the information in the text to arrive at a situation model or expanded networks of knowledge. Readers rely on prior knowledge to make within-text and more global inferences. Of key importance, knowledge contributes to a reader's ability to self-monitor and repair a meaning-making hurdle.

Students in the intermediate grades increasingly read more texts to learn new information. Each discipline has unique core constructs that define how knowledge is built and communicated (epistemology). These constructs are infused into the texts that learners read, write, and use to build the knowledge of that disciplinary content. Although there are several general reading and writing strategies that cross disciplinary boundaries (e.g., asking questions, summarizing), there are unique nuances within each discipline that need to be addressed as one engages in the practices of that discipline.

Although historically, advocates of each discipline have expressed concern that integrating science and social studies instruction with literacy would compromise the learning of each, a body of work over the last 30 years has demonstrated that integration can enhance both literacy learning and content learning in a discipline for all students, including emergent bilingual students. Rather than compromising student achievement, research indicates that integration can accelerate synergistic growth in reading comprehension, academic vocabulary, disciplinary writing, and knowledge building when compared to isolated instruction.

Whether teachers are building their own integrated units or using commercially produced programs, there are common components of effective integrated programs. Effective programs include hands-on experiences and content instruction, opportunities for wide reading, writing for authentic purposes, and repeated opportunities to use target vocabulary. Instruction develops epistemological awareness that engages students in knowledge building consistent with experts in the field of study. Finally, learning is engaging, collaborative, and allows for student agency.

FORM 3.1

Unit Introduction Template

Month	Topic	Content Discipline	Texts	Writing Focus

Big Ideas—Connective tissue or conceptual Velcro. Big ideas transfer to other contexts and manifest themselves in various ways within disciplines. Examples of transferable big ideas are change, exploration, freedom, power, justice, and so forth.

Essential Questions—Essential questions are open-ended. They "hook" the students into wanting to learn more about the topic. Every lesson within a unit should be exploring one of the essential questions cited for the unit. When writing essential questions, teachers should ask themselves, "What should my students remember and be able to do, or reflect on, a year from now?"

Essential Vocabulary (15–25)—Taught, tested throughout and at conclusion of unit

(continued)

Comprehension Strategy Focus—*What comprehension strategies will help students overcome the meaning-making hurdles of the texts encountered in the unit? (Pick 2/3 to teach directly and explicitly: activation and appropriate use of prior knowledge; purposeful predictions; visualization; text structure-narrative, expository-descriptive, compare-contrast, sequential, problem-solution; cause-effect; inference generation; ideational prominence; summarizing; questioning; monitoring; evaluation-critique)*

Skills—Knowledge that students need to arrive at big ideas, answer essential questions; facts, details, procedural processes

STANDARDS: Large-grain learning outcomes

Content Standards:

Reading Standards:

Writing Standards:

Speaking/Listening Standards:

(continued)

56

OBJECTIVES: What are the observable, measurable learning outcomes of the unit?

ASSESSMENTS:

PROJECTS:

FIELD TRIPS:

CHAPTER FOUR

Selecting and Working with Texts and Digital Resources

GUIDING QUESTIONS

- What factors should teachers consider when they select texts for intermediate students?

- How can teachers plan for a good match between students' reading abilities and texts?

- What kinds of instructional support do intermediate students need to access and comprehend a wide variety of texts?

- What factors should teachers consider when selecting texts and planning reading instruction support for emergent bilingual students?

SETTING THE STAGE

Ms. Dimitri (pseudonym) was working with her fourth-grade class on a Colonial Days unit. On Monday, she grouped the students in threes and had each triad study a map and a small assortment of pictures from the Introduction and Chapter 1, "Getting Dressed," from the book *The Scoop on Clothes, Homes, and Daily Life in Colonial America* (Raum, 2020). Ms. Dimitri assigned each triad to write a set of inferences based on the map, pictures, and captions in their assigned collection. On Day 2, the triads made a 3-column table in their notebooks with headings for *Page, Confirmed Inferences*, and *New Learning*. All students had a print copy of the text. Ms. Dimitri read the Introduction to the class, followed by a brief discussion. Together, they looked at the map and discussed the inferences that some of the children previously had made on Day 1. Next, Ms. Dimitri recorded a few confirmed inferences on chart paper as the children recorded them in their notebooks. Additionally, new information from the Introduction was added to the *New Learning* column. Then, she directed the triads to follow the modeled procedure for gathering information from Chapter 1. Each group could decide if they wanted to read the text orally or silently with or without the prerecorded audio recording that Ms. Dimitri had made and placed in their Colonial Days Google folder. After reading Chapter 1, Ms. Dimitri asked each triad to discuss the chapter, confirm or disconfirm yesterday's inferences, and add confirmed inferences and new learning to the table in their notebooks.

THE CHALLENGE OF TEXT SELECTION

If you are like other teachers, you may spend hours looking for "just-right" texts to support your students' reading and knowledge development. The increased demand for students to read complex texts (see NGA & CCSSO, 2010) has created a tension between picking texts that students can read successfully and picking complex texts that promote new learning. Additionally, many school districts today do not adopt core literacy programs that provide all the texts needed for units of study. They also do not purchase science and social studies textbooks. As a result, classroom teachers often are in charge of finding texts for their students.

As a teacher in the intermediate grades you may face a number of challenges when selecting texts for your students. For example, you may have a wide range of reading levels in your classroom. It is not unusual for a sixth-grade teacher to have students in the same class who are reading at a second-grade level along with students reading at a high school level. This challenge is compounded by having to locate texts that match your state's learning standards in the content areas. Budgetary restrictions also make your decisions difficult and limit your choices. Many teachers spend thousands of dollars a year from their personal funds to ensure that their students have appropriate reading materials. Online resources have helped to offset some of these challenges. However, you, like other teachers, probably spend countless hours reviewing reading materials to make appropriate selections for your students. (See Appendix B for a list of text and curriculum resources.)

MATCHING TEXT FORMS TO LEARNING GOALS

The intermediate grades offer you and your students exciting opportunities to participate in a world of print and digital resources that far exceed what most primary teachers utilize in their classrooms. Rather than trying to match your text selection to a preset quantitative balance of fiction and nonfiction, choosing texts to achieve learning goals will *result* in the balance required by your learning standards. Modern literary, science, and social studies standards call for students to read and write a wide range of texts (NGA & CCSSO, 2010; National Council for the Social Studies, 2013; Next Generation Science Standards Lead States, 2013). Therefore, school personnel need to identify, categorize, and provide various print and digital texts to meet the learning goals. A proper balance of text types is *the effect* of deliberate attention to texts needed for building different kinds of knowledge.

We have attempted to list and describe the types of texts found in intermediate classrooms loosely by genre. However, more recent use of the term *genre* acknowledges the situational influences on categorizing a text's genre (Fox, 2004). Therefore, the purpose, context, and the reading response influence the categorization.

Fiction

Authors draw from their imaginations and personal experiences to create fictional texts. Sometimes, they adapt true stories. Most novels and stories adhere to a narrative text structure. A narrative text structure typically includes a setting, characters, a problem for characters to solve or a goal that the characters are trying to achieve, episodes that depict attempts to solve the problem or achieve the goal, and a resolution. When writing fiction, authors tend to elaborate with sensory details. Details and artistic style variation are often valued as indicators of an author's craftsmanship. Fictional genres include realistic fiction, historical fiction, fairytales, fables, tall tales, folktales, mysteries, legends, science fiction, fantasy, and mythology. Fictional genres are typically the vehicle for literary units in classrooms.

Drama

Drama is a fictional text format that uses dialogue and performance to tell a story. Drama includes plays, operas, mimes, and ballets (Banham, 1998). Drama performances may be performed in a theater, on television, in a movie, on the radio, or on the street.

Poetry

Poetry is a form of literary text that is based on the interplay of words and rhythm. Before written language, rhythm and rhyme were used to help people remember information. Early poetry rules for rhyme and meter varied by culture. Although these classical forms can still be found, today's poetry often achieves a rhythmic quality without adherence to traditional, rule-bound structures. The salient feature of all poetry is the use of words to create images and emotion. In today's classrooms, it is valuable to share how songs and poetry can be used for multiple purposes, including appreciating beauty or sending powerful political messages.

Nonfiction

Nonfiction is any prose that is based on facts, data, real events, or real people. Any deviation from real occurrences threatens the text's value and credibility. There are many genres and subgenres of nonfiction. The different text structures used to organize the ideas in nonfiction are one of the challenges involved in reading and understanding it. Additionally, some books, articles, or documents internally switch text structures.

Narrative nonfiction includes biographies, autobiographies, blogs, and magazine and newspaper feature stories (e.g., obituaries, profiles, *New York Times* "Modern Love"). While adhering to facts, authors of these subgenres tend to include more verbose descriptions of events and use stylistic conventions associated with fiction more than other nonfiction genres. Narrative nonfiction also is organized according to a narrative text structure.

The purpose of expository text is to convey information. Textbooks, newspapers, journal articles, and other informational texts are expository texts. The most common text structures employed in expository texts are sequential, problem–solution, descriptive, compare–contrast, and cause–effect. For more information, see Chapter 6 and Chapter 8.

Students need to be exposed to other forms of text that they encounter in their daily lives. Procedural texts include all texts that describe a sequence for how to do something. Recipes, experimental procedures, rules for games, and "how-to" books or posters are commonly utilized procedural texts. Field notes, interviews, newspaper articles, and editorials are also examples of nonfiction texts. Functional texts, such as flyers and schedules, also warrant instruction.

Digital Resources

All of the texts described earlier can be found in either print or digital formats. However, some forms of text are only accessible digitally (e.g., blogs, websites, webpages, social media posts). Districts or grade-level teams need to add lessons on how to read and compose digital texts as part of their curricula.

Primary Sources and Secondary Sources

Nonfiction texts may be categorized as primary or secondary sources of information. Primary sources are firsthand forms of evidence. They include original documents, raw scientific data, photographs, letters, interviews, and other artifacts. Many fifth-grade classrooms in New York do a close reading of the "Universal Declaration of Human Rights" when studying immigration, human rights, and reading the novel *Esperanza Rising* (*www.engageny.org*; Ryan, 2012). See the National Council for Social Studies website to access free webinars describing how to use primary sources effectively: *www.socialstudies.org/inquiry-and-teaching-with-primary-sources.*

Secondary sources include forms of information and commentary from other researchers, books, journal articles, or reviews describing, interpreting, or synthesizing primary sources. Most books used in classrooms are secondary sources, such as *The Scoop on Clothes, Homes, and Daily Life in Colonial America* (Raum, 2020). Even though the book has artifacts and text boxes that contain quotes from the time period (cited in other secondary sources), these count as secondary sources because we are not observing the original source.

MATCHING TEXTS AND STUDENTS

For students in the intermediate grades, interacting with the large volume and variety of texts demanded by the curriculum can be challenging. As a result, we often see students experience what is known as the "fourth-grade slump" (Hirsch, 2003, p. 10). However, the sudden dip in reading performance can happen as early as late second or early third grade, depending on the classroom reading demands.

Several factors contribute to the plummeting reading performance of intermediate students. If students are not able to read texts fluently because of sluggish decoding, lack of automaticity in recognizing high frequency English words, and lack of conceptual vocabulary knowledge, the increased text length and unfamiliar information in the texts can pose overwhelming challenges, resulting in students feeling frustrated and defeated. Homework that should take 45 minutes may take 2 or 3 hours, destroying family recreational time, and causing family discord.

Text Readability Levels

In an earlier section, we discussed the variety of texts that need to be included in the reading diet of intermediate readers. However, to achieve a balanced diet of content and text genres, students will need to read texts that span a wide range of difficulty. Determining a text's difficulty can be challenging and is made even more confusing by the numerous metrics used to measure text difficulty. The CCSS model of text complexity (NGA & CCSSO, 2010) identifies three dimensions for teachers to consider when determining text complexity: qualitative characteristics, quantitative characteristics, and reader and task considerations. This means that looking at a single commercial readability label on a text is only a first step in determining whether a text is appropriate for a student or a group of students. Teachers need to preread the texts and evaluate each text according to the following three dimensions.

Qualitative Characteristics

Qualitative features include levels of meaning, such as whether the text's purpose is explicit or has subtleties that call for critical analysis. Complex levels of meaning may also be influenced by linguistic devices such as figurative language or satire.

Texts written in clear, conversational language are easier to understand than texts that use unfamiliar, archaic, or academic language. Visuals may either support comprehension (e.g., pictures, photographs, maps) or pose obstacles (e.g., graphs, charts). Knowledge demands also influence readability in both narrative and informational texts. Text length is another qualitative feature that affects the readability of texts. Finally, texts with simplistic, familiar, clearly signaled text structures are more readable than texts with nonconventional text structures such as nonlinear time sequences.

Producers of qualitative reading gradients tend to consider many of these features when determining text levels (e.g., Fountas & Pinnell, 2016; Reading A–Z). However, one of the challenges of qualitative metrics is that they often vary from company to company. Additionally, teachers cannot reliably identify what qualitative criteria determined the difficulty level if they only use the text level number (or letter) as a gauge of text complexity.

Quantitative Characteristics

Quantitative measures have been used over time to identify text readability. Different formulas use multiple factors to generate a numerical readability level for a section of text. Most formulas use some combination of sentence length, word length, frequency of English word use, and sentence structure. These factors each contribute to comprehension difficulty. Lexile, one of the most commonly used measures today, uses word frequency and sentence length to arrive at a fine gradient of text difficulty (*www.Lexile.com*). Coh-Metrix is a newer quantitative reporting system that measures text cohesion. Text cohesion includes factors such as word concreteness, sentence complexity, references within a passage (e.g., pronouns), causal connections, and adherence to a narrative structure (e.g., plot line, temporal signal words) (Graesser et al., 2011). According to Graesser and his colleagues, high-cohesion texts explicitly signal the relationship among words, sentences, and ideas so that readers can formulate mental networks more easily. Low-cohesion texts force the reader to do more cognitive work (e.g., retrieve knowledge and connect sections of text). Although teachers do not typically access this metric to determine readability, cohesion is an important factor for you to consider when previewing a text or when organizing a text set for a unit of study.

Reader and Task Considerations

The third dimension of the CCSS Model of Text Complexity (NGA & CCSSO, 2010) acknowledges the role that individual reader factors and differences in reading response tasks play in determining the difficulty of the reading process. This dimension puts the primary responsibility on the teacher to evaluate the readers' comprehension pressure points that influence how complex the text will be for them. In Chapters 1 and 3, we discussed how the pressure points (e.g., decoding, vocabulary, knowledge, motivation, reading purpose, instructional support) work together dynamically to contribute to the comprehension process.

Your lesson plans largely influence whether a text is appropriate for a reader or a group of readers in your classroom. As a result, a text that might be too difficult in one context might be manageable in a different context. For example, having students chorally partner read a text is one way to make a stretch text easier than it would be for students to read the same text independently (Brown et al., 2018). A text's readability is affected by the purpose for reading, the type of instructional support, whether knowledge building is embedded in the unit, and the follow-up reading response task. Only you can make this determination.

Student Reading Levels

Instructional reading levels are useful estimates of reading competency, but they should not dictate the texts that students read in the intermediate grades (Brown et al., 2018; O'Connor et al., 2002). They provide an *estimate* of how well a reader reads and responds to a text at a single point in time. We address reading assessments in detail in Chapter 9.

Identifying Estimates of Student Reading Levels

Instructional reading levels are determined by asking students to perform an unrehearsed reading of an unfamiliar, random informal reading inventory (IRI) passage, benchmark kit text, or computer-based test passages. The reader answers questions after reading. Each assessment uses a different text readability leveling system. Text levels may be reported as grade level (IRI), qualitatively established commercial text level (benchmark kit), or quantitative Lexile band (computer-based test).

Oral reading accuracy percentages and comprehension percentages are considered in tandem to determine an independent, instructional, or frustrational reading level (Betts, 1946). These reading levels were established and defined by Betts (1946) (see Table 4.1). During his era, traditional reading instruction consisted of teachers setting a reading purpose and providing background information, students reading aloud or silently, followed by teacher-led questioning in a whole-class setting. The minimal level of instructional support influenced the seemingly high standards.

- The *independent level* is the highest level at which a student can read the text without instructional support.
- The *instructional level* is the highest level at which a child is likely to benefit from *traditional* whole-class instructional support.
- The *frustration level* is any level at which a child is likely to be frustrated, even with *traditional* whole-class instructional support.

TABLE 4.1. Betts (1946) Criteria for Reading Assessment Performance

Level	Oral reading word recognition	Comprehension questions correct
Independent	99–100%	90–100%
Instructional	95–98%	75–89%
Gray area[a]	91–94%	51–74%
Frustration	90% or lower	50% or lower

[a]Expand your judgment to include additional quantitative indicators (e.g., fluency rate, retelling) when either score is in the gray area to determine the estimated reading level.

Using Estimated Reading Levels Judiciously

Determining a student's instructional band level is diagnostically useful, but it should never be used to constrain students' reading selections. The estimated instructional reading level is malleable and stretches as instructional support, prior knowledge, and vocabulary increase (Brown et al., 2018; Shanahan et al., 2012; Stahl, 2012). Brown et al. (2018) found that third graders who did paired choral reading of texts that were 2–4 years above their identified instructional level made accelerated overall reading progress compared to a control group that engaged in choice independent reading. O'Connor et al. (2002) determined that third graders working in intervention groups made similar progress reading instructional-level or grade-level materials as long as they read more than 55 words correct per minute. Additionally, when students reach a decoding threshold, other comprehension pressure points exert a stronger influence on readability than decoding does (Perfetti & Adlof, 2012; Paris, 2005; Paris & Hamilton, 2009; Wang et al., 2019). For a full discussion, see Chapters 1 and 3. Once basic foundational skills are in place, prior knowledge, vocabulary, and affective factors should influence text selection decisions more than narrowly restrictive leveling systems. It is humiliating and disengaging for students to be excluded from something they want to read because it does not adhere to a narrow, ambiguous readability band.

We recommend that your reading curriculum model influences your text selection. For example, students engaged in integrated units are likely to have greater success when reading texts on a familiar topic than when reading a cold text with unfamiliar concepts and vocabulary. Our opening vignette demonstrated a few ways that Ms. Dimitri scaffolded her students' reading so that they could successfully comprehend unfamiliar, challenging text. Literacy and social studies were integrated. Therefore, academic vocabulary (e.g., culture, customs, colony, colonial, colonists) was familiar. The unit vocabulary was previously introduced in other settings and during the teacher-led book introduction (e.g., place names, Pilgrims). Prereading instruction, modeling, and discussions established a focused purpose for reading and a social mechanism for sharing comprehension. Ms. Dimitri ensured that her students were held accountable for reading by assigning them to read and

TABLE 4.2. Daily Lesson Components

	Primary purpose	Type of text
Teacher read-aloud (whole class) Instruction—Teacher-led Discussion—Teacher-led	• Comprehension • Vocabulary	• Complex text • Compelling, controversial texts
Shared reading/writing (whole class) Modeling—Teacher and student Discussion—Teacher-facilitated	• Community reading or writing of a common text • Comprehension • Vocabulary • Fluency	• Grade-level text • Complex text
Small group Coaching—Teacher Discussions—Teacher- or student-led	• Differentiated strategy/skill groups • Collaborative work/research • Book clubs • Guided instructional level reading for students performing below third-grade instructional level	Variety of text forms and readability levels
Independent (often occurs simultaneously with small-group activities)	• Preparation for book club or small-group activities • Research, inquiry work • Rereading	Variety of text forms and readability levels

Note. Balance components weekly in middle school settings.

discuss the text in small groups. This procedure guaranteed at least two exposures to the content and vocabulary in the chapter "Getting Dressed." Each text encounter involved talking, reading, and writing.

Within reason, we advise you to not abandon difficult texts. However, this does not mean that you, the teacher, should orally read all the challenging texts as your students listen. Instead, you can provide various types of support, depending on the difficulty of the text and the purpose for your students reading it. A wide variety of classroom instructional structures are instrumental in ensuring that all students receive the support they need to read and discuss engaging grade-appropriate texts. We recommend that your weekly schedule of literacy activities include teacher read-alouds, shared reading/writing and discussion of target texts, small-group differentiation for strategic support or collaborative activities based on interest or estimated reading levels, student-led small-group discussions, and independent reading (see Table 4.2).

INSTRUCTIONAL SUPPORTS FOR WIDE READING

Reading a Common Text

There are many texts that deserve to be part of a grade-level curriculum for different reasons. It may be that a text is an award-winning literary classic, contains information that is important for all members of the class to know, or characterizes the human experience of the events in a social studies unit. We will use the term "core" materials to describe materials that all students in the class read as part of a common learning experience. Core materials can be short texts or visual materials that are used by all students in the class to ensure their achievement of the learning goals. Some core texts may serve as an *anchor text*, also called a *target text*, that is a lengthy text that serves as a centerpiece for a unit of study. It is typically read and discussed across multiple weeks.

Core reading emphasizes the significance of creating and maintaining a classroom literacy-learning community that is not segregated by reading level. All students need opportunities to look beyond text levels to appreciate themselves and others as readers. Whole-class interactions enable students to value each other as individuals who bring important contributions to the conversation and task at hand. Being a member of a classwide reading community provides an opportunity for students to read texts that they might not select themselves.

Due to the range in readability of core texts, students need different levels of scaffolding to make the texts accessible. Although the class is listening to or reading the same text, different types of scaffolding may be necessary to enhance student comprehension. Whole- or small-group activities may be used with core texts.

Interactive Teacher Read-Alouds

Interactive teacher read-alouds occur when the teacher reads the text aloud and engages the students in responding to the text. There are many important reasons for conducting interactive read-alouds in the intermediate grades.

First, the teacher read-aloud provides an opportunity for intermediate students to become familiar with challenging texts. The read-aloud's primary purpose is to teach comprehension and sophisticated vocabulary without students bearing the burden of decoding. As listeners, your students can give their full attention to the story or information. A read-aloud is not a technique for calming students after recess with lights off and heads down. It is a time for thinking, visualizing, questioning, fitting new information into an existing cognitive structure, and making inferences. As a result, prior to a read-aloud can be a good time for you to introduce individual comprehension strategies explicitly and then to have students practice applying them during the read-aloud (see Chapter 6). This also is a good time for you to introduce and define key vocabulary (Beck & McKeown, 2001). This is addressed more fully in Chapter 5.

Fisher et al. (2008) reported that during teacher read-alouds, some teachers used think-alouds to model flexible application of comprehension strategies to make sense of difficult texts. The teachers said that they modeled how to use text features to enhance comprehension and how to use context to determine word meanings. They also encouraged students to ask questions, discuss ideas with a partner, and write responses to the text after the read-aloud.

Second, teacher read-alouds introduce and model how students should read, comprehend, and critique text formats that may be new to them (e.g., journal articles, web pages, editorials, primary sources). The students then apply their new learning during shared reading, small-group work, and individual assignments. These core texts are also referenced during writing instruction.

Third, interactive read-alouds in the intermediate grades can facilitate discussions of compelling books that contribute to students' understanding of sensitive or controversial topics. The historical fiction picture book *In the Time of the Drums* (Siegelson & Pinkney, 1999) tells the story of captured Igboland slaves who were loaded under a ship's deck and brought to Georgia. Upon arriving at Dunbar Creek on St. Simons Island, the chained Igbo (Ebo) people committed mass suicide; they chose the hereafter rather than enslavement. The book tells an important story of resistance through the eyes of a young boy who experienced the event. Although the event is disturbing, it also speaks of love and commitment to family, standing up for one's beliefs, and the importance of perpetuating one's cultural heritage. The events are commonly referenced in African American and Gullah folklore. A teacher who crafts where to stop reading, the questions to ask, and discussion prompts can thoughtfully use this book to increase students' awareness of history and human nature.

Often teacher read-alouds are framed within an isolated time block with the class listening passively or answering an occasional question. However, when read-alouds are connected to units of study, they can stimulate small-group activities. For example, intermediate teachers can adapt an instructional activity that Kay employed with her second-grade class. She read aloud to her class *The Story of Ruby Bridges* (Coles, 2010) and then had them watch Disney's 1998 movie *Ruby Bridges*. Afterward, the students engaged in Alvermann's (1991) Discussion Web activity to discuss and present arguments for the two different perspectives that were observed in the movie and book. This activity engaged students in complex thinking, discussing, and writing. See Chapter 7 for procedural directions on implementing the Discussion Web.

Shared Reading

Shared reading is the second type of whole-class literacy context. The texts introduced during shared reading may be slightly beyond the instructional reading level for many students in your class. These challenging texts are often referred to as *stretch texts* or *heavy texts*. Consistent with Vygotsky's (1978) concept of the zone of proximal development, students can work productively with tasks at a higher level of difficulty when you increase the amount of instructional support.

Many people associate shared reading with the characteristics of Holdaway's (1982) Shared Book Experience that uses enlarged texts or "big books" with emergent readers to develop print concepts and other early literacy skills. However, as students pass through different developmental stages, shared reading can scaffold skills and strategies that define each new stage of learning. Although classrooms that use a basal/core reading program still include shared reading as part of their day, many classrooms that heavily rely on a workshop model or small-group reading with leveled readers (e.g., Fountas & Pinnell, 2016; Guided Reading) often omit shared reading.

A few things make shared reading different from an interactive teacher read-aloud, although sometimes the first reading of the shared reading text or sections of the text might be read by the teacher (Schwanenflugel et al., 2009; S. A. Stahl & Heubach, 2005). In shared reading, the students are expected to assume some or all of the responsibility for text reading during the lesson or lesson series. Therefore, all students must have copies of the text or visual access to the text during each text reading. Some teachers use a smartboard to share texts or screen share during virtual lessons.

Based on a survey of teachers, Fisher et al. (2008) determined that comprehension, vocabulary, text structures, and text features were commonly addressed during shared-reading lessons. In these classrooms, shared reading averaged 10–14 minutes and was followed by small-group or independent activities.

FLUENCY-ORIENTED READING INSTRUCTION

Fluency-Oriented Reading Instruction (FORI) and Wide Reading FORI (WRFORI) are shared-reading protocols that have been extensively researched in second-grade classrooms but also work well in third grade (Kuhn, personal communication, March 22, 2021; Schwanenflugel et al., 2009; S. A. Stahl & Heubach, 2005). The research evidence indicated that both protocols promoted the development of fluency, comprehension, and vocabulary. Supporting struggling readers as they read fictional or informational texts with a high volume of words and conceptual density enables a reduction in the learning gaps caused by a diet of short, simple books typically read by low-proficiency readers.

FORI protocols work well with award-winning picture books (e.g., Caldecott, Coretta Scott King) with 400–600 words, rich vocabulary, and complex themes. Many teachers use FORI or WRFORI during their instruction of books written by Patricia Polacco, Jacqueline Woodson, Chris Van Allsburg, and other authors appropriate for intermediate students. FORI incorporates the repeated reading of the same text across multiple days with teacher scaffolding so that students grasp themes and acquire some of the sophisticated vocabulary. In WRFORI, students read three different conceptually related texts. The whole class reads the core 3-day text together. However, the teacher may choose differentiated instruction for a community text or differentiate by reading level by using different texts on the same topic on the last 2 days of the 5-day routine (Kuhn, personal communication March 23, 2021). FORI and WRFORI require 30 minutes to implement (see Table 4.3).

TABLE 4.3. FORI and Wide Reading FORI Protocols

	Day 1	Day 2	Day 3	Day 4	Day 5
FORI	Build background Teacher read-aloud Discuss theme and key ideas	Echo[a] or chorally[b] read Focus on comprehension, author craft, and vocabulary	Supported student reading: Choral reading[b] OR partner reading[c]		Related extension activities (writing, discussion, projects)
Wide Reading FORI	Build background Teacher read-aloud Discuss theme and key ideas	Echo[a] or chorally[b] read Focus on comprehension, author craft, and vocabulary	Extension activities (writing, discussion, projects)	Introduce a new concept-related text Echo,[a] choral,[b] or partner read[c] book #2	Introduce a new concept-related text Echo,[a] choral,[b] or partner read[c] book #3

Note. Based on Schwanenflugel et al. (2009).
[a]Echo reading: The teacher reads a paragraph or a page and the students chorally repeat the reading of that section of text.
[b]Choral reading: Typically, the teacher and the students read the text simultaneously. During paired choral reading two students read the text simultaneously.
[c]Partner reading: The students alternate reading pages of text.

Close Reading

The first anchor standard of the CCSS states that students are to "read closely to determine what the text says explicitly and make logical inferences from it" (NGA & CCSSO, 2010, p. 10). As a result, a practice known as *close reading* has gained prevalence in many intermediate classrooms. Advocates of the CCSS produced publications that strongly influenced how classroom teachers used close reading to support their students' reading performance with complex texts. Most close-reading procedures involve multiple reads of a short text to analyze the text for different purposes across multiple days (Brown & Kappes, 2012; Fisher & Frey, 2014; Shanahan, 2014). Students learn to make annotations on the text to indicate key ideas, questions, and to summarize. Most protocols include directives for teachers to avoid providing background information before the first reading. They advise sticking to text-dependent questions (questions that are answered in the text) during discussions, and recommend keeping discussions and written responses between the four corners of the page. In other words, the focus of close reading is comprehension of the text-based information.

Teachers should apply caution in deciding when and how to utilize close reading (Fisher & Frey, 2014; Hinchman & Moore, 2013). Kay likes to ask the question "Is this activity breathing life into the text or sucking the life out of it?" Keep in mind that the purpose of close reading is to help students deeply analyze a single piece of text. However, this is a time-consuming process, and teachers should evaluate the cost-benefit of close reading.

If you decide to implement close reading, you need to know the following information. Close reading should be related to the unit of instruction; it should not be an exercise on how to read a random text closely. Because close reading does not recommend providing students with background knowledge, and we recognize that background knowledge is essential to comprehension, you need to make sure that your students have the requisite background knowledge for understanding the passage. Close reading should be with a short text or, as Doug Fisher tells teachers who attend his workshops, "If it has a staple, it is not appropriate for close reading." Poetry, government documents, speeches, news articles, or editorials are a few examples of the kinds of texts that merit close reading as part of a unit of study.

Below, we have listed steps for implementing close reading based on a synthesis of the work of others (Brown & Kappes, 2012; Fisher & Frey, 2014; Shanahan, 2014):

- *First reading:* Individual or assisted reading to get the text's gist or to accomplish general understanding as described in the first three anchor standards of the CCSS (NGA & CCSSO, 2010; see Appendix A). This discussion might be led by the teacher using text-dependent questions, with students providing text evidence to support their answers.
- *Second reading:* Students reread and annotate the text for a specific purpose. The annotation is discussed with a partner. This reading might move beyond general understanding and focus on a specific standard related to text structure or the author's craft. The teacher uses text-dependent questions to facilitate a community share in which the students provide text evidence to support their claims.
- *Third reading:* Students reread the text to analyze, evaluate, compare, or critique it. Students might conclude the session with an individual or collaborative written response, Discussion Web (Alvermann, 1991), or small-group discussion in response to an analytic prompt.

Three-Ring Circus

Just because the entire class is reading the same text does not mean that differentiation and small-group teaching should not occur. The three-ring circus is a useful protocol for differentiating the reading of a common stretch text (Cunningham et al., 2000). After the teacher provides a preliminary text introduction to the entire class, they assign the students to read the text in one of three ways. Above-level students read the text independently and do a comprehension follow-up activity. On-level students read the text with a partner. They might be assigned to alternate summarizing or questioning every two or three pages. The teacher coaches the small group of below-level readers as they read the text orally or silently, possibly using a research-based protocol such as the directed reading–thinking activity (Stauffer, 1969; see Chapter 6).

Differentiated Small-Group Literacy Instruction

Differentiated small-group instruction may be teacher-led, student-led, or collaborative. In the primary grades, teachers tend to use instructional reading levels to form literacy groups. This grouping is still useful for any students who are reading below the early third-grade instructional level (e.g., Fountas & Pinnell, 2016; Levels L–M). In the intermediate grades, reading levels are wider and more malleable. Therefore, it is more useful to form temporary instructional groups to teach particular skills or strategies to students who need extra support in specific areas. The extra support might address foundational skills, comprehension strategy application, or composing written responses to demonstrate or extend reading comprehension. Small groups might also be formed to provide developmental support for above-level students in competencies such as advanced word study (derivatives) or sophisticated writing forms and functions.

As demonstrated in the opening vignette and mentioned earlier, small collaborative groups should occur daily as part of a common text's shared reading. However, small groups can also be the context for book clubs and inquiry projects that engage students in reading different texts about a common theme or topic. Either students or teachers can determine membership in these groups. However, students must have frequent opportunities to choose reading material, research questions, and learning partners. More information is provided on discussion groups and inquiry projects in later chapters of the book.

Independent Reading and Writing

Some curricula, such as workshop models, limit students' reading selections by reading levels but in other ways allow a great deal of latitude in what students choose to read during the in-school literacy time frame. Additionally, large blocks of time are allocated for all students to read individual book choices silently during the literacy block while teachers conference individually. Our view of independent reading differs from this model.

Our view of independent reading and writing offers students a controlled choice aligned with models such as CORI and other forms of project-based learning. Students' independent reading or writing is in preparation to share in a book club, actively participate in a discussion, or make a unique contribution to the class's collective knowledge building around a larger topic. We encourage independent open-choice reading at home that is recorded in reading logs. However, during class, controlled choice dominates independent reading and writing.

SELECTING AND ORGANIZING TEXTS FOR INSTRUCTION

Selecting Text Sets

There are multiple approaches to selecting and organizing text sets for instruction. Some teachers like to collect several books of different readability levels around a common broad topic. For example, a classroom might be digging deeply into reading and writing biographies that reflect resilience. Students choose biographies that match their interest and readability levels. Often teachers use sources such as Reading A–Z or Newsela to provide texts at different reading levels that contain the same content. See Appendix B for more resources.

Other teachers focus on an "essential question" and select books that present various approaches to confronting the big question. A fourth-grade unit might focus on the question "How did the colonial patriots' ideals of liberty and equality contribute to the American Revolution?" Initially, there would be sets of texts that students would use to investigate the events and values that led to the American Revolution. The initial question and reading might then be extended to investigate "How have other groups used those ideals as motives for revolting throughout American history?"

We also want to ensure that we account for the diversity of cultural perspectives. All text set selections should reflect multicultural perspectives and attend to which voices are heard or ignored. Some units might focus on the different cultural or political values surrounding a particular topic. For these units, texts would be selected for the primary purpose of presenting a few competing perspectives on a standards-based issue. The C3SSS (National Council for the Social Studies, 2013) standard D2.His.4.3-5 states, "Explain why individuals and groups during the same historical period differed in their perspectives." This inquiry would require text sets that focus on a single time period written from multiple perspectives.

Each text set discussed in this section is a "conceptual text set" because the subject addressed is an abstract, multifaceted concept (Donham, 2013). Other examples of concepts are courage and survival in literary units, adaptation in science, and democracy and immigration in social studies. The students do not simply read about a type of shark and construct a poster or slideshow to share. Conceptual text sets are used "to build substantive understanding of a set of concepts through repetition, elaboration, and examples provided across texts" (Cervetti et al., 2016, p. 764). CORI is one example of a curriculum that uses conceptual text sets.

Students can decode more easily and form deep and lasting vocabulary acquisition when there are repeated exposures to the words across multiple texts. Reading multiple texts about related concepts enables readers to establish a coherent mental representation. Cervetti et al. (2016) determined that students who read conceptual text sets of just six books over 3 days demonstrated greater conceptual knowledge, more knowledge of target words, and stronger retellings than students who read unrelated texts.

Organizing Text Sets

One way to organize text sets is to move from the simplest to the most complex texts. This might involve starting with texts that include a mix of known and new information, pictures and photographs, and use the most conversational language. Gradually, move toward more difficult texts. When students encounter the challenging texts, they are already familiar with the vocabulary and have some easily retrievable prior knowledge to build on.

WRFORI works in the opposite direction. It provides the most support with the first stretch text and then moves more quickly with two follow-up texts that match readers with texts at their instructional level. Whether you start with simple and move to complex or begin with extensive scaffolding of complex text and then provide less instructional support for follow-up texts, the instructional decisions must be informed and intentional.

Lupo and colleagues (2018, 2019) developed the quad text set framework for elementary and middle schools. Although the models look a bit different, they share four common features. They use at least three additional experiences to bolster the reading of a stretch target text. The sequence of activities is adjusted and often interspersed with a shared reading of the target text as needed to provide supplementary information or provide motivation. Table 4.4 provides the quad text set framework features, but keep in mind that after an introduction that builds background knowledge, the other experiences can be manipulated in any way that makes sense to build related content knowledge, spurs interest, and maintains motivation.

TABLE 4.4. The Quad Text Set Framework

Text type and function	Description
Introduction: Build background knowledge	This is a simplistic text with visuals or a video for providing introductory background knowledge.
Target text: New learning	This is the centerpiece for the set. It is a stretch text, often dense, and may be lengthy.
Informational texts: Build additional knowledge	These shorter texts may be interspersed to provide added content information required to enhance comprehension of the target text; they may be matched to reading levels of students, and instruction may be differentiated.
Accessible texts: Motivate, sustain interest	These concept-related texts are "hooks" to connect to students' lives and interests.

Note. Based on Lupo et al. (2018, 2019).

CONSIDERATIONS FOR BILINGUAL STUDENTS

Some of the factors that you need to consider when selecting reading texts for bilingual students are different from the factors we recommended for native English-speaking students. For example, there are additional pressure points that affect bilingual students' English reading, such as their levels of English proficiency in reading, writing, speaking, and listening in academic and social contexts and their L1 knowledge and academic experiences. Finding out what bilingual students know and can do in their L1 and English by contacting their current and former teachers (i.e., bilingual and/or ESL teachers and all-English classroom teachers) is helpful when you select English texts and plan your reading instruction.

In addition, English decoding and readability formulas (such as Betts, 1946) generally are not good measures for estimating how well bilingual students comprehend English texts. Researchers found that bilingual students who received explicit English decoding instruction did as well as native English speakers on English decoding measures (Lesaux & Geva, 2006). However, their accurate decoding did not mean that they always understood the words that they decoded (Shanahan & Beck, 2006; Snow, 2006). Also, bilingual students' performance on English decoding measures often depends on whether the scorer takes into account their accents. Sometimes, bilingual students know what a word means but cannot pronounce it correctly in English. In reference to the comprehension questions that are part of the readability formulas, bilingual students often demonstrate higher levels of comprehension when they are asked questions in their L1 about English texts and/or allowed to use their L1 to answer the questions (García, 1991; García & Godina, 2017).

In a think-aloud study with six bilingual Latinx fourth graders who scored between the 86th and 99th percentile on a standardized reading test in Spanish but at grade level or below grade level on a standardized reading test in English, Georgia and her colleague (García & Godina, 2017) discovered that all but one student had developed effective cognitive strategies that they employed to read in either language, enabling them to read fairly difficult texts in English when they had relevant background and vocabulary knowledge. Based on these findings, we recommend that you explicitly encourage bilingual students to use cognitive strategies acquired in one language to read in the other language; provide cognitive strategy instruction for those students new to it and review it with your other students (see Chapter 6); select English texts for which bilingual students already have the appropriate background and vocabulary knowledge in their L1 or English; and help them to access this knowledge prior to reading the English texts. If they do not have the knowledge, then you need to help them develop it before asking them to read the texts.

Some of the instructional reading methods presented in Chapter 4 are effective with bilingual students. For example, choral reading usually is effective with bilingual students because it allows them to participate and hear the teacher and other students orally read without emphasizing or highlighting their English decoding. Other techniques that help bilingual students include accompanying silent reading with prerecorded audio read-alouds and pairing an English text with an L1 or English video of the story in the text.

With a few adaptations, other instructional reading methods described in Chapter 4 also are effective. For example, interactive teacher read-alouds and shared reading of common texts are more effective with bilingual students when they can see the print that is being read. The print can be on a white board, on a computer, or in shared copies or individual copies of the text. We caution against asking bilingual students to do close reading without making sure that they already accessed or are provided with the appropriate background knowledge. It also may be easier for bilingual students to closely read nonfiction (for which they have the appropriate background knowledge) rather than fiction. English narrative fiction often includes cultural nuances that bilingual students may not understand without teacher intervention (García, 1998).

We also recommend that you employ instructional techniques based on what is known about the English literacy participation and performance of bilingual students. Encouraging bilingual students to write their responses to English texts in their L1 and/or English prior to participating in small groups or the whole group, usually results in higher levels of participation (García, 2003). Also, bilingual students typically will participate more in small groups than in the whole group, especially when they are grouped with other speakers from the same L1 and are allowed to use their L1 and English to discuss what they read (García et al., 2021). Another technique that may help bilingual students is providing them with the L1 version of a text to read before asking them to read the English version.

CONCLUSION

In the intermediate grades, students need to read a wide variety of texts for multiple purposes. Constructing a curriculum of knowledge building requires a balance of different types of text. The balance of different types of texts is the *effect* of a meaningful curriculum. It is not a matter of counting the percentages of fiction and nonfiction texts. We have based our discussion on recent research, the synthesis of the RfU studies (Pearson et al., 2020), and the CCSS (NGA & CCSSO, 2010). However, our readers should use their state standards as guidelines for determining readability expectations for their students. State standards or district curricula tend to do a good job of specifying which genres or text forms (folktales, mythology, historical documents, scientific process writing) are required for each grade level. These guidelines make the job easier for teachers to select particular texts and related assignments. As always, we recommend that you work with your grade-level team to gather multiple perspectives, ensure buy-in, and distribute the workload.

Once the curriculum has been determined, teachers need to know their students. Getting some gauge of their students' instructional reading levels is important. However, we know that the diagnosed reading levels based on an unprepared reading of random texts should only be valued as a rough estimate of a reading range for students who are reading above second-grade level. Therefore, it is ill advised to lose extensive instructional time determining an instructional reading level at this stage of development. The dynamic interaction of the comprehension pressure points exerts a larger influence on a text's readability than decoding alone does. Matching books and students at this stage of development calls for teachers to consider the reader, the task and reading context, and the text's qualitative and quantitative readability measures. In addition to knowing the estimated instructional reading-level band of the students in the class, each teacher must preread each text critically and analyze it based on multiple readability measures of complexity in order to identify potential comprehension challenges.

After a detailed analysis of the text and the formation of conceptual text sets, the teacher can decide what types of instructional support will be needed for the current class of students who will be reading the texts to build knowledge in the learning domain. The variety of instructional supports provided will enable all students to successfully read and respond to challenging texts that are read communally, differentiated texts that they will read in a small group with teacher guidance, and easy texts that they will read independently based on students' interests and to contribute to the classroom investigative process.

CHAPTER FIVE

Vocabulary Development That Supports Comprehension

GUIDING QUESTIONS

- How is vocabulary related to reading comprehension?
- What are the principles of effective vocabulary instruction that influence comprehension?
- How should teachers select words for intentional vocabulary instruction?
- What instructional techniques work well with vocabulary in literary texts?
- What instructional techniques work well with academic vocabulary?
- What instructional techniques support incidental vocabulary learning?
- What vocabulary principles and techniques are effective with emergent bilingual students?

SETTING THE STAGE

The fifth-grade teachers at Malcolm X Elementary School are planning their upcoming social studies unit about the U.S. federal government's structures and functions. During the meeting, they are discussing plans for the unit's vocabulary instruction. At the last meeting, Ms. Bianca agreed to select 15–25 target words from the curriculum and texts they will use during the unit. She presents 22 target words for explicit instruction during the 3-week unit. The team reviews her selections and adds the words *ratify* and *amendment*. This discussion leads to a selection of morphemes (*dem, crat/cracy, leg, jud,* and *poli*) that the teachers can teach during the unit. Mr. Liffey volunteers to develop activities for morphology stations before next week's team meeting. Next, the team discusses options for assessing vocabulary development. Rather than using a traditional multiple-choice test as a pre- and posttest, Ms. Molloy suggests that they try a vocabulary rating scale that she learned about during a professional development session. Before the unit begins, the students self-rate their level of knowledge about the unit's target vocabulary. At the end of the unit, they fill out the rating scale again and validate their knowledge by providing additional information about the terms, such as providing a sentence, definition, diagram, or filling out the information in a graphic organizer. The team agrees to let Ms. Molloy prepare this and to share it at the next team meeting. During the upcoming week, Ms. Bianca and Mr. Maharaj will look in their curriculum guides and their resource folders for other vocabulary activities that the team might want to include in the unit of study.

THE RELATIONSHIP BETWEEN VOCABULARY AND READING COMPREHENSION

A robust research base indicates a strong relationship between vocabulary and comprehension (Anderson & Freebody, 1983; Pearson et al., 2020). For example, vocabulary test scores and reading comprehension test scores correlate in the .85–.95 range (S. A. Stahl & Nagy, 2006). Also, the size of a person's vocabulary is a strong predictor of their reading comprehension. Because vocabulary knowledge is strongly associated with topic knowledge, it is likely that students who know a word's meaning have a network of knowledge surrounding that word.

Without intervention, children who arrive at school with low levels of English vocabulary knowledge are likely to struggle with text comprehension throughout school (Stanovich, 1986).

Researchers have indicated that the development of vocabulary and compre-hension is a reciprocal process (Anderson & Freebody, 1983; Pearson et al., 2020). This means that students with strong vocabulary skills are likely to read and com-prehend more than students with weaker vocabulary skills. As a result, they learn more than the reticent reader, thus increasing their vocabulary knowledge (Sta-novich, 1986). To break this cycle, we recommend knowledge-based curricula and vocabulary instruction.

PRINCIPLES OF EFFECTIVE VOCABULARY INSTRUCTION

Three meta-analyses of vocabulary research conducted over the last 40 years yielded insights regarding effective vocabulary instruction (Elleman et al., 2009; S. A. Stahl & Fairbanks, 1986; Wright & Cervetti, 2016). One of the common find-ings was that generalized vocabulary instruction, including instruction on context clues and morphology, did not produce benefits on standardized comprehension measures. However, explicit vocabulary instruction consistently yielded compre-hension gains for passages that included taught words. Here are some principles of effective instruction:

- Include the printed word, the definition, and contextual examples. Add visuals when possible.
- Engage students in active work with the target words.
- Provide repeated exposures to the target words.
- Strive to develop deeper knowledge through varied activities.

The methods that we describe throughout this chapter incorporate these principles. Vocabulary is an unconstrained skill like comprehension, so knowledge acquisition is incremental and contingent on the context.

Additionally, not all words should receive equal attention or the same type of instruction. Evidence indicates that even brief attention is better than no attention (Wright & Cervetti, 2016). Some words only merit a brief mention before or during reading. Other words will require varied experiences with the word before the students understand the concept (e.g., *irony, theorem, hypocrisy, elements*). When planning instruction, you need to decide how and when you will teach each target vocabulary word. *Before-reading* instruction should address words that are crucial for understanding the text's big ideas. *During-reading* instruction should be brief, essential, and enhance rather than disrupt comprehension. Just as you do not look up every unknown word you encounter during reading, there also is no need to define every word in a student reading assignment, especially if it is unessential and infrequent. More elaborated instruction should typically occur *after reading* or throughout the unit as focus lessons or vocabulary stations.

SELECTING WORDS FOR INSTRUCTION

Choosing which words to teach is the first challenge of vocabulary instruction. Nagy and Anderson (1984) determined that there were about 88,500 words in printed school English. Learners acquire vocabulary *incidentally* during wide reading and *intentionally* through explicit instruction. How do we decide which words deserve our time and instructional attention?

Beck et al. (2002) developed a three-tier heuristic for categorizing vocabulary to aid instructional decision making. Tier One words are basic words that we encounter in daily life—*dog, neighbor, fun, store*. Most native English speakers will not need instruction on these words. Words used by mature language users are Tier Two words—*teal, dome, skillet, bellow*. Tier Two words appear most frequently in written language, less commonly in everyday conversation. Students know the concept and might use a more general word (e.g., *walk*) in place of a Tier Two word such as *stroll*. Therefore, effective instruction may only need to include a definition or synonym, a few examples, and opportunities for repeated use. Tier Three consists of words that are extremely low frequency or that tend to be associated with a specific disciplinary domain—*photosynthesis, democracy, ecosystem*. Tier Three words often relate to unfamiliar and multifaceted concepts that require ongoing learning and experiences before learners grasp the full meaning of the word.

Keep in mind that the tiers are simply a heuristic to guide your thinking about the properties and functions of words as you select words and decide how you will teach them. For example, general academic vocabulary words may be Tier Two or Tier Three (e.g., *similar, survey, criteria, function*). General academic vocabulary includes the words on Coxhead's (2000) Academic Word List (AWL) and Gardner and Davies's (2013) Academic Vocabulary List (AVL). General academic vocabulary often cuts across disciplinary domains. When deciding how to teach a word from the AWL or AVL, consider its function. For example, the definition for the word *sequence* has general applicability across domains. Additionally, students are familiar with the concept of sequence, so you can teach it as a Tier Two word. However, both the concept and application of the word *percent* are domain-specific. They always rely on the learner knowing the implied mathematical relationship. This knowledge requires the in-depth conceptual processing associated with Tier Three words.

Teaching Tier Two and Tier Three words requires time and deliberation. Therefore, select and spend time on the highest-utility words, words that students will see, hear, and use regularly. Often textbooks or state curricula identify large numbers of words for each story or unit. Use your knowledge of your students (including vocabulary pretests) and your goals to generate your list (Stahl & Bravo, 2010; Stahl et al., 2020). Pare down the number of words for elaborated teaching to a manageable number. You can draw attention to about eight words for stories, but you will probably only have time to provide elaborated instruction for three to five words. For disciplinary units, select 15–25 *target words* that you can include in multiple activities across the unit.

TEACHING VOCABULARY IN LITERARY TEXTS

Planning for Instruction

Your first step in planning your instruction is to survey and list the words in the story that are likely to be unfamiliar to your students. Then, sort the words by tier. Most of your words will likely be Tier Two words. However, if you are integrating ELA with social studies or science, your fictional selection may also have some Tier Three terms. Hopefully, those terms were on the list of target words for the unit, and your students have a degree of familiarity with them. This story will provide additional exposure and a deeper understanding of the Tier Three words.

Next, identify whether you will teach each word before reading, during reading, after reading, or not at all. If you are using the text as an interactive read-aloud or shared reading, create a script for how you will teach each word. Introduce any words that are essential to understanding the theme or big ideas of the story before reading. For example, a teacher who was reading Woodson's (2013) book *This Is the Rope: A Story from the Great Migration* retaught the word *migration,* even though the students had been exposed to the word in science and their integrated social studies unit on civil rights.

For brief, point-of-contact instruction during reading, we recommend that you put sticky notes in one color on the pages where the vocabulary items appear. Write the child-friendly definition or student prompt ("Show me how you *tremble*") on the sticky note. Use sticky notes in a different color or size to tag three to five high-utility Tier Two words that you will teach after reading. On these sticky notes, include a child-friendly definition and three example sentences. Preparing the definitions and the sample sentences in advance ensures both time efficiency and precision in accurately representing the vocabulary words.

Teaching Tier Two Words

Beck et al. (2001, 2002) recommended a protocol for teaching Tier Two vocabulary that was part of their comprehensive Text Talk read-aloud procedure. It incorporates three of the principles of effective vocabulary instruction: the definition and

Teaching Tier Two Words (Beck et al., 2001)

1. Display the word, read it, prompt the students to read it.
2. Read the sentence within the text that included the word.
3. Provide a child-friendly definition of the word.
4. Provide three example sentences that include the word and provide a clear example of the word's meaning—for example, "I saw my grandparents, my aunts, my uncles, and my cousins at my family reunion"; "This summer, I will have a reunion with my friend who moved to California"; My mother saw her old friends from high school at her class reunion."
5. Call on three students to generate an oral response to a specific prompt—for example, "Tell us about someone who you would like to see at a reunion and why."
6. Option: Controlled choice vocabulary activities. These quick prompts call for children to consider the features of the target word—for example, "Give me a thumbs up if the item that I am describing is *brittle:* a tree branch, a blanket, a peanut shell, a sheet of ice, an eraser, a dry leaf, a pretzel stick."
7. Recommendation: Use a Word Wizard chart to indicate when students use the target words in their classroom speech or writing during the next week or two.

contextual information, nine repeated exposures to the word, and active engagement.

Teachers who substitute a partner think–pair–share for the three student example sentences reduce the number of exposures to the words and cannot provide corrective feedback as needed. You could have the students write sentences after the protocol as a follow-up activity in a station. We recommend that you use this simple protocol with Tier Two words only, not Tier Three words that require concept development.

It is also a good idea to add the Tier Two words to a vocabulary word wall or a Word Wizard chart (Beck et al., 1982) to increase the likelihood that *you* and your students will incorporate the words in your daily language when possible. The Word Wizard chart is simply a poster that records the target words across the top of a chart and the students' names down the first column. When students use the target words in their conversations or written products during an allocated time period, they receive a check on the chart.

Integrating Vocabulary and Comprehension

The Vocab-O-Gram (Blachowicz, 1986) and Story Impressions (McGinley & Denner, 1987) are two prereading activities that merge the introduction of vocabulary with predicting and setting reading purposes. They work best with short stories, sophisticated picture books, or book chapters.

Vocab-O-Gram

The primary purpose of the Vocab-O-Gram is to introduce the students to familiar and unfamiliar vocabulary that provide clues to the key story elements (Blachowicz, 1986). You define the unknown words for the students. In small groups, the students discuss the terms listed in the heading box and write predictions about the text within the category rows on the diagram. Based on your teaching goals, you can change the categories on the diagram. The whole class discusses the predictions and clarifies vocabulary before the students read the text. See an example of a Vocab-O-Gram in Figure 5.1.

Story Impressions

McGinley and Denner (1987) designed Story Impressions as a prereading narrative comprehension activity. It also supports word recognition and vocabulary knowledge. All students above first grade enjoy and benefit from the activity, but it is particularly beneficial for struggling readers when the whole class is reading the same text. Evidence indicates that all readers (including above- and below-level readers)

Use the vocabulary to make predictions about the story. Words may be used more than once. If there are words that your group is unsure about, write them as mystery words. *Connecticut bleak Puritan trial heretic Aunt Rachel Barbados taxes mysterious fever autumn public punishment harsh blasphemy Blackbird Pond Katherine hopelessness Hannah brigantine suspicion defiantly witchcraft*	
Setting (Where and When)	What might the setting be like?
Characters	What do you think about the characters?
Actions	What might happen?
Resolution	How might it end?
What questions do you have?	
Mystery words	

FIGURE 5.1. Vocab-O-Gram for *The Witch of Blackbird Pond* (Speare, 1958).

who used Story Impressions answered more postreading questions correctly and had higher story recall scores than students in the control groups (Denner et al., 1989; Denner & McGinley, 1992).

To implement Story Impressions, you select 10–20 single words or phrases of up to three words from the story. These must be of key importance to the plot and should also include target vocabulary. Share the words with your students in a sequential, vertical display. Figure 5.2 depicts a Story Impressions list derived from *The Garden of Abdul Gasazi* (Van Allsburg, 1979). Read the list and define any unknown words. In dyads or triads, students discuss and predict what the story will be about based on the list of sequential phrases. Using the phrases in sequential order, the students write a story based on their predictions. Naturally, other information can be added to create a story that includes a beginning, middle, and ending. The students share their stories with the class. Next, they read the published story and follow up with a whole-class discussion.

This activity provides multiple exposures to each vocabulary word as the students hear, read, speak, and write the words multiple times throughout the protocol. It sets the stage for struggling readers and emergent bilingual students to have a successful reading experience. The research evidence also indicates that the comprehension results were not contingent upon how closely the predicted story approximated the published story.

stay with Fritz
↓
Alan
↓
afternoon walk
↓
small white bridge
↓
no dogs allowed
↓
Abdul Gasazi
↓
retired magician
↓
long search
↓
follow Fritz's tracks
↓
awesome sight
↓
nervously climbed
↓
follow me
↓
detest dogs
↓
bellowed Gasazi
↓
change Fritz back
↓
he disappeared
↓
blurted
↓
front yard
↓
felt silly
↓
believe in magic

FIGURE 5.2. Story Impressions for *The Garden of Abdul Gasazi* (Van Allsburg, 1979).

TEACHING ACADEMIC VOCABULARY

This section focuses on teaching academic vocabulary (i.e., words primarily used in academic settings, print publications, and digital media). There are two kinds of academic vocabulary: general academic vocabulary (appears across disciplinary domains) and discipline-specific academic vocabulary (Tier Three).

Many schools select a schoolwide word of the week from a list of general academic words (e.g., Coxhead, 2000). Although well intentioned, this can be problematic. Many general academic vocabulary words are *polysemous,* or have multiple nuances of meaning. Therefore, schools should use caution when teaching a single definition for general academic vocabulary. Additionally, some general academic vocabulary definitions differ by domain and conceptual complexity (e.g., *conduct, volume, element*). When general academic words are conceptually dense, teachers need to employ Tier Three teaching techniques.

In addition to academic vocabulary, the characteristics of academic *language* make disciplinary discourse more challenging to comprehend than stories. So even if you work on teaching the vocabulary and developing knowledge, it is important to provide specific disciplinary support to your students when they are reading and writing academic texts. Nagy and Townsend (2012, p. 93) specify that academic language differs from everyday conversational English because it has more of the following:

1. Latin- and Greek-based vocabulary
2. Morphologically complex words
3 Complex grammatical structures
4. Informational density
5. Higher levels of abstraction

The Simple View of Reading does not account for the characteristics of academic language. A deeper discussion of these features is beyond the scope of this chapter. However, Nagy and Townsend (2012) suggest that acquiring morphological fluency and producing written academic language are promising ways for students to improve their comprehension of academic language.

Teaching Tier Three Words

The salient features of Tier Three words are that they are domain-specific, and students require conceptual development to understand the words. Typically, a simple definition does not capture the complexity of Tier Three words. As discussed in Chapter 4, using integrated units and text sets provides an organic way for students to develop related concepts and repeatedly hear, speak, read, and write a set of target vocabulary.

Students need a combination of experiences and contexts to grasp the meaning of disciplinary vocabulary. Although students need to know the definition for each word, simply getting students to look up glossary or dictionary definitions for words is not effective. Often the students do not understand the definitions. Additionally, it is not cognitively engaging.

There is no set formula for determining the correct number of exposures or the best type of experiences. Vocabulary learning is incremental, so students enter and leave the unit with individual vocabulary levels and networks of knowledge about each word. It is wise to administer preassessments, formative assessments, and posttests to capture vocabulary knowledge and development (see Stahl & Bravo, 2010; Stahl et al., 2020). These simple activities can fit seamlessly into your classroom routine. Additionally, they ensure that you are not spending time teaching vocabulary that your students already control.

The routine for teaching Tier Three vocabulary differs from teaching Tier Two because you are developing conceptual knowledge. Marzano's (2009) *six-step process* provides varied, active repeated exposures for learning words, as shown in the text box below.

Building Conceptual Vocabulary

In order to gain the conceptual knowledge associated with Tier Three words, students need to apply the words in multiple contexts. You will want to include a range of activities that call for hearing, reading, writing, speaking, and applying the words. It is easy and effective to include interactive word walls and class-constructed hypermedia dictionaries for all units. Four-Square Concept Maps are popular and easy to implement; keep the routine thought provoking by varying your prompts. You can adapt other activities and word games to units as appropriate.

Six-Step Process (Marzano, 2009)

1. Provide a definition, explanation, or example of the word.
2. Students restate the definition, explanation, or example in their own words in their vocabulary notebooks.
3. Students construct a visual representation of the word.
4. Students engage in a variety of activities that help them deepen their understanding of the target vocabulary.
5. Students engage in small-group discussions that call for the use of the target vocabulary.
6. Students play games that include the target words.

For example, semantic feature analysis fits well with the content in some units but not in others. However, within each unit, some activities should explicitly relate target words to each other. You can use these activities to fulfill Marzano's six-step process. Although we provide descriptions of a few vocabulary activities that work well for developing conceptual vocabulary, to expand your vocabulary instruction toolkit, we recommend that you review resources that focus solely on vocabulary (e.g., Blachowicz & Fisher, 2014; S. A. Stahl & Nagy, 2006; Templeton et al., 2015; Stahl Vocabulary Webinar Series Strand 21, 2018, available at *www.youtube.com/watch?v=hkde6xLrglI*).

Interactive Word Walls

Display word walls for target words associated with a unit of study on the wall, part of a bulletin board, or a poster. The content must be visible from a distance. Unlike high-frequency word walls, you do not need to organize these words alphabetically. Arrange the words to illustrate relationships between the words using webs or graphic organizers. The content expands across the duration of the unit as you add student-generated material.

Hypermedia Dictionaries

Assign responsibility for defining a target word to each student or pairs of students at the beginning of the unit. Select a platform that allows for sharing and embedding multimedia, such as Quizlet, Google Doc, or a flashcard application. The students add content to their dictionary entries throughout the unit.

Possible Sentences

Possible Sentences is a prereading or previewing activity (S. A. Stahl & Kapinus, 1991). You choose about six target words or concepts that will appear in the assigned text. Then, you write these words in column 1. Next, you write four to six related words that are likely to be familiar to the students in column 2. Provide the students with a brief introduction to the assigned text. Then, you provide a brief oral definition for each unknown word in column 1. Assign students to create two or three sentences using two or more words in each sentence that they might expect to see in their assigned reading. At least one word in each sentence must come from column 1. Next, ask a few students to read their sentences and write them on the board. Do not discuss or correct the original sentences. Then, the students read the assigned text. After reading the text, the class returns to the possible sentences on the board, and the class discusses whether each sentence is accurate based on their comprehension of the text. If the sentence is not accurate, the class discusses how they can correct it. Then the students return to the sentences they originally wrote and modify them to ensure that they accurately represent what they read.

Four-Square Concept Map

To begin this activity, students fold a piece of paper into fourths. Then, they list information about a target word in each square. You should determine what they tell you about the target word. Possible prompts/choices are a dictionary definition, a student-generated definition, a visual image, a synonym/antonym, examples, nonexamples, related words, and etymology. It is essential to vary the prompts so this activity does not become stale for you and your students. After students acquire experience with each prompt, they can choose from a menu of prompts.

Semantic Mapping

Semantic mapping activities can be used before, during, and after a unit of instruction or a single text. Mapping extends the students' ability to classify information and see relationships among words. Teachers often use it at the beginning of a unit as a brainstorming activity. To create a semantic map, students generate words related to the unit's focus. Then they organize the terms into categories. This map can serve as the class word wall, with students adding more words as they proceed through the unit. Students should not do this activity independently. Like most vocabulary work, the discussion is a crucial aspect of the mapping activity (S. A. Stahl & Nagy, 2006).

Semantic Feature Analysis

Semantic feature analysis facilitates students' comparison of vocabulary items that belong to a common class or category (e.g., transportation, geometric figures, governmental branches). It provides a visual representation of the commonalities and differences in vocabulary items in the same class. Semantic feature analysis works well as a review activity at the end of a unit. Discussion is imperative because there are always ambiguities, and the discussion usually deepens students' knowledge of the terms in the same class. When possible, we recommend that you leave empty spaces for students to add additional terms and features (see Figure 5.3).

SUPPORTING INCIDENTAL VOCABULARY DEVELOPMENT

Due to the high volume of words that students encounter during their school years and the limited number of words teachers can teach, students must acquire vocabulary knowledge incidentally. Swanborn and de Glopper (1999) determined that students learn about 15% of the unknown words they encounter. This means that students can learn 2,250 words a year if they read for 25 minutes a day. In order to learn that number of words incidentally, the texts must include unknown words, and students would need to read about 150 words per minute. Students gradually

	Craters	Moons	Rings	Evidence of water	Storms	Volcanic activity		
Mercury								
Venus								
Earth								
Mars								
Jupiter								
Saturn								
Uranus								

Use a + to indicate that the planet has that feature. Use a – to indicate that the planet does not have that feature. Come to a group consensus.

FIGURE 5.3. Semantic feature analysis for planets.

accumulate partial information about words that, with repeated exposures during wide, independent reading, increases over time. Teachers can support incidental vocabulary learning by using instructional units and text sets containing overlapping vocabulary (Cervetti et al., 2012, 2016), instructing students on how to use context clues, and systematizing morphology (meaningful word units) development.

Contending with Context Clues

During intermediate-grade classroom visits, we frequently hear teachers prompting their students to use the context to figure out what a word means. Unfortunately, explicit clues are rare in authentic reading material. Beck et al. (1983) identified a continuum of four contextual categories in natural texts. At one end of the continuum are *misdirective* contexts that can mislead the reader to an incorrect definition. Next along the continuum are *nondirective* contexts that do not provide any clues to the word's meaning. Continuing along the continuum, we encounter *general* contexts or clues that only indicate general information (e.g., a mood, an object, an action). At the other end of the continuum, we reach *directive* contexts that include synonyms or definitions that provide clues to the meaning of the word. Confirm that the context *is* directive before you prompt your students to use context to define an unknown word. Utilizing context requires background knowledge and inferencing skills. It often leads students to misleading guesses about vocabulary items (S. A. Stahl & Nagy, 2006).

Stahl and Nagy (2006) proposed a three-pronged approach to using context. First, develop word consciousness so that students become interested in words and know when they do not know a word's meaning. Second, focus on the goal of comprehension by incorporating instructional protocols like reciprocal teaching (Palincsar & Brown, 1984) and Questioning the Author (Beck et al., 1997). These protocols emphasize comprehension monitoring to determine when a word or phrase hinders comprehension, and they use rereading and discussion to figure out the word's meaning. Finally, you can help your students to develop a level of contextual awareness that enables them to distinguish when they know enough about a word to proceed with their reading and when they need to seek the assistance of a dictionary or a more knowledgeable other.

Managing Morphology

Morphemes are the smallest meaningful units in words and include bases, affixes, and Greek or Latin derivatives. Students demonstrate *morphemic awareness* when they manipulate morphemes to infer the meanings of unfamiliar words in isolation. Levesque et al. (2018) determined that the employment of *morphemic analysis* had the most direct influence on comprehension. This finding implies that the most effective instruction engages students in manipulating morphemes to create and define new words in context. Derivative morphemes are the morphemes that change the part of speech (*migrate, migratory, migration*). Therefore, students need to distinguish between the different meanings and the syntactic utilization of words with a common base. Students accomplish this through manipulations of morphemes and engaging in academic reading and writing that requires them to use these forms functionally. This model yields a developmental trajectory of word learning that improves over time (Levesque et al., 2018; Nagy & Townsend, 2012).

Often schools approach morphology haphazardly, with each teacher addressing morphemes as they see fit. This approach results in overteaching some common morphemes and never teaching less common or more complex morphemes. Other schools buy a workbook or computer program to teach isolated vocabulary, including some units on morphology. As with all vocabulary, morphology is best taught systematically in alignment with related content. It works well when a district ELA committee selects a standard developmental morphology list (e.g., *Words Their Way* [Bear et al., 2020]) and creates a plan that systematizes explicit, contextualized, and thorough instruction. In these cases, the affixes and Greek/Latin bases are often introduced in ELA and then retaught when they appear in disciplinary content materials as the teachers in the vignette planned to do.

The research on the relationship between morphology instruction and its impact on general comprehension is mixed (Keiffer & Box, 2013; Nagy & Townshend, 2012; Wright & Cervetti, 2016). Morphologically complex words become more frequent as students advance in grades and read academic texts (Nagy & Townshend, 2012). Additionally, higher facility with morphology increases reading fluency, which allows more cognitive capacity for comprehension. Kieffer and Box (2013) found that morphological awareness made indirect contributions to the comprehension of emergent bilingual students and native English speakers via morphologically complex academic vocabulary (contained at least one morpheme) and reading fluency. Nagy and Townsend (2012) hypothesized that knowledge of morphology increased in importance across the middle and high school years as disciplinary texts included more morphologically complex words.

CONSIDERATIONS FOR BILINGUAL STUDENTS

A major factor that adversely affects the English reading comprehension of bilingual students (both current and former emergent bilingual students) is unfamiliar English vocabulary. Many of the instructional recommendations and protocols described earlier in this chapter should be effective with bilingual students if you remember to use the ESL/bilingual principles in the text box on page 27. Just providing oral definitions of unknown English words is likely to be problematic for bilingual students, so instructional protocols such as Possible Sentences may not be effective with them. Instructional protocols that require additional English vocabulary knowledge, such as semantic mapping, also may not be that effective with bilingual students.

One way to increase the English vocabulary knowledge of bilingual students is to tap into their L1 vocabulary knowledge. If students know the L1 equivalent of an unknown English word, then helping them to match the L1 equivalent with the unknown English word is a promising way to increase their English vocabulary. Giving students yes–no vocabulary checklists in their L1 and in English is a quick way to find out which words they already know in each language. You can create the English checklist based on your future instruction and give it to all your students as a preinstructional measure (see Stahl & Bravo, 2010, for checklist examples). If you do not know your students' L1, then working with their bilingual teacher or a school staff member who knows the L1 is one way to create the equivalent L1 checklist.

Given the large number of English words that bilingual students may not know in an English text, you need to have a method for determining which words to teach. First, we recommend that you identify the text structure for the story or section of text that the students will read. Then, identify the vocabulary items in the text that are critical for understanding the meaning of the text in accordance with the text structure. These are the words that you want to make sure your students know. If you need to limit the list further, choose the words according to the following criteria:

- Words frequently found in other English texts
- Words that students will need to know 5 years from now
- Words that students can use to learn other important words (e.g., from *civilization*, they can learn *civics* and *civil*)

If you have students whose L1 shares cognates with English (e.g., French, German, Greek, Italian, and Spanish), then teaching your students how to unlock the meaning of English cognates when reading should be helpful. Table 2.1 in Chapter 2 provides online cognate resources along with English–Spanish cognate examples. Because 75% of emergent bilingual students in the United States are Spanish speakers, we present cognate instruction for Spanish-speaking bilingual students as an example. In a study with bilingual third graders, Georgia and her colleagues discovered that the students improved their ability to identify Spanish–English cognates when their teacher gave them a cognate definition and examples; had them identify all the cognates in their Spanish reading and English instruction in mathematics, science, and social studies; and had them practice identifying similar and different word parts in Spanish–English cognates (García et al., 2020). To do the latter, they used two colored pens: one color to underline the parts that were similar, and another color to circle the parts that were different. To illustrate what they did, we

Steps for Teaching Cognates (García et al., 2020)

1. Provide students with a cognate definition and multiple examples of cognates. A cognate definition that you can adapt is the following: *Cognates are words in two languages (e.g., English and Spanish) that look alike or almost alike and that mean the same thing or almost the same thing.*

2. Have students practice identifying cognates in their reading, mathematics, science, and social studies instruction.

3. Have students identify the word parts in cognates that are similar and different.

4. Have students circle all the cognates on an English passage prior to reading it.

5. Show students how many cognates there actually are in the passage. Then, have them read the passage with the cognates correctly circled on it and try to use the circled cognates to figure out unknown English vocabulary.

6. Work with students individually or in small groups on how to use the cognates to figure out unknown English vocabulary while reading.

7. Most importantly tell your students to read for meaning! If use of a cognate does not make sense, then don't use it!

8. Show and teach them about false cognates—words that look like cognates, but that do not have the same meanings, such as *embarrass* and *embarazada* (which means "pregnant" in Spanish) and *pie* and *pie* (which means "foot" in Spanish). You can find lists of false cognates on the Internet. Use the false cognates to show your students how these words do not fit the meaning of the reading passage, and why it is important to read for meaning!

have indicated the similarities and differences in the words *battery* and *batería* by putting in bold the parts that are similar, in italics the parts that are different, and by using – to indicate missing letters: **bat**_tery_, **bat**–*ería*. In a study with Spanish-speaking fourth graders, Georgia reported that after modeling and providing the students with specific practice on how to use cognates while reading English texts, the students were able to use cognates to figure out unfamiliar vocabulary when reading in English (García et al., 2020). Based on Georgia's cognate work with bilingual third and fourth graders (García et al., 2020), we recommend that you teach cognates to bilingual students using the steps in the text box on page 93.

CONCLUSION

There is longstanding robust research evidence that substantiates the strong relationship between vocabulary and comprehension. Knowledge of words typically indicates a network of knowledge related to a topic. Research also indicates that general vocabulary instruction does not tend to produce benefits on standardized comprehension measures (Elleman et al., 2009; Wright & Cervetti, 2016). Therefore, investing in a commercial vocabulary package or program is not likely to yield increases in reading comprehension. However, vocabulary instruction consistently yielded comprehension gains for passages that included taught words. This good news enables teachers to feel confident that tailoring vocabulary instruction to their curriculum and their students will yield positive outcomes.

Meta-analyses of vocabulary instruction also provide clear instructional guidance. Students need to learn the definitions for words, but looking up a list of words in a dictionary or glossary is not an effective means of learning new vocabulary. Providing a child-friendly definition and having students create dictionaries or word walls stating the definition in their own words is more likely to lead to word ownership. In order to learn new words, students need multiple exposures to the words. The number of different exposures needed varies by word and student. Additionally, the word-learning activities should be varied. Students need opportunities to hear, read, write, and speak the words in multiple contexts. Similarly, a range of assessment activities provide help in gauging your students' knowledge and incremental vocabulary development before, during, and after instruction (Stahl & Bravo, 2010; Stahl et al., 2020).

It is impossible to teach students all the unknown words that they will encounter. Therefore, teaching students to use context and morphology effectively for making meaning is important in the intermediate grades. Word consciousness and comprehension monitoring are essential tools for recognizing and figuring out unknown words.

Unfamiliar vocabulary can often pose a comprehension barrier for bilingual students reading English texts. Integrated disciplinary units tend to provide experiential, visual, and organic repeated exposures to vocabulary that are supportive to all students, especially emergent bilinguals. Additionally, teaching your students how to unlock the meaning of English cognates is helpful for students whose L1 shares cognates with English.

Vocabulary knowledge is intricately intertwined with knowledge building and reading comprehension. Although it is embedded within the comprehension process, like the teachers at Malcolm X Elementary School, we must approach vocabulary instruction with deliberation and intentionality. Although the vastness of the task can at times seem overwhelming, try to keep in mind that as an unconstrained skill, your students' vocabulary growth is multifaceted and long term.

CHAPTER SIX

Strategy Instruction for Narrative and Expository Texts

GUIDING QUESTIONS

- What does research tell us about cognitive strategy instruction?
- What are cognitive strategies and why are they important?
- What are the essential instructional techniques for developing cognitive strategies?
- How should teachers implement strategy instruction with narrative texts?
- How should teachers implement strategy instruction with expository texts?
- How should teachers implement dialogic cognitive strategy instruction?
- What are instructional strategy protocols for students in grades 3–6?
- What are the considerations for implementing strategy instruction with bilingual students?

SETTING THE STAGE

Four fifth graders of varied reading levels sit around a small table. Jonathan is the student leader today. He begins the discussion by asking the small-group participants to read silently the next four pages of *An Elephant in the Garden* (Morpurgo, 2010) and to raise any questions they have about what they read. The student sitting next to him, Raphael, asks, "Why is the nurse being so mean to the old lady? She should pay more attention to her." Cindy replies, "I think the nurse is in a hurry. She's taken care of the old lady for a while and knows that she isn't well." Lois responds, "Nurses always have a lot to do, so she could be in a hurry. But why doesn't she want her son to talk with Lizzie, the old lady?" Jonathan asks them to read the next four pages to see if their questions are answered. With Jonathan's guidance, the students silently read more of the book, stopping to discuss specific monitoring and comprehension strategies until the 30-minute period ends.

OVERVIEW OF RESEARCH

In the above vignette, the students raised questions and posed tentative answers, utilizing a cognitive strategy or mental tool, to interact with and comprehend the text (Almasi, 2003; Baker & Brown, 1984). Throughout the 30 minutes, the students employed other cognitive strategies. They briefly summarized what they read before making predictions about what would happen next in the book; visualized when they needed to create a picture in their heads to better understand what was happening; generated inferences about the motivation of a character; and used context to figure out unfamiliar vocabulary. According to the federal What Works Clearinghouse practice guides on reading comprehension (Kamil et al., 2008; Shanahan et al., 2010), the evidence for explicitly teaching students in grades 3–6 how to use cognitive strategies while reading is strong. Table 6.1 identifies the research-based cognitive strategies that frequently are taught to students in grades 3–6 to improve their reading comprehension. These strategies are high-utility tools that support reading comprehension in all content areas (Shanahan & Shanahan, 2008). In the younger grades, teachers often use leading questions to guide their students' strategic thinking. However, as students in the intermediate grades read more complex material with unfamiliar concepts, it is important for them to learn how and when to utilize the cognitive strategies independently.

Teachers' employment of other instructional strategies or techniques also resulted in improvements in grade 3–6 students' reading comprehension. Table 6.2 shows the instructional techniques that the federal clearinghouses (Kamil et al., 2008; Shanahan et al., 2010) and the National Reading Panel (2000) recommended teachers employ with students in grades 3–6. These are instructional "routines and procedures" to help students comprehend texts (Kamil et al., 2008, p. 17).

Although there may be some overlap between the strategies and techniques presented in Tables 6.1 and 6.2 and those presented in basal reading series, our recommendations for how you, the teacher, and your students discuss and implement them are likely to be different. The students in the opening vignette were participating in "dialogic cognitive strategy instruction," a combination of cognitive strategy instruction and dialogic reading instruction. According to Wilkinson and Son's (2011) review of strategy research, cognitive strategy instruction resulted in improvements in students' reading comprehension when it was dialogic and flexible. Dialogic reading instruction occurs when teachers and students actively engage in collaborative discussion and when students demonstrate agency through independent decision making (Wilkinson & Son, 2011, p. 361). Flexible strategy instruction occurs when students implement cognitive strategies according to their comprehension monitoring, the specific demands of the texts they are reading, and the contexts in which they read. Students do not use all the strategies every time they read nor do they use the strategies in a set sequence.

In fact, researchers reported that students' knowledge of specific cognitive strategies was not what led to improvements in their reading comprehension and

TABLE 6.1. Research-Based Cognitive Strategies for Students in Grades 3–6

Cognitive strategy	Definition and explanation	Examples (inferences are underlined)
Drawing inferences	Authors often do not state everything in the text. When you, the reader, fill in the missing information, you make three types of inferences: You combine information (1) within the text, (2) across the text, and (3) from the text and your background knowledge.	1. *Anaphora* is an inference that requires combining information within the text (e.g., "Sarah was mad at John because <u>he</u> wasn't nice to <u>her</u>"). 2. An inference across the text involves combining ideas within the text. For example, in the first paragraph, the text introduces the decline of the Roman Empire. Several paragraphs later, the text states that the Roman Empire became so big geographically that it was difficult to govern. The reader has to infer that <u>its large size was one reason that the Roman Empire declined.</u> 3. Some inferences require the reader to combine text information with background knowledge. For example: *Text:* "Mr. Spiggly decided he wanted a small dog. He was 75 and didn't want the dog to die before he did." *Background knowledge:* The lifespan of small dogs is longer (12–18 years) than that of big dogs (7–12 years). The inference is that <u>Mr. Spiggly wanted a small dog because its typical lifespan is longer than that of a big dog.</u>
Monitoring and using fix-up strategies	Monitoring is checking your compre-hension as you read. When you realize you don't understand what you are reading, you should use fix-up strategies to improve your compre-hension, such as rereading, reading ahead, and reading more slowly.	"Wait, I don't understand this section. I'm going to reread it more carefully. Oh, now I get it."
Purposeful predictions	Based on what you already read, heard, or saw, you make a prediction about what is going to happen next.	"The old lady has a German accent. She gets emotional when she talks about February 13th. My prediction is that the story she wants to tell took place in Germany during World War II."
Questioning and answering questions	Asking questions about issues you don't understand in the reading, looking for or thinking about the answers as you read, and providing answers to the questions	In the opening vignette to this chapter, the fifth graders wondered why the nurse didn't want the old lady to talk to her son. They read on to see if they could find answers to their questions.
Summarizing	Briefly stating in your own words the primary or main ideas in the reading	A student used 52 words to identify the main ideas and supporting details in a 250-word expository text.
Text structures	When students identify the organizational structure of narrative and expository texts, they improve their understanding and recall of the texts and their ability to communicate this information.	• Students completed a story map that includes the story grammar elements. • After reading a text about global warming, the students completed an outline of superordinate causes of global warming and specific subordinate effects of each cause.
Visualizing	Picturing in your head what you read	A student imagined the large elephant in a small garden. The elephant's head was way above the garden fence. There wasn't enough room for the elephant to turn around.

Note. Based on Kamil et al. (2008); NRP (2000); and Shanahan et al. (2010).

TABLE 6.2. Research-Based Instructional Techniques

Instructional technique	Narrative text	Expository text
Activating and developing appropriate prior knowledge	Students think about and share relevant information about the narrative and genre. When they do not have the knowledge, the teacher provides it. When they activate irrelevant knowledge, the teacher corrects it.	Students think about and share relevant information about the topic(s) and text structure(s) in the text. When they do not have the knowledge, the teacher provides it. When they activate irrelevant knowledge, the teacher corrects it.
Finding main ideas and levels of importance	For example, students can be taught to identify the author's purpose for writing the text, key story elements, the genre and topic of the text, and any themes, morals, or lessons in the text.	Students identify the key ideas in the text, text section, and/or in each paragraph. They can determine the levels of superordinate and subordinate ideas.
Retellings	Students recount the key features of the narrative according to the text structure of the genre.	Students recount the key features of the text according to its text structure. (descriptive, sequence, problem–solution, etc.)
Graphic organizers	Students employ visual depictions of the genre's structure to highlight the organization and content of the narrative text.	Students employ visual depictions of the explicit or implied text structure to highlight the organization and content of the expository text.
Collaborative learning	Students read and discuss texts in small-group settings including book clubs.	Students read expository material in cooperative settings and engage in inquiry to build knowledge.
Using context	The student doesn't know what *gramophone* means in the following passage: "We had a gramophone at home, a windup one with a big trumpet—you do not see them like this anymore, only in antique shops. . . . So Marlene Dietrich's voice was always in the house" (Morpurgo, 2010, p. 19). The student uses the surrounding text to figure out that "a gramophone is a music player."	"These actions are designed to suppress voting. Requiring voters to show IDs before they can vote is voter suppression," read the student. "I have not ever heard the words *suppress* and *suppression* before. However, since this article is about how new rules are making it harder for people to vote, I think *suppress* must mean to keep somebody from doing something."

Note. Based on Kamil et al. (2008); NRP (2000); and Shanahan et al. (2010).

motivation to read (Kamil et al., 2008; Rosenshine & Meister, 1994; Stahl & García, 2015; Taylor, Pearson, García, Stahl, & Bauer, 2006). Rather, when students participated in flexible and dialogic cognitive strategy instruction, researchers attributed their improved reading comprehension and reading motivation to their close reading, increased comprehension monitoring, and improved thinking about text.

Recently, other researchers concluded that students' utilization of cognitive strategies to comprehend texts in specific disciplines or content areas, such as science and social studies, was not sufficient to increase the students' learning from the disciplinary texts (Biancarosa et al., 2020; Cervetti et al., 2012; Connor et al., 2017; Pearson et al., 2020; Shanahan & Shanahan, 2008). They called for teachers to include specific knowledge about the disciplinary contexts when they worked with students on utilizing strategies to read in the disciplines. Disciplinary knowledge includes the types of information and inquiry experiences emphasized in the respective content areas, how the knowledge is conveyed or organized, and epistemic knowledge or how knowledge is generated in a field (see Chapters 1 and 3). We deal with some aspects of disciplinary knowledge when we discuss strategy instruction with narrative and expository or informational texts later in this chapter.

COGNITIVE STRATEGY INSTRUCTION TO IMPROVE STUDENTS' TEXT COMPREHENSION

Earlier in the school year, Ms. Cooper, the teacher of the four students in the opening vignette, spent time reviewing how students should monitor their reading comprehension and utilize six cognitive strategies (summarization, prediction, inference generation, text structure, questioning, and visualization) that most of them had learned earlier and practiced in grades 2–4. In the whole-group setting, she demonstrated how the students could identify and utilize each of the strategies to facilitate their reading comprehension. Then, she worked with the students in small groups to initiate dialogic strategy instruction. Below, we indicate the goals that Ms. Cooper kept in mind and the process that she employed to further her students' knowledge and use of cognitive strategies while reading.

Self-Regulation

One of Ms. Cooper's instructional aims was to facilitate her students' development of self-regulation for reading. Self-regulation refers to students' ability to set goals for their reading, to monitor their reading, and to independently employ strategies to repair and enhance their reading comprehension as necessary (Stahl & García, 2015, p. 81). Self-regulation requires that students be aware of their own reading strengths and difficulties; the reading demands of the text and the activity or task for which they read; and the role of the context in which they read. According to Almasi (2003), self-regulation is promoted when students know the purpose for employing strategies, are able to use a range of strategies, have developed metacognitive knowledge or self-awareness so that they know when they are having comprehension problems, can evaluate the comprehension demands of a text and reading activity or task, and are motivated to use strategies (p. 13).

Declarative, Procedural, and Conditional Knowledge

To promote students' self-regulation of strategies, we recommend that you, the teacher, explicitly teach three types of information about each strategy: declarative, procedural, and conditional knowledge. Declarative knowledge is what the strategy is or does. For example, summarization involves briefly stating in your own words what was read. It requires you to synthesize the information that was read into much fewer words and sentences. Procedural knowledge is how you implement the strategy. For instance, to summarize a narrative text, you need to make sure that you state what happened according to the important features of the text structure of the story or the story map (e.g., the setting, the characters, the goal or problem, the plot, the resolution, and the theme). To summarize an informational text, you need to state what happened according to the text structure or explicit organization of the text or the author's implied text organization (e.g., to describe, to explain, to compare). Conditional knowledge is knowing when and why it is appropriate to use a particular strategy. For example, it often is appropriate to briefly summarize the text before making a prediction (*the when*) so that the prediction is based on what was read in the text (*the why*).

Gradual Release of Responsibility

To teach your students how to employ strategies, we advise you to utilize the gradual release of responsibility (GRR; Pearson & Gallagher, 1983; Pearson, McVee, & Shanahan, 2019), as shown in Figure 6.1 and Table 6.3. First, we recommend that you *explicitly explain or review* an individual strategy by identifying the *declarative, procedural, and conditional knowledge* for it. Then, while reading a text aloud,

Task	Share of responsibility for the task				
Explicit explanation of individual strategy: declarative, procedural, and conditional knowledge					
Model the strategy while reading					
Collaborative use of strategy					
Guided practice of strategy					
Independent application of strategy					

Teacher   Student

FIGURE 6.1. Teacher and student roles in implementing the gradual release of responsibility (Pearson & Gallagher, 1983; Pearson et al., 2019).

TABLE 6.3. Implementation of the GRR with the Prediction Strategy

GRR steps	Teacher	Teacher and students	Individual student
Explicit teaching	"Today we are going to work on using prediction to improve our reading comprehension."		
Declarative knowledge	"A purposeful prediction is when we think about what might happen next in a story or in an informational text based on clues in the text or our own experience."		
Procedural knowledge	"We make purposeful predictions before we begin reading and at stopping points while we read. To make a prediction before reading, we look at the title/cover and think about what the story or text might be about. Inside the text, we make predictions based on what we know about the topic, the genre, the text structure, and what we previously read. For example, we know that informational texts often have headings that provide a big idea that is followed by explanations and examples."		
Conditional knowledge	"We make predictions to help monitor our thinking about the text, to help connect new information with what we already know, and to help us remember what we read. We don't make predictions for text we already read."		
Modeling of strategy	"My first prediction is about the cover. The title is *Magnets*. I predict that the book will teach me about magnets and what makes things stick to magnets. I know that some kinds of metal stick to magnets. The first chapter is called 'Magnets and Magnetism.' When I look through the first few pages of the chapter I see the words *force*, *attract*, and *repel* in bold. So I think the chapter will teach me how these words relate to how magnets work."		

Collaborative use	1. "Now, let's look at the next section of the chapter together. I want you and your partner to decide on a prediction, and write it on the sticky I gave you." (Discussion of a few of the students' predictions and what evidence they used to generate the prediction.) 2. "I'm going to read the next few pages, and I want you to confirm or disconfirm the prediction [write the words on the board]. Confirm means your prediction was correct [put a plus by the word], disconfirm means your prediction wasn't correct [put a minus by the word]. With your partner, I want you to put a plus on the sticky if your prediction was on target and a minus if it wasn't on target." 3. "Now, let's discuss which predictions worked and which predictions didn't and why."
Guided practice	4. "Now let's look at the next chapter, I want you to write your own prediction on a sticky." 5. "One at a time, please read your prediction, and I will put it on the board." 6. "As I read aloud a few pages of the book, listen to see if your prediction was confirmed or disconfirmed." 7. "Okay, let's put pluses and minuses by the predictions and discuss them."
Independent use of strategy	1. "Now, let's preview the last chapter. I want you to write a prediction on your sticky." 2. "Listen as I continue to read aloud the book. Decide if your prediction is confirmed or disconfirmed by putting a plus or minus by it." 3. "Put your name on the sticky and turn it in."

103

you *model* or show your students how to implement the strategy. Next, you *collaboratively work* with your students by asking them to use a specific strategy with the text you just read aloud and by *scaffolding* (i.e., supporting) their use of the strategy. We recommend that the students share their strategy use with partners, and then the partners share their strategy use with the whole class. Throughout you should scaffold students' strategy work by highlighting what they are doing well and what needs to be changed. Then, you should give your students *guided practice* by having them select and try out a strategy with a section of text you read aloud. Work with them to decide if they used the strategy correctly or incorrectly, and then discuss their use of the strategy in partners and/or with the whole class. Lastly, let them *independently apply* the strategy to a text they read silently or that you or a student read aloud. Collect their work so you can see how each student is implementing the strategy. After students have learned how to employ each strategy, we recommend that you use the GRR to show them how to use *multiple strategies* while reading a text. You also should provide your students with the opportunity to employ individual and multiple strategies with a variety of texts, including narrative and expository texts. Throughout your instruction, it is important to remember that the goal of strategy instruction is for students to utilize appropriate strategies to aid their reading comprehension, not for the students to demonstrate their strategy knowledge.

Preparation for Cognitive Strategy Instruction

Before initiating cognitive strategy instruction with a text, there are a number of things that you, the teacher, need to do. First, you should select a text that you and your students will use. The text needs to be difficult enough to warrant the use of cognitive strategies, but easy enough for the students to comprehend when they effectively employ cognitive strategies. Next, you need to identify the disciplinary context of the text (literary, science, or social studies). Then, you need to determine how the text is organized, or the text structure. For example, the sequential text structure, which often characterizes texts in science and social studies, shows the order in which processes or events occur. Clue words for the sequential text structure include *first, second, third* (etc.), *next, then,* and *finally.* Understanding the text structure that organizes expository text should help your students to identify and learn the main ideas in the text and the relationships among the ideas.

If your students are not familiar with text structures, then you should use the GRR to teach them text structures. Here is where graphic organizers can be very helpful because they not only highlight the main ideas in the text but also show the relationship among the ideas. In addition, they present a visual image of how the text is organized. Here is an example of a graphic organizer for sequential text:

1	⇨	2	⇨	3

Although we list graphic organizers as a recommended instructional technique (see Table 6.2), you have to be careful not to overuse them. When students predominantly are given graphic organizers to outline what they read, they often do not learn how to take notes on their reading. Graphic organizers highlight the main ideas in texts but do not always provide sufficient space for students to list all the important supporting details. Some graphic organizers, like the Venn diagram shown below, are too simplistic, and may result in students not indicating all the relevant information (Wolsey & Lapp, 2017). We discuss graphic organizers and text structures in more detail later in this chapter and in Chapter 8.

Before implementing strategy instruction, be sure to preread the text to identify the types of prior knowledge that your students need to comprehend the text. If your students do not have the appropriate prior knowledge for the discipline, text focus, and text structure, then you should provide it. Without this type of knowledge, it will be difficult for your students to comprehend and learn from their reading because you will not be facilitating their integration of new knowledge with already known knowledge.

In addition to considering your students' prior knowledge, you need to identify any potential meaning-making hurdles that your students are likely to encounter. Cognitive strategies are the tools that good readers use to overcome meaning-making hurdles. For example, throughout Ms. Cooper's unit of instruction, she and her fifth graders have worked on inference generation, particularly how characters' actions and words can help to identify characters' motives. Therefore, an instructional focus on inference generation related to the characters' motives in *An Elephant in the Garden* (Morpurgo, 2010) might be very helpful for Ms. Cooper's students.

Lastly, you need to decide when you and your students are going to read the text (before you work on the strategies, as you work on the strategies, or both?). Another decision is how you and your students will do the reading: Are you, the teacher, going to read the text aloud to them, are they going to read it silently as you read it aloud, are they going to read it collaboratively with classmates, or are they going to read it silently to themselves? These decisions should be based on your careful prereading of the text to determine how much and what kind of support your students will need to accomplish the goals of your unit of study.

IMPLEMENTING STRATEGY INSTRUCTION WITH NARRATIVE TEXTS

After you identify and read the narrative text you are going to use, you need to identify the text's focus (what it is about) and its type of literary text or genre: fable, fairytale, fantasy, fiction, folktale, historical fiction, mystery, poetry, prose, or science fiction (see Bauman & Bergeron, 1993; Buss & Karnowski, 2000). Then, we recommend that you identify the text structure that characterizes the genre. For example, fiction usually involves a story map with a setting, the protagonist or major character, the goal of the protagonist, other key characters, the initiating event, the plot (or repetitive events), and the protagonist's goal attainment or lack of goal attainment. Often, there is a theme and moral or lesson. Understanding the text structure will help you to decide on the instructional techniques (see Table 6.2) that you will ask your students to implement and to determine where they might face comprehension problems and would benefit from employing cognitive strategies (see Table 6.1).

The next two steps are to (1) implement the first instructional technique in Table 6.2— activate your students' prior knowledge about the text's literary genre, text structure, and narrative topic and inhibit irrelevant prior knowledge—and (2) use the GRR to work with your students on selecting and employing appropriate individual strategies and multiple strategies with the selected text. If your students do not have much knowledge about the text's literary genre, its text structure, and the narrative topic, we recommend that you provide them with this knowledge before beginning your cognitive strategy instruction.

Below, we present two examples of how Ms. Cooper worked with her fifth graders to employ cognitive strategies with the book *The Hobbit* (Tolkien, 2013). *The Hobbit* is an example of fantasy genre—imaginary fiction with roots in oral storytelling and folklore, which typically includes elements of magic or witchcraft (Buss & Karnowski, 2000).

Prior to the instruction below, Ms. Cooper already had employed the GRR to teach her students how to employ the cognitive strategies in Table 6.1. She also had activated her students' prior knowledge about fantasy fiction, its text structure, and tales of adventure.

Ms. Cooper began her instruction by reading aloud the first 10 pages of Chapter 1 as her students silently read the pages along with her. In the examples below, the students are working in pairs and each student has a copy of the book and a bookmark with the strategies from Table 6.1 listed on it.

Example 1: Students' Identification and Use of a Single Cognitive Strategy

MS. C: (*to the whole class*) Okay, talk quietly with your partner about which strategy you could use to understand the setting at the beginning of the story.

RITA: When you say setting, do you mean where the hobbit lives?

MS. C: Yes, where the hobbit lives.

JAMES: (*to another boy, Kobe*) It says he lives in the ground.

KOBE: Yes, but it also says it isn't nasty or dirty. Then, it describes a long tunnel.

JAMES: There are nice things in it, too.

KOBE: So, which strategy? (*Students look at the bookmark.*)

JAMES AND KOBE: (*simultaneously*) Visualization!

KOBE: We have to make a picture of where he lives in our minds.

MS. C: Okay, let's talk about the strategy you all selected and why. . . . Now I want you all to visualize where the hobbit lived.

Example 2: Students' Use and Identification of Multiple Strategies

MS. C: Are there sections of the story that you didn't understand? (*Reads and points to the instructions written on the board.*) "1. Point out an example of what you didn't understand to your partner. 2. Use strategies to figure out what you didn't understand. 3. Write on your sticky the strategies that you used to figure it out."

VIOLET: I didn't understand why the dwarves all went to Mr. Baggins's house.

LUISA: Hmm, I didn't either. Let's reread the pages just before the dwarves arrived. Maybe, this is the answer. It's on page 7. It says (*reads aloud*): "With the spike on his staff he scratched a queer sign on the hobbit's beautiful green front door."

VIOLET: That's it, I think. The dwarves all saw the sign and knew that Gandalf had chosen Mr. Baggins.

LUISA: Yeah, it doesn't actually say that, but I think that is the answer.

VIOLET: So, what strategy did we use? We asked a question and looked for an answer.

LUISA: Yes, and we made an inference because the answer wasn't in the story. Let's write down two strategies: We asked a question and we made an inference to answer it.

VIOLET: We also reread when we didn't understand.

LUISA: Okay, we used three strategies. Let's write them down.

MS. C: Okay, let's discuss what you didn't understand and the strategies that you used.

IMPLEMENTING STRATEGY INSTRUCTION WITH EXPOSITORY TEXTS

Before implementing strategy instruction with expository texts, you need to decide on the disciplinary focus of the text: science or social studies? Science usually focuses on the natural world (Connor et al., 2017; Next Generation Science Standards Lead States, 2013), while social studies focuses on the human experience and includes the topics of "civics, economics, geography, and history" (National Council for the Social Studies, 2013, p. 17). Then, you need to identify the focus of the text (what it is about) and its text structure.

How to Determine Expository Text Structure

To identify the text structure, you should examine the author's communicative purpose, the relationship among ideas, and clue words in the text. Science and social studies include some of the same text structures, such as: cause and effect, comparison and contrast, description, problem–solution, and sequence. For instance, a descriptive text in science on mammals is likely to identify the animals in this category (e.g., humans, dogs, cats, horses); whereas, a descriptive text in social studies is likely to identify the mountain ranges in a country. Clue words can help you to determine text structure. Descriptive clue words include *for example, for instance,* and *in addition.*

Sometimes, authors employ multiple text structures to explain a topic. For instance, a science text on erosion might include descriptive text structure to show the different types of erosion, cause–effect text structure to explain how erosion occurs, and problem–solution text structure to identify what can be done to eliminate or curtail erosion. When this occurs, we recommend that you break the text into separate sections, often indicated by headings or subheadings, and focus on the text structure that characterizes the section you and your students are reading and discussing.

Unfortunately, text structures in expository texts are not always easy to determine. Sometimes, authors write inconsiderate texts (Armbruster, 1984); that is, they do not write their texts according to specific text structures, and the reader has to infer the text structure.

Activation of Students' Prior Knowledge

After you have chosen an expository text and identified its disciplinary content, focus, and text structure, you should activate your students' prior knowledge about the text's discipline, text structure, and focus. This is most seamlessly approached if your unit of literacy instruction is synchronized in some way with your disciplinary units of instruction (see options in Chapter 3). If your students do not have much knowledge about the text's disciplinary content, focus, or text structure, then we recommend that you provide it *before* beginning your cognitive strategy instruction. Interrupting your and your students' reading of a text to provide necessary background knowledge can disrupt students' comprehension and become tedious, as was shown in the vignette about teachers' use of the book *Number the Stars* (Lowry, 1989) in Chapter 3.

EXAMPLE OF COGNITIVE STRATEGY INSTRUCTION IN SCIENCE

Below is an example of how Mr. Rodriguez helped a group of fourth-grade readers employ cognitive strategies and one of the instructional techniques in Table 6.2 (graphic organizer) to facilitate their comprehension of an expository text on climate change. Mr. Rodriguez found a short NASA article on climate change on the Internet (*climatekids.nasa.gov/climate-change-evidence*), printed copies for all his students, and had his students silently read it. Before the students began their discussion, Mr. Rodriguez already had used the GRR to teach them how to employ single and multiple strategies with different types of texts and how to use graphic organizers for science topics. He also activated their prior knowledge about Earth's climate.

MR. R: Okay, you've already read the first two pages of the text. What did you learn about climate change?

MYNA: It sounds scary to me. I live by the bay, and if the water rises more, my house will flood.

DAN: That is a scary prediction.

SUSAN: Yeah, but how do we know that the water is going to rise more? Maybe, it's going to stop. My uncle says that climate change isn't real.

LUÍS: Here it says that scientists have proof of climate change (*reads the text aloud*): "Scientists have been observing Earth for a long time. They use NASA satellites and other instruments to collect many types of information about Earth's land, atmosphere, ocean and ice. This information tells us that Earth's climate is getting warmer."

SUSAN: Does it actually say that? I didn't see that information when I read it.

LUÍS: Look, you have to combine the information in the sentences to see what the scientists are saying. You have to make inferences. When it says "they" here, it's talking about the scientists in this sentence. "This information" is about the information that NASA collects.

SUSAN: Oh, I didn't do that.

MR. R: Okay, based on what you read, I want you to work in pairs to list on the cause and effect graphic organizer the reasons that scientists think the climate is getting warmer.

DAN: Is that what the scientists call the evidence for climate change?

MR. R: Yes. Good use of context to figure out the word *evidence*.

IMPLEMENTING DIALOGIC COGNITIVE STRATEGY INSTRUCTION

Wilkinson and Son (2011) and the authors of the federal Clearinghouse for Adolescent Reading (Kamil et al., 2008) reported that students' reading comprehension was significantly improved when they actively engaged in the selection and use of cognitive strategies (independent of their teacher) while reading. Georgia and her colleagues (2021) also found that fourth-grade bilingual students (Spanish–English) who participated in dialogic cognitive strategy instruction over an academic year outgained other bilingual fourth graders (who participated in dialogic text discussion or a treatment control) on a standardized reading comprehension test in English. The opening vignette in this chapter illustrated what dialogic cognitive strategy instruction looked like when students effectively implemented it independent of the teacher. Below, we draw from Georgia and her colleagues' (2021) study to explain how you, the teacher, can do this.

Before implementing dialogic cognitive strategy instruction, you first need to use the GRR to teach your students how to employ cognitive strategies singly and multiply with a variety of texts. Then, we recommend that you give your students bookmarks with the cognitive strategies listed on them. Next, we advise you to put your students in heterogeneous small groups (groups of students with mixed reading levels) of four to five students and assign one of the strong readers to be the initial group leader. Prior to having each group work with a text, we encourage you to model the small-group discussion by working with one group while the rest of the class watches. Initially, you serve as the group's leader. Prior to modeling the small-group work, identify the text you are going to use, read it, and mark it with stickies to indicate where you want to stop and discuss the use of specific strategies to repair or facilitate the students' comprehension. Read aloud three to four pages, and then ask the students in the small group to identify a strategy that should help them to better comprehend the text, stopping to lead a discussion of the particular strategy and how it helps or does not help the students to comprehend the text. Continue to read aloud the text, and stop and discuss strategies until all the students in the small group have participated. The next day, have the student leader, with your help, work with the group to read aloud and discuss the next three to four pages, while the rest of the class watches.

Next, tell your students that when they participate in small groups, they are going to read a few pages in their texts silently before discussing their use of strategies. On subsequent days, meet with each small group, as the other students quietly do other work. Before each group meets, give the students stickies to put on pages where they encounter comprehension problems. Support each leader as they lead a discussion that identifies and discusses the appropriate use of strategies for understanding a specific section of text. Video-record several of the more successful groups; show the videos to your students; and have the students rate the discussions according to whether everyone in the group talks, the students stay focused, and the students treat each other with respect. Next, hold a whole-class discussion on how the students could improve the work of the small groups. The next step could be for students to develop and use their own checklist to evaluate the effectiveness of the small-group work. Some teachers reported that when students used their own checklists to evaluate the effectiveness of small-group work, their small-group discussions improved. Also see the evaluation and Fishbowl processes described in Chapter 7.

INSTRUCTIONAL STRATEGY PROTOCOLS

There may be times when you may prefer to implement an instructional strategy protocol or combine it with your cognitive strategy instruction. Below, we provide brief descriptions of four instructional strategy protocols: directed reading–thinking activity (DR-TA), reciprocal teaching (RT), collaborative strategic reading (CSR), and transactional strategies instruction (TSI). We discussed the most complex integrated strategy repertoire, concept-oriented reading instruction (CORI), in Chapter 3.

Directed Reading–Thinking Activity

The DR-TA is an instructional reading comprehension protocol developed by Stauffer (1969). It is a good starting point for teachers and students due to its simplicity. The DR-TA guides students to think about their reading prior to reading the text, during their reading of the text, and after reading the text. The DR-TA can be implemented with the whole class, small groups of students, or individual students. Reading researchers who evaluated the effectiveness of the DR-TA reported that second, third, and fourth graders who participated in DR-TA outperformed other students on reading comprehension measures (Baumann et al., 1992; Biskin et al., 1976; Stahl, 2008).

To use the DR-TA, teachers should first preselect a narrative or expository text, read it, and mark places in the text where they think students' reading comprehension will be facilitated when students make and confirm text-based predictions (Stahl, 2008; Stahl & García, 2015). According to Reading Rockets (2021), *D* refers to the first step in the protocol, or *Direct*, in which teachers direct students' reading and thinking about the text or text selection. For example, before students read a section of text, teachers encourage students to use the text's title, cover, illustrations, chapter headings, text headings, subheadings, bold vocabulary, prior knowledge, and text structure to make predictions about what a single section of text is about. These predictions also help students to set specific purposes for their reading. In this step, students must *justify* how they made their prediction. This ensures that students are not making guesses. *R* refers to the second step in the protocol, or student *Reading*. Students read to a preset point in the text. Next, teachers ask them open-ended questions to help them confirm or disconfirm their predictions up to that point, and make revised or new predictions for the next section of the text. *T* refers to the *Thinking* students do to identify proof in the text that validates or disconfirms their original predictions. The *A* refers to the activity, or teacher–student discussion of the text. The discussion after each section of text covers key elements in that section, not just prediction validation. The process is repeated for each section of text. For more information on how to implement the DR-TA, see Reading Rockets at *www.readingrockets.org/strategies/drta*.

Reciprocal Teaching

RT originally was developed to improve the expository reading comprehension of middle school students who were poor readers (Palincsar & Brown, 1984). Since its initial use, teachers have effectively implemented RT with students in grades 1–8 to improve their reading comprehension of narrative and expository texts (Hacker & Tenant, 2002; Stahl & García, 2015).

   In RT, teachers first explicitly instruct students on how to use one of four cognitive strategies (questioning, summarizing, clarifying, and predicting) while reading part of an authentic text in a whole-class setting (Palincsar et al., 1989). After students learn how to use each strategy, the teacher posts the strategies and models how the students should use the strategies when they read the texts in heterogeneous small groups of four to six students. Initially, the teacher leads the students in their use of strategies in the small groups. Once the students are comfortable employing the strategies while reading and discussing texts in small groups, the teacher assigns students to be the teachers in the small groups. The first student assigned to be the teacher leads the other members of the small group in their use of the four strategies to discuss their understanding of one section of the text. The students in each group take turns performing the role of teacher, leading their peers through the four strategies for each section of text, until every student has had a turn as the teacher. Most teachers provide students with posters or "cheat sheets" to support them in their use of strategies and turn-taking while implementing RT. More information on how to implement RT is provided in several resources (Hacker & Tenant, 2002; Lubliner, 2001; Palincsar et al., 1989).

Collaborative Strategic Reading

CSR initially was based on RT and was employed to improve the reading comprehension of expository texts by emergent bilingual students or students with learning disabilities at the middle school level (grades 6–8; Klingner & Vaughn, 1996). However, elementary teachers also have successfully used CSR to improve the reading comprehension of students with a wide range of reading levels in grades 4–6 (Kling-ner et al., 1998).

Currently, teachers implement CSR by teaching students to conduct a preview of the expository text prior to reading it; to identify clicks (what they understand) and clunks (what they do not understand) while reading a text; to determine the gist of each section of text; and to wrap it up (after reading) (Bremer et al., 2002). Bremer and colleagues explained that during preview, students are asked to make predic-tions about an expository text based on their knowledge of the topic and by look-ing at the headings, subheadings, and illustrations in the text. Through "click and clunk," teachers instruct students on how to monitor their reading and use fix-up strategies. When teachers ask students to identify the gist, they ask students to tell what or who a paragraph is about in 10 words or less. Teachers instruct students to wrap up the reading by asking them to pretend they are the teacher and to identify questions about the text that the teacher might include on a test. The teacher also asks the students to write down the most important ideas in the text.

According to Bremer et al. (2002), the four strategies are taught to students before they are asked to participate in cooperative groups. For the latter, the teacher assigns students to participate in heterogeneous reading groups of four students, with one student assigned to be the leader (who tells the group members what to read and which strategy to discuss); another student is the clunk expert; a third stu-dent is the gist expert; and the fourth student calls on the other students to read the text and share information. As the students work in their groups, the teacher circu-lates to provide guidance. Afterward, in a whole-class session, the teacher reviews how students enacted the strategies and performed in the cooperative groups. You can find more details on implementing CSR in Klingner et al. (2012) or by exploring the IRIS module (*https://iris.peabody.vanderbilt.edu/module/csr*).

Transactional Strategies Instruction

TSI is a complex multiple-strategy program in which teachers instruct primary and intermediate students on how to use a large number of strategies as they read (Pressley et al., 1992, 1994). Although originally created to improve students' read-ing comprehension of expository texts, it also has been successfully employed with narrative texts. TSI includes the four RT strategies (clarifying, predicting, ques-tioning, and summarizing) plus "comprehension monitoring, confirming (verifying), disconfirming," use of fix-up strategies (e.g., rereading), invoking prior knowledge, "problem solving, think aloud, using text or picture clues, and visualizing," text structure, personal response to text, and making connections, among other strate-gies (Stahl & García, 2015, p. 85). Teachers are supposed to use explicit instruction, modeling, the GRR, and scaffolding to help their students employ multiple strate-gies to improve their reading comprehension as they read "real" or authentic texts.

In addition, students are taught to set goals and to make plans for their reading. TSI also has students work in student-led small groups to resolve comprehension issues and to discuss their interpretations of texts. Because of the large number of strategies, and the fact that teachers are supposed to explicitly teach each strategy over a period of time and use student-led small groups to enact TSI, it can take a long time for teachers and students to effectively implement TSI. Nonetheless, when it has been implemented well, there is evidence that students in TSI significantly improved their reading focus, engagement, and performance compared to students in business-as-usual groups. More information on implementing TSI can be found in Brown and Coy-Ogan (1993) and Pressley et al. (1992).

CONSIDERATIONS FOR BILINGUAL STUDENTS

A number of researchers reported that bilingual students improved their reading comprehension in English when they received some form of cognitive strategy instruction (García et al., 2021; Klingner & Vaughn, 1996, 1999; Padrón, 1992). When Georgia and her colleagues (García et al., 2021) worked with teachers of Latinx bilingual fourth graders in a high-poverty school district on dialogic strategy instruction, they asked the teachers to shelter their English strategy instruction by using ESL techniques, to use the home language (i.e., Spanish) to preview and review when they read or discussed English texts, and to let the students use all their linguistic resources (home language, English, and/or translanguaging) when they met in partners or small groups to discuss their reading or strategy use and when they wrote about their reading (for more information, see Chapter 2). We advise you to do the same. If you don't know the home language of your students, you obviously can't use it to preview and review English texts, but if there are other adults in your class who know the home language, you could ask them to do this. You also could ask students who are proficient in English and their home language to work with you on providing previews and reviews of English texts and to tell you what students are discussing or writing when they use their home language or translanguage. If you are teaching students to use strategies in their home language, because students may vary in their home-language proficiencies, you should follow the same techniques explained above but substitute the home language for English and vice versa.

It also is important for you to realize that bilingual students may use strategies unique to their bilingual status to discuss, explain, or clarify their reading comprehension (for more information, see Chapter 2). For example, they may paraphrase or explain what they read in one language by using the other language or by translanguaging (using all their linguistic resources). Bilingual students' employment of these strategies should be encouraged, not discouraged, because bilingual students often show increased comprehension when they are allowed to use them (García & Godina, 2017).

Lastly, when you work with bilingual students, it is important to find out if they already learned or know how to use strategies when reading in one of their languages. If so, they should be able to transfer this expertise to reading in their other language. Sometimes, all you need to do is remind them that they can use the cognitive strategies that they already learned in one language while reading in the other language.

CONCLUSION

Strategy instruction includes cognitive strategy instruction and instructional (strategy) technique instruction. Cognitive strategies refer to the mental tools that individuals employ to think about, interact with, and comprehend texts. Instructional techniques are teaching practices that facilitate students' comprehension of texts when they read. Researchers reported that when teachers instructed grade 3–6 students on how to flexibly employ cognitive strategies and employed instructional techniques with them, the students' reading comprehension improved.

Teachers need to teach cognitive strategies so that students develop self-regulation; that is, students should select and use cognitive strategies according to their reading goals and performance; the demands of the text, task, or activity; and the context in which they read. The aim of self-regulation is for students to independently select and use appropriate cognitive strategies to comprehend what they are reading, not to demonstrate their knowledge of cognitive strategies.

The GRR, which includes explicit instruction on declarative, procedural, and conditional knowledge, is an effective way for teachers to instruct students on how to use strategies while reading. However, before working with students on selecting and using cognitive strategies with texts, teachers need to select a text that warrants cognitive strategy instruction; preread it to determine the prior knowledge that needs to be activated or provided regarding the text's disciplinary context, topic focus, and text structure; and identify potential comprehension problems. They also need to decide if students are going to read the text before or while implementing cognitive strategies and how the text is going to be read (e.g., by the teacher or a student reading aloud or through silent student reading).

Teachers also should provide students with opportunities to employ strategies with narrative and expository texts. Prior to reading both types of texts, students need to have the appropriate background knowledge for the topic focus and text structure. When narrative texts are used, students also need to know about the genre of the text prior to reading it. Similarly, when expository texts are used, students need to know about the text's disciplinary context before reading it. When students do not have the appropriate background knowledge, then teachers need to provide it.

Dialogic cognitive strategy instruction is an effective way for students to implement cognitive strategies. This instruction involves collaborative dialogue with the teacher and/or with students in heterogeneous, student-led, small groups to identify and use cognitive strategies while reading.

There are several instructional strategy protocols that teachers may want to consider implementing, such as the directed reading–thinking activity, reciprocal teaching, collaborative strategic reading, or transactional strategies instruction. When implemented correctly, they resulted in the increased reading comprehension of grade 3–6 students compared to students in business-as-usual or control group instruction.

Several researchers reported that the implementation of cognitive strategy instruction with current and former emergent bilingual students resulted in improvements in the students' English reading comprehension. However, teachers should use the information in Chapter 2 to help adapt their instruction for current emergent bilingual students. For example, their instruction needs to be sheltered when it is in English. Teachers also should provide previews and reviews of English texts by having someone use the students' home language; allow students to choose how they want to respond and discuss texts when in partners or small groups (i.e., in English or the home language or by translanguaging); and recognize that if students already know how to use strategies in one language, they should be able to use them in the other language but might need encouragement.

CHAPTER SEVEN

Dialogic Learning
The Power of Discussion, Argument, and Debate

GUIDING QUESTIONS

- Why is discussion a critical component of comprehension instruction?
- What discussion components influence students' comprehension?
- What discussion formats work well in each disciplinary area: literary, science, social studies?
- What should you consider when working with emergent bilingual students on text discussions to promote their reading comprehension?

SETTING THE STAGE

Ms. Dimitri's fourth-grade students had a lively discussion about the relationship between two characters in *Sophia's War* (Avi, 2012). At the 5-minute wrap-up buzzer, a few students realized that Pascal had not contributed to the conversation, so as taught, they invited him to share. "I don't have anything to say," he responded. Two of the boys simultaneously raised their voices, egging him on to share: "How can you not have anything to say after all the stuff that we said already!" and "Say something! Just say what you think!" Ms. Dimitri calmly complimented the group for trying to include everyone and reminded them that it is each person's right to "pass" if they choose not to add something. Then she quietly asked Pascal if he would like to share his thoughts. Pascal stated, "I think Sophia was offended by how John acted to her." Ms. Dimitri immediately affirmed his observation, "What an interesting view! Would anyone like to follow-up on Pascal's comment?" In moments, she had recognized the group's fulfillment of its obligation to be inclusive, honored Pascal's right to "pass," and validated Pascal's contribution as worthy of a new discussion thread.

THE VALUE OF DIALOGUE

Comprehension is an in-head activity. However, speaking, writing, and creating a product are observable and measurable ways to share what we have comprehended with others. Additionally, when we explain ideas or defend a position to another, we deepen our conceptualization of those ideas and consolidate the information into our existing cognitive network (Kintsch, 1998). Listening to multiple perspectives from peers is the training ground for young readers to begin mentally considering multiple perspectives. In a dialogic exchange, the participants add each other's ideas to the pages of the text and stretch their comprehension. This process aligns with the theory that comprehension is socially constructed (Vygotsky, 1978). In the text box below, we provide definitions of some terminology used throughout this chapter.

Although many teachers label their class activity as a "discussion," Nystrand et al.'s (1997) study found that 90.79% of 1,151 interactions in English and social studies classrooms in eighth and ninth grades did not include discussion or a democratic exchange of ideas around a topic. Most classroom exchanges were recitations with teachers asking 92–98% of all questions. On average, 85% of each class period was devoted to lecture, initiate–response–evaluate (IRE) questioning, and seatwork.

Setting time aside for rich discussion can be difficult under daily time constraints in classrooms. As a result, many interactions might fall into a recitation routine. However, incorporating open-ended questions (*how* and *why* questions); follow-up questions; high-level, test-released questions (see Appendix C); and quick think–pair–shares (partners discuss a whole-class question) can mitigate the effects of the traditional recitation exchange (Blything et al., 2019; McTighe & Lyman,

---

Definitions of Dialogic Learning Terminology

- **Conversation:** An informal exchange of ideas between two or more people that tends to wander from topic to topic (Backer, 2018).

- **Dialogic learning:** A general term that includes educational practices in which students and teachers socially exchange words, texts, or other media in service to building knowledge.

- **Discussion:** An interaction between two or more people that focuses on a topic or question. Discussions also reflect the democratic values around participation, equality, and freedom (Backer, 2018; Reznitskaya et al., 2009).

- **Recitation:** The teacher *initiates* a question, a student *responds*, and the teacher *evaluates* the acceptability or accuracy of the student's response (IRE) (Cazden, 1988).

1988). However, keep in mind that think–pair–shares are not a replacement for discussions that prompt deep thinking and the expression of multiple voices.

Typically, it is crucial to consider both the content of the discussion and the interaction process when evaluating a classroom discussion. Research evidence has proven that simply increasing student talk will not automatically result in higher levels of comprehension (Murphy et al., 2009). Deliberately matching your instructional goals with a discussion format that is aligned with your purpose is essential.

INFLUENTIAL COMPONENTS OF DISCUSSION FORMATS

First, we will identify some discussion formats that you can put in your toolkit to meet different instructional purposes. Most of the approaches that we address have evidence to substantiate their effectiveness with all students, including emergent bilingual students and striving readers (see Table 7.1). In a meta-analysis and research review, Soter et al. (2008) identified several common characteristics from discussion protocols that promoted high-quality talk about text and that were highly effective in promoting students' comprehension in the intermediate grades. Salient characteristics of the most effective discussions included: a prediscussion activity to promote responses; teacher choice of text; teacher control of the topic; student control of interpretive authority and turn-taking; teacher use of the GRR to introduce teacher-led or peer-led small groups; small-group structure; heterogeneous ability grouping; reading that occurs before the discussion; and a content or process postdiscussion activity.

Stance

Rosenblatt (1978) introduced the term *stance* to categorize the mindset of readers during the reading experience. Readers with an *efferent* stance read to gather information. Although often associated with expository text, readers who anticipate being questioned after reading narratives also read with an efferent stance. The *aesthetic* stance is when the reader vicariously shares the characters' lived human experience (feelings, thoughts, actions). The *critical analytic* stance focuses on a dilemma or problem, in which justifications for different action responses are made based on text evidence and reasoning (Wade et al., 1994).

These stances set the tone for particular discussion formats. Most discussion formats are likely to include a mixture of stances with a central purpose dominating. The stance influences the role of the teacher, interpretive authority, topic threads in the discussion, and the dynamic between the text and the reader. As teachers, you want to align your discussion format with your instructional goals and your reading purposes.

TABLE 7.1. Discussion Format Characteristics

	Dominant stance	Leader	Interpretive authority	Control over turns	Control over topic	Text type	Grouping
Recitation[a]	Efferent	Teacher	Teacher	Teacher	Teacher	Narrative Expository	Whole class or small group
Instructional conversation[b]	Efferent	Teacher	Teacher	Students–teacher	Teacher	Narrative	Whole class or small group
Questioning the author[a,b]	Efferent	Teacher	Students–teacher	Students–teacher	Teacher	Narrative Expository	Whole class or small group
Book club/literature circle[a,b]	Aesthetic	Students	Students	Students	Students	Narrative	Small group
Collaborative reasoning[a,b]	Critical reasoning	Teacher–students	Students	Students	Teacher–students	Narrative Expository	Small group
Science writing heuristic	Critical reasoning	Teacher–students	Students	Students	Teacher–students	Expository	Small group and whole class
Discussion Web	Critical reasoning	Students	Students	Students	Teacher–students	Narrative Expository	Small group

Note. Analysis adapted from [a]Chinn et al. (2001) or [b]Soter et al. (2008).

Who Is in Charge?

Leadership

Most whole-class discussions are teacher-led. However, small-group discussions can be teacher-led, teacher- and student-led, or student-led.

Regardless of the discussion protocol selected, teachers need to model effective discussion practices in their everyday classroom discussions (e.g., the use of open-ended questions, follow-up questions (uptake), active listening, and equitable inclusion). There is evidence that student talk and management difficulties in small groups tend to imitate and reflect interactions in the whole-class teacher-controlled recitations and discussions (Almasi, 2003; Chinn et al., 2001).

Students need explicit instruction on how to participate in small-group discussions. Teachers and students should collaboratively formulate a few guidelines for discussions. During mini-lessons, students can role-play how to address Chatty Charlie, Shy Shiloh, and Bossy Bailey. (See Table 7.2 for mini-lesson suggestions.) Maloch (2004) observed a teacher who effectively used her whole-class shared-text reading sessions to teach, model, and provide guided practice in performing the small-group practices that students would employ during their upcoming small-group discussions.

Authority

Once the discussion begins, three forms of authority are in play: interpretive, control of turns, and control of the topic. Interpretive authority is aligned with the stance and the leader's leverage in framing the discussion. In protocols such as questioning the author (QtA; Beck et al., 1996, 1997, 2009), the teacher and students share authority as they discuss the text and ask questions to determine the author's meaning. The readers' lived experiences and personal responses contribute

TABLE 7.2. Mini-Lesson Topics

Content	Process
Author's craft	Sharing airtime
Theme	Disagreeing constructively
Strategy application	Gatekeeping
Applying disciplinary knowledge	Active listening
Identifying evidence	Uptake and other forms of questioning
Building an argument	Pacing
	Self-evaluation

value to an aesthetic text interpretation in literature circles and book clubs. In critical stance discussions such as collaborative reasoning (CR; e.g., Chinn et al., 2001; Reznitskaya et al., 2009), the students use evidence and reasoning to generate a position or conclusion. Logistics such as who controls turn-taking and moving from one topic thread to a new topic thread also provide evidence of student authority, engagement, and thinking.

SELECTING A DISCUSSION FORMAT

Due to space constraints, we are unable to address all types of discussion formats. However, we address six discussion formats in this chapter that have undergone years of study regarding student comprehension. The Discussion Web (Alvermann, 1991) employs research-based practices but does not have research substantiation. Because every text, teacher, and group of students are different, there will be variations in how you decide to implement these discussions in your class. We placed each discussion format in a single content area where it is used most commonly. However, you can adapt most of the discussion formats to other disciplinary areas.

We recommend that you select and adjust the discussion formats to match your teaching goals. For example, if you are addressing the first three anchor CCSS standards (see Appendix A, "Key Ideas and Details") and you and your students are new to small-group discussions, you might choose an instructional conversation (IC; Goldenberg, 1992/1993; Saunders & Goldenberg, 1999). This format would be a good choice because it has clear guidelines for teachers to follow, strong teacher scaffolding during the discussion while creating a dialogue rather than an IRE recitation. You and your students might not feel ready to jump into a literature circle in which the students own the responsibility for managing topics and turns in the discussion.

DISCUSSING LITERARY TEXTS

Generally, the purpose of literary texts is to describe the universality of the human experience. Discussions about these texts invite students to share how the stories relate to their life experiences or influence their views of the world. Literary texts typically have one or more universal themes (e.g., fairness, honesty, resilience, betrayal) that are central to comprehension. Therefore, teachers often use IC, book clubs/literature circles (BCs/LCs), and CR with literary texts. IC provides the most teacher support, while BCs/LCs provide the least teacher support and emphasize the aesthetic experience of the text. Teachers and students collaborate to gather evidence as they grapple with a big question when engaging in CR.

Instructional Conversation

The IC format was designed, implemented, and researched in classrooms with high percentages of low-income minority students, including English learners (i.e., emergent bilingual students; Goldenberg, 1992/1993; Saunders & Goldenberg, 1999) and students with special needs (Echevarría & McDonough, 1993). After reading a narrative text, the IC is implemented to extend the students' understanding of the story. The design includes attention to instructional elements and conversational elements. The teacher focuses the conversation on the theme and key ideas by using high-level questioning and instruction to stretch the students' thinking about the text. Ideally, the students self-select their turns, but initially the teacher may need to call on students to respond.

Elements of Instructional Conversations
(Goldenberg, 1992/1993)

INSTRUCTIONAL ELEMENTS

- Emphasize a theme or key concept.
- Activate prior knowledge and provide necessary background information.
- Provide explicit instruction of skills, concepts, or author's craft.
- Promote more complex language by utilizing sophisticated vocabulary from the text and using discourse moves to help students expand their contributions.
- Elicit the students' referral back to the text for providing reasons to support an idea, argument, or position.

CONVERSATIONAL ELEMENTS

- Use open-ended questions that have the possibility of more than one correct answer.
- Uptake the students' comments with follow-up questions and by initiating new threads of conversation.
- Model (and teach) active listening that builds connectivity between turn-taking rather than parallel talk wherein students only consider their own thoughts.
- Create a challenging, compelling discussion that is balanced within a positive, affective climate.
- Encourage self-selected turn-taking.

You can increase the effectiveness of IC for emergent bilingual students by prompting students to write in a literacy log before the IC (Saunders & Goldenberg, 1999). These writing prompts should call for students to relate something in the story to their personal lives. Adding the literature logs to the IC routine significantly improved theme identification for limited-English-proficient, Latinx students, but not for former English learners, Latinx students with higher English proficiency, who, as a group, continued to outperform the limited-English-proficient students on theme identification. However, IC participation did yield higher comprehension for all the participating students when compared to a control group. Saunders and Goldenberg (1999) advised that two instructional elements could have contributed to the IC students improved comprehension: the choice of a highly engaging text for fourth- and fifth-grade Latinx students and the English learners' participation in a unique transitional program between transitional bilingual education and the all-English classroom that provided them with increased teacher support and instruction.

A collaborative special education and general education classroom in Brooklyn implemented IC with the book *This Is the Rope: A Story from the Great Migration* (Woodson, 2013) from their integrated curriculum. After reading the story, the teachers prompted the students to write a personal experience based on the book: "Describe something that a family member has passed down to you (or your parents) and why it is special." The teachers provided examples such as recipes, photographs, and traditions as well as artifacts. The special education teacher supported the nine special education students as needed. All students wrote for about 20 minutes and then shared their stories with a partner (10 minutes). Then the class was divided into two heterogeneous groups where each teacher led a discussion to connect how the students' stories were similar and different from the main character's experience (20 minutes). The following day, the teachers divided the class into two new heterogeneous groups and conducted two ICs based on a single lesson plan that focused on ensuring that the students understood the family's journey and the symbolic representation of the rope.

Book Clubs and Literature Circles

BCs/LCs mimic adult discussions about books students have read. The goal is for students to control all aspects of the BC/LC while engaging in high-level, interactive talk about the text. In order to accomplish this goal, you need to do the preparation suggested in the section "Leadership," above. Although the lack of teacher control in a BC/LC may result in discussions that summarize events in the texts or analyze the characters, aesthetic responses tend to dominate the free-flowing student-led discussions (Soter et al., 2008)

Scaffolding BC/LC

SHORT-TERM SCAFFOLDING

Garas-York et al. (2013) describe some short- and long-term scaffolding that are needed so that students function independently in a BC/LC. Many teachers provide students with cheat sheets that include question stems or probes that they can use generically or with specific texts. Additionally, students might prepare for their discussions by writing response journals, coding questions or ideas within the text, inserting Post-it notes to indicate discussion points, or completing a double-entry journal to record quotes from the text in the left column and reflections in the right column. These scaffolds might be open-ended or focused on a reading purpose, such as character traits or motivation.

Less effective but very popular is the assignment of roles (e.g., leader, time-keeper, visualizer, questioner, word wizard) for students to enact during the discussion (Daniels, 2002; Garas-York et al., 2013). The purpose of assigning *rotating* roles is to scaffold the individual cognitive processes required when reading and discussing a text before expecting students to juggle all processing simultaneously. Therefore, students only need to practice each role one or two times. Assigning roles is *not* effective or aligned with the intention of a BC/LC when perpetuated over time.

LONG-TERM SCAFFOLDING

Long-term scaffolding requires that teachers use the GRR to steadily increase the level of students' thinking during the conversations (content) and the sophistication of their discourse moves (process). Rather than a teacher steadily withdrawing responsibility for the group linearly, the GRR needs to look more like a dance with an up-and-down exchange of responsibility as the teacher continues to raise expectations for the students or alters the task in some way (Pearson & Gallagher, 1983). Stahl (2009) found that the most effective teachers worked with individual groups, then sat outside each group before circulating among multiple simultaneous discussion groups. These effective teachers also repeated this cycle over time with ongoing discussion goals in comparison to teachers who made a single transition from sitting with a single group to circulating among multiple simultaneous discussion groups.

In the same study, the most effective teachers took advantage of self- and peer-evaluation mechanisms more frequently than less effective teachers did. These mechanisms included self- and peer-evaluation checklists of every discussion (see Figure 7.1), classwide video discussions of individual groups, and evaluations of fishbowl discussions.

During the fishbowl activity, a single discussion group sits in an inner circle, and other class members sit in an outer circle. The outer circle uses the class evaluation checklist to evaluate multiple features or a single feature of the inner circle's

Interact with the Text

Work together to clarify and answer questions about the text.
Work together to understand.
Use strategies (predict, summarize, visualize, clarify, question) to help understand the text.
Address themes.
Ask significant questions.
Connect specific pieces of text with personal experience.
Provide evidence supporting multiple perspectives.
Reread parts of the book.

Interact with Each Other

Be prepared.
Ask questions.
Take turns talking.
Give everyone a chance to talk.
Listen actively and respond to each other.
Be respectful.

Group Member	Rating	Reason
Yourself		

+Excellent ✓+Very Good ✓Good ✓−Needs Improvement −Not Acceptable

FIGURE 7.1. Student self- and peer-evaluation template.

book discussion. For example, you might prompt the outer circle to look for examples of *uptake*, a follow-up question or a new thread of comments that directly link to the content of another student's comment that occurs in the inner group's discussion. After the inner group's discussion, the outer circle reports what they observed, and the two groups exchange insights. A Google search of "fishbowl conversation" will yield many fishbowl conversation videos in all grade levels and subject areas.

Setting Up a BC/LC

TEXT SELECTION

Students should have agency in selecting the book they will be reading and discussing. When planning for a BC/LC, you might select three or four texts that are connected regarding content, theme, or author. It is a good idea to include texts that vary in readability levels and are available as audiobooks. Provide a brief book talk describing each book, including the estimated difficulty level. Allow the students to submit the names of their first, second, and third choices. Based on the students' book selections, build heterogeneous groups of four to six students who can interact well together.

SCHEDULING BC/LC MEETINGS

It can feel overwhelming to fit a BC/LC into a demanding literacy schedule. However, you can use flexibility to organize the components into your existing literacy block (see Table 7.3). Ongoing mini-lessons ensure student growth in the discussion process. It is important to allocate time for students to read the texts during the literacy block (independent reading or guided reading replacement) or elsewhere during the school day. In order to ensure success, some students will need support and opportunities to rehearse what they will say in their small-group sessions (Maloch, 2005). Students can prepare with an instructor, mentor, or peer.

Additionally, students need time to complete a self-evaluation of individual and group interactions followed by a brief whole-class community share at the end of each small-group discussion. In the opening vignette, Ms. Dimitri used a 5-minute warning buzzer to signal that students should wrap up their discussions and

TABLE 7.3. Sample BC/LC Schedules

Sample 1	Sample 2
Mini-lesson (5–10 minutes)	BC/LC discussion (20–30 minutes)
Reading preparation *or* BC/LC discussion (20–30 minutes)	Classroom debrief *or* mini-lesson (10–15 minutes)
Classroom debrief (5–10 minutes)	Reading preparation (15–20 minutes)

complete their self-evaluations. As this becomes routine, it will consume little time and assure the sustenance and developmental growth in healthy discussion practices. Book clubs for a single book should not extend beyond 3 or 4 weeks.

Collaborative Reasoning

CR is a postreading discussion format with a long and robust research history of use with elementary students (e.g., Chinn et al., 2001; Reznitskaya et al., 2009). Compared to control groups, CR participants demonstrated statistically significant improvements in reasoning skills, as well as expanded oral argument strategies over time as they reused strategies that classmates employed (*snowballing*), and they increased the quality and quantity of written arguments in text responses that addressed a big question (Chinn et al., 2009: Jadallah et al., 2009; Reznitskaya et al., 2009). CR yields these outcomes when students read and respond to literary or expository texts.

CR has also been utilized successfully in classrooms with emergent bilingual students. Zhang et al. (2013) found that after participating in CR discussions, fifth-grade emergent bilingual students demonstrated statistically significant improvements compared to a control group in listening, speaking, reading, and writing in English. On a transfer writing task in response to reading, the CR students wrote longer responses with more sophisticated vocabulary and included higher levels of reasoning, more evidence to support their claims, and more counterarguments than the control group (Zhang et al., 2013).

After students read a complex text (e.g., chapter, article, short story), the teacher prompts a big-idea, yes–no question. This question serves as the centerpiece for CR. The teacher sits on the side as the students use evidence from the text and argumentation strategies to support their position.

Ms. Dimitri's class was reading the novel *Sophia's War* (Avi, 2012) as part of their Colonial Days–Revolutionary War integrated unit. The book tells the story of a 12-year-old girl, Sophia, whose rebel, patriot family is housing a dashing, young British Lieutenant John André. In Chapter 22, John André refuses Sophia's request to advocate for her imprisoned brother/rebel soldier, William. After the students partner-read the chapter, Ms. Dimitri organized the class into small heterogeneous groups of five to six students and posed the question "Should Sophia feel betrayed by John André's refusal to provide any involvement or support regarding William's imprisonment?"

GIRL 1: Yes, she should feel betrayed. He played her music and was nice to her. She trusted him.

BOY 1: No. She decided to tell him stuff. She made her own decisions.

GIRL 2: She shouldn't feel betrayed. If I were him, I wouldn't help. I have my own family to worry about. It is not his fault. He has his own responsibilities.

GIRL 1: (*asking Ms. Dimitri, as she looks in the book*) Ms. Dimitri, what does *deceased* mean?

MS. DIMITRI: Not alive anymore, dead.

BOY 2: I want to add on to [unintelligible]. . . .

GIRL 3: I agree with [Girl 2]. It is not his job. It is his job to protect *his* side and kill the rebels. Sophia thinks he should protect her family!! Why would she think that? (*Indignant tone.*)

GIRL 1: But before, he said (*reading from text, p. 87*), "I give you my pledge. If there is anything I can do for you, you need only ask."

GIRL 1, GIRL 2, BOY 2: (*All talk over each other, incomprehensible.*)

BOY 2: That's not relevant.

GIRL 1: I have my opinion, you can disagree.

During the discussion, the students felt comfortable selecting and publicly declaring opposing positions. They used text evidence and reasoning to support their positions. They listened to each other and linked their responses. They used argumentation discourse moves such as "I want to add on" and "I agree with."

The opening vignette in this chapter occurred at the end of the above discussion. Despite the open exchange, Pascal would not express his position and ideas without support and encouragement from the teacher. He serves as an example of the essential ongoing role teachers need to play in supporting both individual students and groups in developing their discussion skills. In addition, teachers can strongly influence whether students value the discussion input from their peers who struggle in speaking English, reading, or following class rules (Maloch, 2005)

The vignette also reinforces three considerations for using CR with emergent bilingual students (Zhang & Stahl, 2011/2012). First, emergent bilingual students need more time to compose their responses mentally, so premeetings and rehearsals with mentors may be helpful (Maloch, 2005). Second, like Pascal, many emergent bilingual students may be reluctant to elaborate on their ideas. It is not uncommon for them to deliver short responses and wait for the teacher's evaluation. Finally, for longer texts, it is a good idea to include a more structured conversation (IC, QtA) and written response logs before asking them to participate in the CR discussion.

DISCUSSING SCIENTIFIC TEXTS

Scientific texts are often expository texts that explain scientific findings or scientific information. When reading and discussing these texts, a reader is likely to apply an efferent stance. However, many scientific texts are procedural texts that explain a process involved in building new scientific knowledge. In these cases, the author and the readers need to apply scientific reasoning, evidence, and argumentation to substantiate the value of the findings.

Questioning the Author

QtA helps students actively search for meaning during the first reading of a difficult text (Beck et al., 1996, 1997, 2009). Researchers used QtA with narrative and expository text successfully. However, the protocol leans strongly toward an efferent stance with the critical stance as a secondary lens. Teachers and students grapple through text segments during their first reading, using teacher-generated "queries" to analyze the difficult portions. The teacher plays a vital role throughout the discussion as a facilitator and participant in the meaning-making process. As a result, QtA is supportive when students are reading new genres; texts that include abstract, complex scientific ideas; or primary historical sources with archaic language forms. QtA has been used successfully with upper elementary and middle school students.

Elements of Questioning the Author

- **Planning:** The teachers read the text before teaching in order to identify the major understandings, relate the text to curriculum needs, anticipate potential student difficulties, segment text, and develop queries.

- **Queries:** Queries help propel the discussions and facilitate students' construction of meaning during reading, unlike questions which tend to test recall after reading. Initiating queries make the author's message public, follow-up queries provide focus and integrate content, narrative queries relate to the special nature and structure of narrative text.

- **Discussion:** A set of six "moves" are used by teachers to help orchestrate student ideas and make improvisational decisions during a dynamic discussion. "Moves" in response to student comments: *marking* a student's comments for emphasis, *turning back* to the students or text, *revoicing* or rephrasing.
  More direct teacher "moves": *modeling* is making in-head processes visible, *annotating* is providing missing information to fill in gaps in the text, and *recapping* is summarizing the major points that the students have constructed.

- **Initial implementation:** Desks are arranged in a *U* shape to facilitate discussion. Students are introduced to the idea of author fallibility and participate in a think-aloud demonstration.

Argumentation in Science-Based Inquiry

Scientific inquiry intertwines the processes of thinking, discussing, and writing. Kim and Hand (2015) defined scientific argumentation as "the act of organizing evidence and theory to support and rebut an explanatory conclusion, model, and prediction for the purpose of justification and persuasion of one's ideas to others" (p. 223). The science writing heuristic (SWH; Chen et al., 2016; Hand et al., 2016; Kim & Hand, 2015) approach engages elementary students in posing questions, gathering data, making claims, producing evidence to support their claims, checking to see what others say (both peers and experts), and reflecting on how their own ideas have changed. Although the students are engaged in scientific activities, the focus of SWH is to use argumentation to develop their understanding of the scientific process. Chen et al. (2016) contended that argumentation in science requires both social negotiation and epistemic understanding of scientific argumentation. Students learn that oral and written argument exchanges build scientific knowledge. Teachers use argumentation to teach students that challenging or disagreeing with the text or your peers (or the teacher!) is part of the scientific process, not a personal attack.

Most classroom science curricula use the NGSS (Next Generation Science Standards Lead States, 2013) or state science standards to design units of study. For example, NGSS Standard 3 LS2-1 calls on students to "Construct an argument that some animals form groups that help members survive." In SWH, students investigate multiple sources or build a model to explore their big question. To attain the above NGSS standard, small groups of students would select an animal to answer the question "How does forming a group help a *group-selected animal* survive?" Teachers might provide an animal option from multiple ecosystems to expand learning opportunities. Then, each small group would study reference materials and establish preliminary claims. The small group would come to a consensus in selecting preliminary claims. Further research would occur to enable them to gather more *evidence* and *elaborate* on their claims. Collectively the group would create a cohesive argument based on evidence to substantiate each claim.

Next, the students would draft their claims and evidence for a PowerPoint slide presentation, on chart paper, or on a poster for a first-round oral presentation to the whole class. During the whole-class discussion, their peers critique the oral presentations by challenging, defending, supporting, or rejecting either the evidence or the reasoning and cohesion of the argument. During this discussion, the small group might elaborate on claims challenged or defend claims that their peers reject. As the students use models and written graphs or diagrams to demonstrate their ideas, they build epistemological understanding. Peer critique of evidence also expands their understanding of what counts as scientific proof. After this round of discussions, each small group begins a revision process based on their peers' feedback and digs more deeply into scientific resources. The peer-review discussion process follows each revision. There might be multiple rounds of peer review for complex investigations before the class accepts the final project (Chen et al., 2016).

Several SWH research findings align with the findings of CR studies. First, sustained practice is vital in yielding increases in the sophistication of social negotiation, discourse moves, and snowballing (Chen et al., 2016; Reznitskaya et al., 2009). The teacher is available in both formats to provide scaffolding, redirection, wait-time, or uptake as the situation merits (Kim & Hand, 2015). Additionally, both CR and SWH found relationships in the development of oral arguments and their transfer to written arguments (Chen et al., 2016; Hand et al., 2016). In SWH, there were also increases in the students' usage of epistemological behaviors in argumentation and knowledge building (Chen et al., 2016). Evidence indicated that SWH contributed to an increase in Iowa Tests of Basic Skills scores in language and science for students in classrooms with a high implementation of SWH, especially those students who receive free and reduced lunch (Hand et al., 2016).

DISCUSSING SOCIAL STUDIES TEXTS

Teachers can use most of the research-validated discussion formats that we have previously described in social studies. However, like for science, teachers must adapt the critical reading process and epistemological discourse to the values of the discipline. Evidence includes texts, graphics, artifacts, primary sources, and more. A social studies critique considers the source of the evidence (e.g., author background, website, journal), the context, and existing corroboration. In social studies, the purpose of the discussion is often to develop solutions, share voices, and create change.

Students often participate in a debate to explore solutions to a problem. However, in the elementary years, they will need teacher guidance and structures to help them use evidence to support their positions rather than plucking random facts to support opinions. Additionally, the intermediate grades are a time to develop the social negotiation skills described in the SWH process. Social negotiation is also required to solve challenges in society.

Discussion Webs

The Discussion Web (Alvermann, 1991) is a discussion format that brings together reading, talking, listening, and writing. It provides a valuable scaffold for preparing students to engage in more formal debates.

The Discussion Web graphic organizer is an H-shaped visual with the question in the middle and spaces for pro–con evidence on the two vertical legs. During the whole-class discussion, you can prompt a deeper discussion and analysis of the arguments that each group presented to address the source of evidence, the context,

Discussion Web Steps for Social Studies (Alvermann, 1991)

1. Have students read or view multiple sources that present conflicting information on an issue.

2. Introduce the discussion web with a pro–con (yes–no) question.

3. Place students in partnerships. Direct the partners to take turns jotting down arguments for both positions. They do not have to fill in all the lines but there should be equal amounts of evidence for each position.

4. Combine two partnerships to form new groups of four students. The new groups compare their arguments for each position. Then they must come to a consensus on one position or the other. However, there will be an opportunity for dissenting voices to be heard.

5. Give each group 3 minutes to select a single best reason to support their conclusion. Each group should pick a spokesperson to share that argument with the entire class. Each group shares their position and their best argument for that position with the class. They should also mention any dissenting viewpoints that have not been mentioned by others.

6. Finally, each individual writes a personal position statement.

and the level of corroboration within the sources read. For example, after reading a pro–con Newsela article set, a fifth-grade class used the Discussion Web to foster a discussion on the question "Do we need voter ID laws?" This was the students' first experience with a Discussion Web. Therefore, the teacher chose the Newsela feature that included two parallel articles on the topic written by different people. Rather than having an open-ended search for multiple perspectives, the article set supplied practical constraints on working through the discussion process for the first time. After the students finished the Discussion Web activity, the teacher led a discussion on how the authors' professional positions might have influenced their perspectives and why it is important to investigate sources of evidence (see Figure 7.2).

Debates

The Discussion Web is a supportive introductory activity for preparing students to engage in more formal debates. Malloy et al. (2020) incorporated debates into three fifth-grade, state-mandated social studies units. The teacher extended the mandated topic to encompass a related current problem and resolution. For example, during their Industrialization unit, the students debated a resolution related to the environmental challenges of disposing massive amounts of discarded, mass-produced

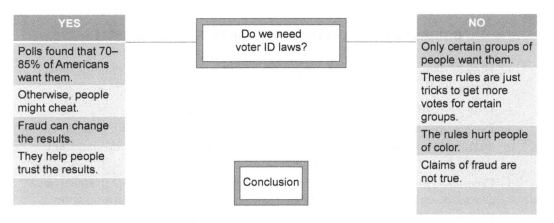

FIGURE 7.2. Discussion Web. Adapted from Alvermann (1991).

stuff. The teacher divided the students into two groups. As in the Discussion Web, all students had to prepare both affirmative and negative arguments to defend or challenge the resolution. Next, the teacher randomly assigned each group to defend a position. Both sides presented their opening position statements with the opportunity for the negative side to propose a counterresolution. A 90-second cross-examination followed each opening argument. Then, each side presented a 1-minute final statement of its strongest argument points. Finally, each student created an individual written argument based on their personal stand on the resolution.

The teacher and researchers used the state writing rubrics for evaluating the oral debates and written arguments. The 4-point rubric included the following elements: (1) a clearly stated position, (2) evidence with elaboration, (3) a logical, cohesive organizational structure, and (4) clear, expressive language. Over time, the students shifted from using opinions to evidence and reasoning. The organizational structure of their arguments also improved. The students' writing improved most in the areas of focus and organization.

The teacher in the study modified her instruction between each debate. Her modifications can be helpful for anyone who wishes to initiate debates in the intermediate grades. The teacher added additional modeling and oral argument rehearsals. She also created and shared some common sentence starters for the students to use in each debate section. Additionally, her students gathered evidence from multiple sources, so she taught them note-taking skills and provided graphic organizers to help them organize their research in alignment with each pro–con position. The students used the tools to organize their evidence for both the debate and their written position paper.

As teachers, we have an obligation to educate our students to view multiple sides of a problem. Critically evaluating sources and presenting the information in reasoned, cohesive oral and written arguments are valuable life skills.

CONSIDERATIONS FOR CONDUCTING DISCUSSIONS WITH BILINGUAL STUDENTS

There are several recommendations to remember when conducting discussion groups with emergent bilingual students. First, as noted in the reviews of IC (Saunders & Goldenberg, 1999) and CR (Zhang & Stahl, 2011/2012), emergent bilingual students often will participate more if you let them write what they are going to say before calling on them to participate. Writing in English, in their L1, or by translanguaging (using their L1 and English) gives them the opportunity to plan their participation. The latter seems to reduce their anxiety about making errors in their oral English, forgetting English words, or speaking English with an accent.

Second, due to emergent bilingual students' developing English proficiency, they may participate more when they are given the chance to use their L1 to discuss what they read in English. If you do not speak their L1, then we recommend that you organize them in small groups or pairs with other students who speak their L1 but who vary in their English proficiency. You should encourage the students to use their L1 or to translanguage (use both their L1 and English) to discuss what they read in English. Then, ask the students who speak better English to share with you what was said in the discussion groups.

Lastly, you need to know how your bilingual students (current and former emergent bilingual students) are interpreting English text if you are to help them improve their English reading comprehension. Because they are from different cultural and linguistic backgrounds than native English speakers, they may develop interpretations of English texts that are different from what you and the authors expected. Therefore, it is important for you to establish a respectful climate in your classroom so that your bilingual students feel comfortable sharing their interpretations of English texts with you at the same time that you and your native-English-speaking students feel comfortable sharing with them the evidence and procedures that you employed to arrive at your interpretations of English texts.

CONCLUSION

Dialogic approaches are based on sociocultural constructivism theory, the idea that human interaction builds knowledge (Vygotsky, 1978). Talking about a text helps solidify our understanding of what the text said. When students share their ideas about a text and their related experiences with others, it enhances the comprehension of the speaker and the listeners. This interaction paves the way for them to see a text's message from multiple perspectives independently.

When teachers thoughtfully match the discussion format with the lesson's purpose, their students can understand the text more deeply. Different discussion formats influence what students look for in a text and how they talk about it. The format also influences whether the teacher or students take the lead in determining who talks, what the group talks about, and who has interpretive authority.

Some common elements of effective discussions lead to high-level thinking about texts (Soter et al., 2008). It works best for teachers to allocate some control over the choices of texts to align them with the learning standards. Small-group structures allow for the most student talk. In most cases, the text needs to be read before, not during, the discussion. Typically, it works best for teachers to provide the prompts for discussions. However, the students assume responsibility for turn-taking and interpretive authority in the most effective discussions. Groups can be either teacher-led or student-led, but there needs to be ongoing teacher involvement in scaffolding the students' ability to engage in high-level, interactive talk with each other. There is commonly a follow-up written composition activity. Just as writing or taking notes can help students prepare for the discussion, the discussion also serves as a rehearsal for writing a more formal response to reading and sharing knowledge. Self- and peer evaluations contribute to the ongoing development of high-quality student discussions.

Regardless of disciplinary content, discussions that lead to comprehension and knowledge building share some common indicators. First, the best discussions have high quantities of interactive student talk. However, quantity is not enough. Authentic questions tend to yield uptake, elaborated explanations, and exploratory talk that lead students to deeper understanding, reasoning, and epistemological grounding (Chen et al., 2016; Nystrand et al., 1997; Soter et al., 2008). Additionally, across the disciplines, some common words and phrases (e.g., *because, agree, maybe, think, how, why*) are indicators of student reasoning.

To increase the participation of bilingual students, we recommend that you let them write (in their L1, English, or English and their L1) what they plan to say before they participate in class discussions. Also, we recommend that you group them with other L1 speakers of varying English proficiency and let them discuss the texts in their L1 or through translanguaging. Before the group meets, ask one of the more English-proficient students to pay attention to what is said in the group and to be prepared to share with you what they said in the group.

Finally, it takes time and patience to foster dialogic expertise. All of us have facilitated student discussions that fell flat, appeared to waste valuable time, or ended chaotically. However, the secret is to readjust, self-evaluate, and persist. Video is your friend. As with most teaching activities, collaborating with colleagues helps. The results are worth the effort.

CHAPTER EIGHT

Disciplinary Writing Instruction

GUIDING QUESTIONS

- Why should teachers emphasize disciplinary writing for students in grades 3–6?
- What general instruction should teachers implement to support disciplinary writing?
- How should teachers instruct their students about disciplinary writing in ELA, science, and social studies?
- How do integrated disciplinary literacy programs in science, social studies, and ELA teach disciplinary writing?
- What are the considerations for bilingual students when teaching disciplinary writing?

SETTING THE SCENE

Mr. Walsh is meeting with a small group of fifth graders about writing a historical essay. He previously had the students in his fifth-grade class read two texts on the Civil War, and use a compare–contrast graphic organizer to take notes on what they read. Now, Mr. Walsh wants the students to use their notes to write a historical essay that compares what the two texts say about the Civil War. However, one of the students, Julie, is confused because the two texts differ in their interpretations of the Civil War:

JULIE: They don't say the same thing. How do I know what to write about the causes of the Civil War?

TRENT: Yeah, this text says it's about the rights of the states. That's bull.

MR. WALSH: Eric, what does the other text say?

ERIC: It says that the Civil War was about slavery.

ARNETHA: This text doesn't even mention slavery.

MR. WALSH: Who wrote the different texts? What do you know about the authors and when they wrote the texts?

In the scene above, when Mr. Walsh asked his fifth graders to write about texts with different points of view on the Civil War, he encouraged them to think and write like historians. VanSledright and Kelly (1998) explained that historians view history as interpretations of past events rather than as absolute facts. According to De la Paz et al. (2016), historians "do not have all [the] records from every perspective at any given point in time, [so they] do some amount of imagining and make tentative conjectures based on . . . historical sources" (p. 32). To estimate how much corroboration exists for historical interpretations, historians critically evaluate the origins of interpretations and the contexts (or time and place) in which they originated.

Mr. Walsh also facilitated his students' text comprehension when he asked them to write about what they read (Vacca & Vacca, 2004). Fordham et al. (2002) reported that writing about a topic "requires deeper processing than reading alone entails" (p. 151). Vacca and Vacca (2004) pointed out that "writing facilitates learning by helping students explore, clarify, and think deeply about the ideas and concepts they encounter in reading" (p. 353).

OVERVIEW ON DISCIPLINARY LITERACY

Since the introduction of the CCSS (NGA & CCSSO) in 2010, there has been an increased focus on reading and writing informational texts in grades 3–6. Although students in these grades benefit from general content-area reading and writing strategies, these strategies are not sufficient for them to comprehend, write, *and learn from* disciplinary texts (Jones et al., 2019; Shanahan & Shanahan, 2008). Goldman, Snow, and Vaughn (2016) explained that disciplinary literacy now requires students to do more than recall and write summaries of what they read. To learn and write in the disciplines, students need to understand nonliteral language in texts, determine the meaning of unfamiliar words and conceptual constructs, analyze text structures, recognize intertextual references, integrate information from several texts, solve problems using text-based information, critique arguments within texts, and build arguments for claims based on evidence provided in texts (p. 256).

In addition, literacy in each of the disciplines (i.e., literature, mathematics, science, and social studies) reflects different cultural communities; that is, how people think, talk, read, and write in each discipline varies in terms of its organization and what is valued and emphasized (O'Brien et al., 1995; Shanahan & Shanahan, 2014).

Although specific disciplinary literacy goals before grade 6 were not listed in the CCSS (NGA & CCSSO, 2010), many education experts believe that if teachers wait until grade 6 to introduce and teach disciplinary literacy, it will be too late for students to acquire the disciplinary knowledge and skills that they need to address college and career standards (Shanahan & Shanahan, 2014). By grade 6, all students should be engaged in disciplinary writing; that is, they should be writing about what they read in disciplinary texts and learn from inquiry activities in the specific disciplines, integrating information from texts, videos, and inquiry projects when appropriate (Shanahan & Shanahan, 2014).

GENERAL INSTRUCTION FOR DISCIPLINARY WRITING

To participate in disciplinary writing, students need to recognize and utilize the text structures or organizational structures that disciplinary experts employ to organize their thinking and writing in the discipline. Researchers reported that when students in grades 3–6 used text structures to guide their reading, recall, and written summaries of material read, their text comprehension and learning improved (Armbruster et al., 1987; Meyer et al., 2018; Williams, 2005). To teach or review text structures, and the clue words that signal the respective structure, we recommend that you utilize the three types of knowledge (declarative, procedural, and conditional) and GRR (presented in Chapter 6).

Expository Text Structures

In Chapter 6, we introduced you to three text structures that disciplinary experts frequently employ to write expository texts (i.e., nonfiction texts that provide information): description, sequence, and cause and effect. In this chapter, we identify two additional text structures that often are used with expository texts: compare–contrast and problem–solution (Hess, 2008; National Research Council, 2012). The compare–contrast text structure identifies the similarities and differences in two or more items, processes, people, or events. Key clue words or phrases include *both, similar to, alike, same, different, in contrast, unlike, whereas, on the other hand* (Hess, 2008). The problem–solution text structure identifies an issue, conflict, or problem; indicates an action or "an attempt to solve the problem"; and "the results of the attempt to solve the problem" (Armbruster et al., 1987, p. 332). Clue words include *problem, conflict, issue, question, reply, response, action, answer, improve, solution, resolve* (Armbruster et al., 1987; Wolsey & Lapp, 2017). Table 8.1 shows the five text structures employed in expository texts, the respective clue words, and the organizational purposes.

TABLE 8.1. Text Structures, Clue Words, and Frame Examples

Text structure	Clue words	Organizational purpose	Frames
Description	*for example, such as, another type, for instance*	Explain characteristics of an object, an event, a person, or place.	There are three types of rocks along the river bank. Some rocks are _____. Others are _____. Another type is _____.
Sequence	*first, second, third; then, next, finally, last*	Events, procedures, or processes explained in order of occurrence.	To set a thermostat, first, you should _____. Next, you need to _____. Then, you should _____, Last, you should _____.
Compare–contrast	*both, however, in contrast, like, same, different*	Present similarities and differences.	There are similarities and differences in elephants and whales. They both are _____. In addition, they are _____. However, they are different because _____.
Cause–effect	*cause, if . . . then, therefore, led to, resulted in*	The sources of a cause and the results are explained.	There are various types of erosion. Water erosion results in _____. Wind erosion causes _____. If _____, then that leads to _____. _____ three types of erosion _____ the Grand Canyon.
Problem–solution	*problem, solved, response, so, because, as a result, therefore*	Identification of a problem and how it is resolved.	A problem that the American colonists had was that _____. So, they _____. Eventually, they solved the problem by _____.

Note. Based on Armbruster et al. (1987); Hess (2008); and Wolsey and Lapp (2017).

Narrative Text Structures

Narrative texts are common in ELA, and increasingly appear in social studies and science. Authors use narrative texts to tell a story or share an experience. Narrative texts employed with students in grades 3–6 include short stories, novels, biographies, drama, and informational articles or books written in narrative form.

In this section, we briefly review the narrative text structure for fiction: the story grammar (frequently called story structure or story map). The story grammar will vary according to the genre or type of story and the story's complexity. However, there usually are three parts to a story: a beginning, middle, and end. Also, stories include the following elements: setting, characters, a conflict (initiating event or goal to be obtained), plot (episodes describing how the events unfold or the goal is pursued), and a resolution (how the conflict has ended). The author's message or purpose for writing the story is conveyed through a theme or moral. There also is a narrator who tells the story, indicating the point of view.

Frames

A frame is a cloze-type paragraph for which students provide the missing content words. Frames highlight the respective clue words for a text structure and model summary writing based on the text structure. You can use frames as initial support for students' disciplinary summary writing, but over time, should work with your students so that they no longer need the frames. Examples of frames for specific types of expository texts are shown in Table 8.1.

You also can use a frame to help students plan their narrative writing and/or analyze or recall what they read. For example, Figure 8.1 shows a frame that Ms. Kosovski gave to her fourth graders to help organize their personal story writing.

Graphic Organizers

In Chapter 6, we reported that graphic organizers were one of the instructional techniques that the federal What Works Clearinghouses (Kamil et al., 2008; Shanahan et al., 2010) recommended that you employ with students in grades 3–6. Teachers often use graphic organizers to help students identify the main ideas in expository texts and to show the relationships among the main ideas and supporting details. Graphic organizers also help students identify the key story elements in narrative texts. Sometimes, teachers ask students to employ a graphic organizer to take notes on what they read or to explain their results in an inquiry project. In addition, students can use graphic organizers to plan and write summaries of what they read, plan and write essays about what they learned in science or social studies, and plan and write texts.

We showed a graphic organizer for sequence in Chapter 6. Figure 8.2 shows a compare–contrast graphic organizer that compares Venus and Earth. Figure 8.3 (on page 144) provides a problem–solution graphic organizer on women's fight for the right to vote, or suffragism.

In Chapter 6, we briefly discussed some of the limitations involved in using graphic organizers. Additionally, you need to make sure that the graphic organizer you design, adapt, or use matches the text structure in the text or the implied text structure. To get the most benefit out of graphic organizers, it also is important for your students to already know how to synthesize or take notes on what they read, so that they do not just copy information from the text into the graphic organizer.

INTEGRATED ELA AND WRITING INSTRUCTION FOR GRADES 3–6

To plan your disciplinary writing instruction for ELA, we suggest that you and your colleagues focus on (1) the types of writing that professional writers do and (2) the ELA standards for grades 3–6 required by your state. According to the

The title of my story is _____

_____.

It takes place (when and where) _____

_____

_____.

The main character is _____

_____.

The other characters are _____

_____

_____.

The main character is upset because _____

_____

_____.

The character tries to fix (resolve) the problem by _____

_____

_____.

The other characters respond by _____

_____

_____

_____.

The story ends when _____

_____

_____

_____.

The theme/lesson of the story is _____

_____

_____

_____.

FIGURE 8.1. Frame for students' story writing.

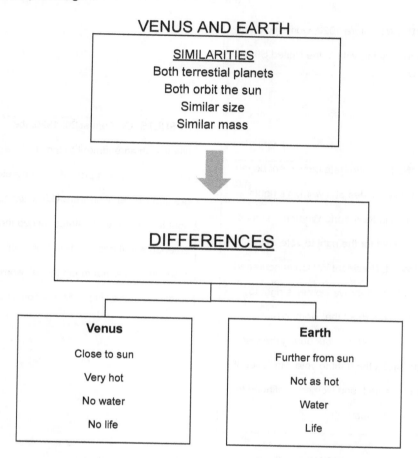

FIGURE 8.2. Compare–contrast graphic organizer.

website Annenberg Learner (2021), writing professionals employ writing "to narrate, describe, request, explain, evaluate, and argue." To illustrate state writing standards for grades 3–6, we show the Arizona ELA writing standards in Table 8.2. In the table, we also included several of the CCSS (NGA & CCSSO, 2010) writing standards, which expanded those in Arizona.

Although literary analysis is a CCSS (NGA & CCSSO, 2010) ELA standard, it does not appear until grade 6. In designing ELA instruction for students in grades 3–5, you need to prepare them for the emphasis on literary analysis in grade 6. The aim of literary analysis is to evaluate the author's craft or how the author employed literary elements to convey the meaning of a text. According to Robinson (2019), key components of literary analysis for narrative texts include the language, plot(s), mood, setting(s), theme(s) or main idea(s), point(s) of view, narrator(s), conflict(s), and characters. However, the writing that you assign your students to enhance their

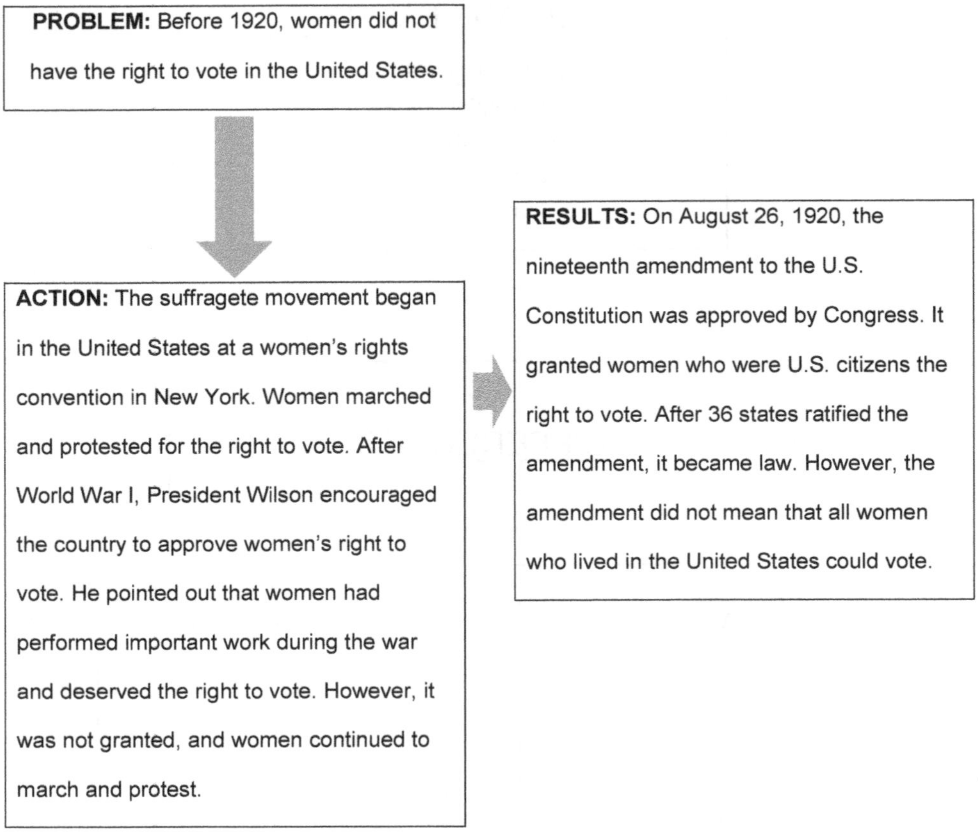

PROBLEM: Before 1920, women did not have the right to vote in the United States.

ACTION: The suffragete movement began in the United States at a women's rights convention in New York. Women marched and protested for the right to vote. After World War I, President Wilson encouraged the country to approve women's right to vote. He pointed out that women had performed important work during the war and deserved the right to vote. However, it was not granted, and women continued to march and protest.

RESULTS: On August 26, 1920, the nineteenth amendment to the U.S. Constitution was approved by Congress. It granted women who were U.S. citizens the right to vote. After 36 states ratified the amendment, it became law. However, the amendment did not mean that all women who lived in the United States could vote.

FIGURE 8.3. Problem–solution graphic organizer.

understanding of literary elements and the author's craft will depend on their age. The assignments could be as simple as writing personal responses in a literature response log about what students liked or did not like in a reading (see Goldenberg,1992/1993; Saunders & Goldenberg, 1999), to more complex ones, such as identifying and responding to the author's theme, or after participating in a study of an author's writing, writing their own narrative texts using some of the same literary elements as a specific author.

Once you decide on what to emphasize in your disciplinary writing instruction for ELA, we recommend that you use the three types of knowledge (declarative, procedural, conditional) and the GRR presented in Chapter 6 to model and guide your students on the types of writing that you want them to do. Sharing and analyzing mentor texts related to the assignment also should be helpful. For example, if you are working on the role of point of view in narrative fiction, you could present

TABLE 8.2. Arizona ELA Writing Standards for Grades 3–6, with CCSS Additions

Writing task	Third	Fourth	Fifth	Sixth
Opinion and explanatory pieces with supportive evidence, linking words, and conclusion	X	X		
Opinion and explanatory pieces with supportive evidence, linking words, *precise vocabulary,* and conclusion			X	
Argumentative and explanatory pieces with supportive evidence, linking words, precise vocabulary, and conclusion				X
Maintain a formal style in argumentative and explanatory writing				X
Introduce a topic clearly and group related information in paragraphs and sections; include formatting (e.g., headings), illustrations, and multimedia when useful to aiding comprehension		X		
Narrative with clear event sequence, descriptive details, dialogue, and words to indicate change in time	X	X	X	X
Draw evidence from literary or informational texts to support analysis, reflection, and research			X	
For literary nonfiction: Trace and evaluate the argument and specific claims in a text, distinguishing claims that are supported by reasons and evidence from claims that are not				X
Conduct short research projects that address different parts of a topic		X		
Conduct short research projects to build knowledge through investigation			X	X
Collect information from sources to answer a question	X	X		
Writing organized for a task, audience, and purpose	X	X		
Revise writing based on adult and peer feedback	X	X		
Plan, draft, revise and edit to produce clear and coherent writing			X	X
Demonstrate sufficient command of keyboarding skills to complete a writing task			X	X

Note. Italics indicate CCSS (NGA & CCSSO, 2010) wording or standards.

your students with the traditional fable of the three little pigs (Seibert, 2001) and have them work in pairs to complete a story map to identify the point of view in the story and how it affects the plot and theme. Then, after discussing this with the whole class, present them with the same general story but from a different point of view. For instance, you could present them with the version of the three little pigs told from the wolf's point of view (Scieszka, 1989), and ask them to work in pairs to complete a story map to identify the point of view in it and how it affects the plot and theme. Then, after a whole-class discussion, you could assign them to read another fable, and depending on their ages, work in pairs or small groups (1) to rewrite it from a different point of view or (2) to complete a compare–contrast graphic organizer and write an explanatory essay about the role of point of view, using the two fable versions as evidence for their claims. We refer you to two resources for nonfiction and literary books to help you find mentor texts and additional instructional ideas for students in grades 3–6 (Buss, 2002; Buss & Karnowski, 2000).

INTEGRATED SCIENCE AND WRITING INSTRUCTION FOR GRADES 3–5

Educational researchers who integrated students' science instruction with literacy instruction reported that when students wrote about their inquiry or hands-on science projects as they implemented them, their understanding, recall, and learning about science improved (see Chapter 3). For science writing, it is important to remember that the student's job is to employ precise language, visuals, and graphics, and "use appropriate and sufficient evidence and scientific reasoning to defend and critique the validity and reliability of claims and explanations about the natural world, or methods for collecting data and evidence" (Arizona Department of Education, 2016, p. 5). We recommend that you follow your state's standards for appropriate inquiry projects and related writing tasks. As an example, we refer you to Table 8.3, in which we present the types of science inquiry projects, research questions, and science writing tasks approved by the state of Arizona for students in grades 3–5. Chapter 7 also provided examples of how scientific argumentation combines discussion and the formulation of written scientific arguments and proofs.

INTEGRATED SOCIAL STUDIES AND WRITING INSTRUCTION FOR GRADES 3–5

The State of Arizona did not provide the same type of information for integrating writing instruction into social studies as they did for science. To provide guidance on how to integrate writing into your social studies instruction for grades 3–5, we drew from California's combined writing and history/social studies standards. For

TABLE 8.3. Arizona Science Inquiry Projects and Writing Tasks for Grades 3–5

Grade level	Inquiry topic	Research question	Writing tasks and investigations
3	Sound	"Is there always a vibration when there is sound?" (p. 9)	• Write claim (prediction or hypothesis) in science notebook based on readings, videos, and preliminary observations. • Conduct investigations and record observational notes in lab record. • Revisit and revise claim in science notebook based on inquiry evidence.
4	Light	"When you flip the light switch, what happens that makes the lights turn on or off?" (p. 10)	• Do preliminary drawing of how a light bulb lights and write claim in science notebook. • Look at others' drawings, videos, readings; do experimentation, discussion. • Do new drawing and update/revise claim in science notebook.
5	Space—moon	"Why did it look like the shape of the Moon changed over time?" (p. 12).	• Write claim based on moon observations in science notebook. • Work with others to develop and test hands-on model. • Match drawings with actual phases of the moon in science notebook.

Note. From Arizona Department of Education (2016).

example, in grade 3, students are expected to read a variety of historical texts and do the following:

- "Write both opinion and informative/explanatory texts about history/social science topics . . . , [and] with guidance and support from adults, . . . produce writing . . . appropriate to the task and purpose;"
- "Engage in planning, revising, and editing and use technology to produce and publish writing;"
- " . . . conduct short research projects that build knowledge about a topic" (California Department of Education, 2017, p. 27).

In grades 4–5, students are supposed to "effectively convey opinions and information; . . . summarize and explain the content of text by using precise language and domain-specific vocabulary; . . . begin comparing and contrasting . . . primary sources and . . . secondary sources" (California Department of Education, 2017, p. 28). In grade 5, students are supposed to "conduct research projects on the same event or topic by employing and listing multiple sources, including texts and online resources" (p. 28).

To provide an actual example of integrated writing and social studies instruction in grade 5, we drew from Ferretti et al.'s (2001) work. In this case, a history teacher and a writing teacher collaborated to provide fifth graders with a series of historical questions, historical texts on the western expansion in the United States during the 1900s, and writing strategy instruction. The teachers placed the fifth graders in small heterogeneous groups to investigate how and why an emigrant group (farmers, miners, or Mormons) moved westward. The students investigated the overall question: "Should these emigrants have gone west?" (Ferretti et al., 2001, p. 62). The historical aims of the research project were for the students to understand (1) "the importance of providing a true and accurate account of a historical event," (2) how "to evaluate bias in evidence," (3) "how to corroborate sources," and (4) how "to qualify . . . conclusions when there is contradictory evidence" (Ferretti et al., 2001, p. 62). Students were provided with primary sources (i.e., diaries, drawings, photographs, memos, letters) and a secondary source (a commercial video). Their end product was a multimedia project presentation about the selected group with written texts and images that portrayed a narrative or a "story of people who encountered a problem that required them to take some action with positive and negative outcomes" (Ferretti et al., 2001, p. 63). After analyzing their results, Ferretti et al. (2001) concluded that the integrated disciplinary instruction resulted in "gains in students' knowledge about the period, and improvements in the students' understanding of historical context and historical inquiry" (p. 69).

DISCIPLINARY WRITING INSTRUCTION WITH SCIENCE OR SOCIAL STUDIES INSTRUCTION IN GRADE 6

Sometimes, sixth-grade state disciplinary literacy standards in science and/or social studies are addressed in middle school grade bands (i.e., grades 6–8). For example, Arizona did not produce separate science or social studies writing standards for grades 6–8 that were linked to college and career-readiness standards. The expectation appeared to be that the content-area teachers would adapt and implement the literacy standards according to the content they were teaching. Beerer (n.d.) explained, "The writing standards do not differ by content area, but assume that the writing will be specific to the content of the discipline" (p. 3).

LEARNING FROM INTEGRATED DISCIPLINARY LITERACY PROGRAMS IN SCIENCE, SOCIAL STUDIES, AND ELA

In this section, we review two integrated disciplinary programs that explicitly taught disciplinary writing to students in grades 3–6. The first program, Seeds of Science/Roots of Reading (SSRR; Cervetti et al., 2012), focused on integrated literacy and science instruction. The second program, Catalyzing Comprehension through Discussion and Debate (CCDD): Word Generation (CCDD, 2021a, 2021b, 2021c), developed and implemented integrated literacy programs in several disciplines (i.e., language arts, mathematics, science, and social studies). Here, we focus on their integrated literacy instruction in history for grade 6 (called Social Studies Generation; Duhaylongsod et al., 2015), with some discussion of the history program's implementation in grades 4 and 5, followed by a brief discussion of their integrated literacy instruction in ELA for grades 4 and 5, called WordGen Elementary (CCDD, 2021a, 2021b, 2021c). We discuss the ELA program after the history program because less information was provided about its writing component and its effectiveness.

Science Writing in Seeds of Science/Roots of Reading

In SSRR, teachers explicitly taught fourth graders how to take notes and write scientific reports about what they were learning in science (Cervetti et al., 2012). The focus of the integrated science and literacy lessons was on "light, light interactions, and light as energy" (p. 638). The integrated curriculum emphasized students' "academic and technical vocabulary, involvement in sense-making talk around their investigations, and their ability to communicate their growing understanding in talk and writing" (p. 636). The curriculum consisted of four inquiry units with 10 sessions (45–60 minutes each) in each unit. Although the developers wanted the fourth graders to read trade books about light, they could not find enough trade books on this topic, so they wrote some of the books. In total, the fourth graders read nine books about light. Cervetti et al. (2012) explained that the texts were the sources for "targeted vocabulary" related to light (e.g., "absorb, block, characteristic, emit") and academic words that students used to talk and write about their inquiries (e.g., "analyze, claim, data"; p. 639).

Two of the 10 sessions in each inquiry unit focused on writing in science. The writing strategies emphasized were "summarizing, evaluating claims and evidence, and making explanations from evidence" (Cervetti et al., 2012, p. 639). Throughout the writing instruction, the teachers used the GRR to explicitly teach and guide students' summary and explanatory writing.

Students were taught summary writing according to the following process. After reading a book, students made scientific hypotheses based on the book, completed an empirical investigation, collected evidence, and revised their hypotheses based on the evidence. Then, they planned their summary writing by working together to create a giant concept map posted on a classroom wall. Next, they identified the key words or most important words from passages in the book to create main idea statements about important parts of the book. For each of the main idea statements, they selected supporting details from the group concept maps. Then, they used the main idea statements and supporting details to write their summaries.

The teachers also taught the fourth graders how to write scientific explanations based on the data tables they had created for their inquiries. In the explanations, students identified claims and provided evidence for them.

When the findings for SSRR were analyzed, the participating students outperformed those who were in the control group (the instruction-as-usual group) on measures of science writing. In their writing, the students in SSRR demonstrated more science concepts, more use of science vocabulary, more evidence, and appropriate introductions for science writing compared to the writing of students in the control group. Areas in which there were no significant differences in students' writing included definitions of the science vocabulary and the conclusions.

CCDD: Word Generation for History

The developers of CCDD: Word Generation for History considered it developmentally inappropriate to ask students in grades 4–8 to read primary sources to evaluate and find evidence for claims (Jones et al., 2019). Their aim was to introduce elementary (grades 4–5) and middle school (grades 6–8) students to historical thinking (Duhaylongsod et al., 2015). To offset difficult reading, they wrote the short texts that students read in the program.

The organization of the integrated literacy programs in history at the elementary and middle school levels was similar, but the programs differed in their length and in the writing tasks that students completed. For example, fourth and fifth graders participated in twelve 10-day units for 45–50 minutes per day (Duhaylongsod et al., 2015); whereas, middle school students (grades 6–8) participated in six 5-day units for 45 minutes per day (Goldman et al., 2016). At the end of each instructional unit the fourth and fifth graders wrote a "take a stand" paragraph, whereas the middle school students wrote a "take a stand" essay.[1] The curricular units are available at *http://wordgen.serpmedia.org*.

Both the elementary and middle school history programs began with debatable questions and Readers Theatre. The debatable question (also listed as the unit's purpose) was posed at the beginning of the unit. For example, a sixth-grade unit on ancient civilizations related to Greece asked: "Was it better to be an Athenian or a Spartan?" (Goldman, Snow, et al., 2016, p. 261). However, before students did any work related to the question, they were introduced to a modern-day interpretation of the question through Readers Theatre. In the case of Athens versus Sparta, the sixth graders read a fictitious account of middle school students who were discussing the advantages of attending two high schools: One high school emphasized academics but not sports, while the other high school emphasized sports but not academics. According to Goldman, Snow, et al. (2016), the aims of the Readers Theatre were to increase student engagement and introduce the students to an important issue in social studies—for example: How do schools "or social units such as city-states organize themselves around different priorities, with consequences for people's lives?"

---

[1]An actual example of a sixth-grade unit on Egypt is available at *https://irp-cdn.multiscreensite.com/7a45b809/files/uploaded/SoGen_6.1_student.pdf.*

(p. 261). The students worked in pairs to analyze the pros and cons of attending each high school, and to identify the speakers in the Readers Theatre who were likely to hold the respective positions. The Readers Theatre also introduced six key vocabulary terms ("democratic, elitist, competitive, ostracize, individualism, and conformity"), which students worked in pairs to define, used orally, and repeatedly saw in their readings on Greece (Goldman, Snow, et al., 2016, p. 261).

After the students completed the Readers Theatre, they read brief texts about ancient Greece, Sparta, and Athens, for which they worked in pairs to take notes on "the advantages of living in one city" versus "the other, and from the points of view of various stakeholders, such as soldiers, women, and slaves (Goldman, Snow, et al., 2016, p. 261). Sometimes, their note taking was guided by sentence starters and/or questions related to the debatable question.

Before planning their oral debates about living in Athens or Sparta, the students were given a list of facts to use as evidence to support opposing positions in the debate. Goldman, Snow, et al. (2016) explained that the sixth graders were provided with the evidence so that they "focus[ed] their attention on the more sophisticated skill—choosing evidence to support a claim—rather than getting bogged down [by] . . . searching for evidence in lengthy texts" (p. 261). They organized their notes according to "a structured format," so that they included claims about which city was better, facts with warrants (i.e., evidence that supported claims), and "anticipated counterarguments and possible responses" (p. 261).

After the debate, the sixth graders used a flow chart to plan their writing. Then, they wrote an essay, in which they used evidence to support their argument about which city they preferred to live in. The developers considered the debate and essay to be similar to the work of historians because both required students to synthesize the information they had learned.

In terms of results, analyses of the classroom program transcripts indicated that students acted like historians by making claims and supporting them with arguments and evidence, taking into account different perspectives. Although students' warrants often were historically inaccurate, the developers argued that "once students gain experience and confidence . . . generating warrants in historical writing, they are in a stronger position to improve those warrants with . . . accurate interpretation . . . in later grades" (Duhaylongsod et al., 2015, p. 603).

CCDD: WordGen Elementary for ELA

The ELA version of CCDD for grades 4 and 5 was organized into twelve 2-week units of 40- to 50-minute daily lessons (CCDD, 2021c). The aims of the units were to increase the students' "background knowledge and academic vocabulary" and improve their "argumentation, analytic reasoning, perspective taking, reading to find evidence, oral discussion, and writing" (CCDD, 2021c). Each unit focused on an open-ended question, which had been selected to engage the students (e.g.,

"Should the school day be longer?" [CCDD, 2021c]). A video newscast introduced the question. After viewing the newscast, the students read the findings from two written interviews (conducted by two students) with experts on the topic. Next, the students debated and/or discussed the question with their classmates. Similar to the CCDD program in history (Duhaylongsod et al., 2015), the students participated in a Readers Theatre in which they read the script aloud to hear the characters' perspectives on the topic. Then, they discussed the characters' perspectives. Next, they read short informational texts related to the question. Students took a stand on the question, and after considerable student discussion, wrote a persuasive letter or essay about it. Throughout the unit, they learned the definitions of five or six academic words, and employed the words in their writing.

CONSIDERATIONS FOR TEACHING DISCIPLINARY WRITING TO BILINGUAL STUDENTS

Due to differences in receptive (listening and reading) and productive (speaking and writing) English development, bilingual students often will demonstrate greater comprehension of English texts and English instruction when you allow them to respond by writing in their L1 or by translanguaging (i.e., use words from their L1 in their English writing). When you assign bilingual students to summarize what they learned from an inquiry project, you do not want to penalize them when they cannot remember a key English word or do not know it. If you do not know what they wrote in their L1, you can ask another student or adult who reads the L1. Another way to deal with this situation is to assign students from the same L1 but of different English proficiency levels to work together when writing in English. Afterward, we encourage you to have the students list new English words and their L1 counterparts in a bilingual vocabulary notebook for future use (see Chapter 5 on vocabulary instruction).

It also may be helpful to find out how much writing experience your bilingual students had in their home countries or languages. Although English writing tends to be direct and linear, this may not characterize good writing in other languages and cultures. Understanding the different writing styles that are valued in different languages and countries should help you to know what to explicitly emphasize in your writing instruction.

A technique that we introduced in Chapter 3 that should be helpful for your disciplinary writing instruction with bilingual students is the posting of "student friendly" objectives (Echevarría et al., 2012, 2016). For example, if you are teaching electricity in third or fourth grade, the science and writing objectives listed in the box below might be appropriate. Remember to post your objectives, to orally read them, to have your students orally read them, and to review them throughout your lessons.

> **Science Objectives**
>
> Work with your partner to complete a drawing of how an electric light turns on.
>
> Label your drawing with these words: *electricity, circuit, switch.*
>
> **Writing Objective**
>
> With your partner write a three-sentence explanation of how an electric light turns on.

Many of the other bilingual considerations in Chapters 2 and 3 also apply to bilingual students' disciplinary writing instruction. As long as you use bilingual and ESL techniques to make your integrated disciplinary instruction comprehensible (see Chapter 2), bilingual students should benefit from disciplinary thematic instruction because it provides them with increased instructional time and different contexts in which to deepen their background knowledge and academic vocabulary, two areas that should aid their disciplinary writing.

In fact, WordGen Elementary (2021) has been effectively employed with emergent bilingual students. In classrooms that included both emergent bilingual students and native-English-speaking students, the bilingual students attained gains similar to those of their native-English-speaking classmates. Additionally, they made greater gains in academic language than the native English speakers. The current WordGen Elementary website includes resources that teachers can use with bilingual students, such as family newsletters in Arabic, Chinese, English, or Spanish; picture vocabulary cards in Spanish and English; unit introductions in Spanish; debate and writing prompts in Spanish and English; and English captions for the news video.

CONCLUSION

Elementary school teachers should introduce their students to disciplinary writing, so that by middle school, students have some experience writing in the different disciplines. Two benefits of disciplinary writing are that it facilitates students' disciplinary reading and results in improved disciplinary learning.

General instructional techniques that teachers can use for disciplinary writing include teaching students how to use text structures to write expository (e.g., description, sequence, cause and effect, compare–contrast, problem–solution) and narrative texts (e.g., story grammar for fiction). Instruction on frames and graphic organizers also should help elementary students to organize their disciplinary writing, reading, and thinking.

State standards and the CCSS (NGA & CCSSO, 2010) provide guidance on how teachers can implement disciplinary writing instruction in the ELA for students in grades 3–6, and in science and history/social studies for students in grades 3–5. Science and history/social studies state standards for grade 6 typically are included in the middle school standards. Examples of how teachers could use the state standards to guide their disciplinary writing instruction in ELA, science, and history/social studies were shared.

To provide additional instructional examples, integrated disciplinary literacy programs for students in grades 4, 5, and 6 were presented. The first was SSRR, which integrated science and writing. The second was CCDD: Word Generation, which integrated history and writing instruction, and the third was CCDD: WordGen Elementary, which integrated disciplinary writing instruction with ELA.

Considerations for working with bilingual students include giving them the opportunity to use L1 words for unknown English words when they write in disciplinary inquiry projects. We also encourage you to find out how much writing your students already have done in their home languages and countries and the styles of writing that are valued in their languages and countries. Lastly, many of the recommendations in Chapters 2 and 3 for working with bilingual students also apply to disciplinary writing. One of the integrated disciplinary literacy programs—WordGen Elementary—has been effectively employed with emergent bilingual students.

CHAPTER NINE

How to Assess Intermediate Students' Reading Comprehension

GUIDING QUESTIONS

- What types of assessments help teachers understand their students' reading comprehension?
- What are the different features of summative, interim, and formative assessments?
- Which types of assessments lead to improvements in teachers' reading comprehension instruction and students' performance?
- What are the benefits of a reading comprehension assessment system?
- How should school grade-level teams approach planning for interventions for intermediate students who need supplementary literacy support?
- What do school personnel need to know about assessing the English reading comprehension of bilingual students?

SETTING THE SCENE

Ms. Winters is waiting for a grade-level teachers' meeting to begin. The school principal just handed her a list of test scores that her fourth graders obtained on the state's required ELA assessment, which they took last spring. She is talking to two other fourth-grade teachers (Ms. W = Ms. Winters):

Ms. W: These test scores are from last spring. They are so old. They don't tell me what my kids need to improve their reading comprehension.

Ms. J: What about how they did on the DRA [Developmental Reading Assessment]? We just got those scores back for the fall.

Ms. W: Well, the DRA scores are more recent. They do provide an estimate of each student's instructional reading level, but they still don't tell me the type of instruction that each student needs.

MR. T: Jan was telling me the other day that she's using formative assessment. She said she attended a PSD [professional staff development] session on it over the summer. Maybe you should talk to her. She said it was helping her figure out what to teach her students.

MS. W: (*Sighs.*) I guess I'd better talk to Jan. I wonder if we could work together on formative assessments?

In the above vignette, the three teachers are discussing the types of reading comprehension assessments that school personnel employ: summative assessments, interim assessments, and formative assessments. Table 9.1 describes each assessment in terms of its purpose, the types of information that the assessment provides, and its audience. Our aims in this chapter are to help you assess your students' reading comprehension, identify which assessments to use for which purposes, work with other school personnel to develop and implement a reading comprehension assessment system, learn how to plan interventions for those students with reading comprehension difficulties, and provide considerations for the reading comprehension assessment of current and former emergent bilingual students.

TABLE 9.1. Different Types of Reading Comprehension Assessments

	Summative	Interim	Formative
Major purpose	Evaluation of a student's reading comprehension according to standards/ compared to other students	Evaluation of student progress at key points during the year; inform reading and instructional levels; placement decisions in classroom or school	Feedback on individual student performance to inform teacher's instruction and to inform individual students
Designer	National or state experts; commercial test designers	Commercial test designers or reading experts	Groups of classroom teachers or individual teachers
Frequency	Once or twice/year	Periodically throughout school year (typically, three times)	Daily, weekly, or monthly per student
Information provided	How well students attain standards/compare to other students	Student reading and instructional levels; how students compare to other students	How well individual students perform and respond to teacher's instruction, attain standards
Examples	NAEP, state-standards test, New Meridian, Smarter Balanced; Gates–MacGinitie test; Stanford Achievement Test	DRA, Fountas and Pinnell's benchmark assessment; informal reading inventories; computer-adapted tests	Documentation of student responses to teacher's instruction
Major audience	National, state, district, school personnel; parents/guardians	District and school personnel; teachers; parents/guardians	Classroom teachers; students; school personnel; parents/ guardians

Note. Based on Bunch (2012) and García and DeNicolo (2016).

ASSESSING STUDENTS' READING COMPREHENSION

A major difficulty that teachers face when they assess their students' reading comprehension is that the processes that students utilize to comprehend texts are hidden inside their brains. The sociocultural influences that shape how humans think, process, and interpret texts also are invisible (National Academies of Sciences, Engineering, and Medicine, 2018). In addition, reading comprehension is incremental and contextual; it is not an all-or-nothing occurrence. To figure out what happens when students do *not* comprehend what they read, we refer you to Figure 9.1, or the cognitive model for reading comprehension assessment (Stahl et al., 2020, p. 9).

Word Recognition That Hinders Reading Comprehension

We begin with the top part of Figure 9.1: Phonological Awareness, Decoding and Sight Word Knowledge, Fluency, and Automatic Word Recognition. When a student demonstrates difficulty comprehending English text, we recommend that you consider this question: Does poor decoding hinder the student's reading comprehension (Stahl et al., 2020, p. 9)?

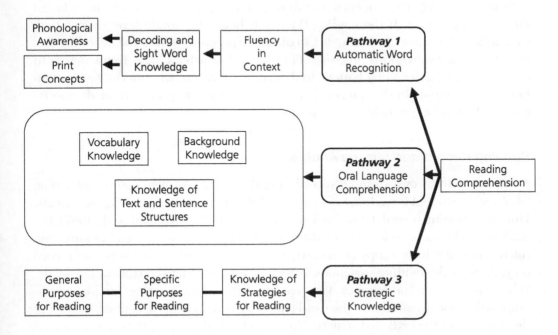

FIGURE 9.1. The cognitive model. From Stahl et al. (2020). Copyright © 2020 The Guilford Press. Reprinted by permission.

Listening versus Reading Comprehension

A simple way to estimate whether a student's comprehension is limited by their decoding is to compare how well they comprehend a text when it is read to them (i.e., when they are listening) to how well they comprehend it when they read it independently. If they demonstrate strong listening comprehension, but weak reading comprehension, then they may need additional decoding instruction and/or support.

Detecting Word Recognition Obstacles

If a student struggles with word recognition, comprehension will be compromised (LaBerge & Samuels, 1974). The arrows along Pathway 1 of the cognitive model trace a diagnostic trail to help you determine where the word recognition process may be weak. The first step is to determine the student's reading fluency in context. This can be done by determining the student's reading rate of grade-level material (words correct/minute). Using the same reading passage, you should gauge the student's reading prosody (expression and phrasing) with a simple prosody scale (see Stahl et al., 2020). You may use classroom materials, a benchmark kit, or a measure such as the *Dynamic Indicators of Basic Early Literacy Skills, Eighth Edition* (DIBELS; University of Oregon, 2020) to gather this information. A fluency norm (e.g., Hasbrouck & Tindal's [2017] Oral Reading Fluency norms) will help you determine whether the student's overall word recognition automaticity is on target for their grade level. If the reading fluency is below the grade-level expectation, then follow the arrows in Figure 9.1 to diagnose precisely where the decoding and high-frequency word skills process is faltering. Administer a high-frequency word assessment and a decoding battery to determine which word patterns need attention. Most students in the intermediate grades will not require further diagnostic tests at the level of phonological awareness.

Running Record and Miscue Analysis

A miscue analysis or a running record of oral reading can help you to determine whether the student is reading for meaning while simultaneously reading accurately. During a running record (Clay, 2013) or miscue analysis (Goodman et al., 1987), the student orally reads an instructional-level text that they have not read before. You, the teacher, also have a copy of the text, and as the student orally reads, you record on your copy the reading variations (errors) or miscues that the student has made. When you analyze the miscues, you pay attention to whether they are visually or graphophonetically similar to the words misread, semantically acceptable (i.e., kept the meaning of the text), and structurally or syntactically appropriate (i.e., reflected the correct grammatical form). You also indicate when the students corrected their oral reading. The error/miscue analysis helps the teacher understand the extent to which the student read for meaning and whether the student self-corrected errors that did not make sense in the reading context. To conduct running records or miscue analyses, you can use authentic texts or the texts and forms included in informal reading inventories (IRIs) such as Lesley and Caldwell's (2016) *Qualitative Reading Inventory,* Fountas and Pinnell's (2010) *Benchmark Assessment System,* or Beaver and Carter's (2019) *Developmental Reading Assessment, Third Edition.* Immediately after the student orally reads the text, the teacher asks the student to retell what was read and to answer comprehension questions, as described in the next section.[1]

Limited Background, Vocabulary, and Syntactic (Structural) Knowledge

In Figure 9.1, Pathway 2 addresses oral language comprehension. Unlike Pathway 1, Pathway 2 is not developmentally linear. Take a look at the large center box with three interior boxes inside it, labeled Vocabulary, Background Knowledge, and Knowledge of Text and Sentence Structures. You should address a second question: Is the student's comprehension adversely affected by limited background knowledge, vocabulary, and knowledge of text and sentence structures (Stahl et al., 2020)?

Oral and Written Retellings

An oral or written retelling is one way to evaluate whether students activated the appropriate background knowledge, knew the key vocabulary in the passage, understood how the text was structured, and comprehended the syntax or sentence structures in the passage. Schema researchers reported that when students activated inappropriate background knowledge, they typically made distortions and elaborations in their written retellings consistent with the background knowledge that they had activated (Anderson et al., 1977; Pearson et al., 1979; Steffensen et al., 1979). Other researchers reported that when students did not know specific vocabulary items in reading passages or did not know how to read sentences with independent and dependent clauses, their oral retellings did not include the vocabulary or information from the clauses (García, 1991; García & Godina, 2017; Jiménez et al., 1996). Similarly, we can expect that students' retellings will omit other text features that they do not understand, such as text structures, auxiliary features (maps, tables, diagrams), and future and conditional verb tenses.

An advantage of the written retelling is that you can administer it to more than one student. Also, to make the analysis easier, you can have students write the retelling according to a graphic organizer. Follow-up questions can capture specific

[1] For more information on how to conduct and analyze running records, we refer you to *http://scholastic.ca/education/movingupwithliteracyplace/pdfs/grade4/runningrecords.pdf.*

information. However, a disadvantage is that students' poor writing may interfere with what they convey to you about their comprehension.

HOW TO CONDUCT A STANDARDIZED RETELLING

You should select a passage for an oral or written retelling that is at the student's approximate instructional level and that would not take more than 3–5 minutes for the student to read aloud. Before students read the passage, you should tell them that after reading it, you are going to ask them to orally retell or write everything that they read. You will get a more complete oral or written account if you ask the students to pretend that they are retelling or writing about the passage to another student or adult who has never read the passage. You also should tell the students that you want them to tell you everything that is in the passage.

When students do an oral retelling, we recommend that you let them retell as much as they can before you provide any prompts or ask any questions. Possible prompts or questions for narrative fiction include the following:

- "How did the story begin?"
- "What was the problem in the story?"
- "How did the story end?"

For informational text, the following prompts or questions are relevant:

- "What was the reading about?"
- "What were the main ideas in it?"
- "What did the author want you to know or learn?"

If students are missing key information in an oral retelling, you can ask them to tell you what else was in the story or text. You should indicate the prompting that you provided on your score sheet.

HOW TO EVALUATE AND SCORE A RETELLING

When you evaluate students' oral and written retellings for background knowledge, you will want to look for distortions and elaborations to see if students' utilized the appropriate background knowledge. In terms of vocabulary, when you preread the passage that you select for students to read, you should make a list of the key vocabulary that you expect to see in their retellings. If the words do not show up in your students' retellings, then you can ask them follow-up questions to see if they know the words. Similarly, when you preread the passage, you should identify the explicit or implied text structure applicable to the section of text that you assign students to read and the key sentence structures that should affect their retelling. Then, when you read and score their retellings, you will need to look for key elements of the applicable text structure—elements of the story grammar if they read narrative fiction and key points and clue words if they read informational text. You will also need to see if they present the correct time frame for the text and information from the dependent or independent clauses.

You can use IRIs, which provide texts and scoring rubrics for oral and written retellings, or use authentic texts and your own scoring rubric. If you develop your own scoring rubric, before the students read the passage, you should identify key elements in the passage that the students should include in their retellings. For narrative fiction, these are the genre, components of the story grammar, and theme/moral of the story. For informational text, it will be the explicit or implicit text structure, the main ideas, and the subordinate details that support the main ideas. To help you record your students' retellings, we provide forms for narrative text (Form 9.1) and informational text (Form 9.2) at the end of the chapter.

Many commercial companies include holistic rating scales. We do not recommend that you use them because they provide limited diagnostic information and teachers' rating consistency on them is low. The following rubric is an example of a holistic rating scale that is not specific enough to be useful in analyzing the reader's comprehension (Stahl & García, 2015, p. 152):

- "Excellent": The retelling is complete: It "includes all [the] important information and supporting information."
- "Satisfactory": The retelling includes all the "important information" but some details are omitted or there are a few misunderstandings that do not interfere with the overall comprehension.
- "Minimal": Some information from the passage is included, but important information is missing or misunderstood.
- "Unsatisfactory": There is inaccurate information or it lacks important text information, or there is "no response."

Comprehension Questions

Oral miscue analyses or running records and oral and written retellings typically include follow-up comprehension questions. You can specifically ask questions to target concerns about students' background knowledge, vocabulary knowledge, and knowledge of text and sentence structures or information that they did not cover in their retellings.

A useful way to know if students comprehended a story or informational text is to ask them a series of comprehension questions after they finished reading the story or informational text. The questions and students' answers can be oral or written.

Students' answers to comprehension questions indicate not only where their comprehension went awry but also where it was effective.

In developing comprehension questions, you want to ask questions that are reading or passage dependent; that is, to answer the questions correctly, students need to have read the story or the text. You do not want to ask them questions that they can answer just based on their prior knowledge.

You also want to ask questions that require students to make different types of inferences for the texts they read. Here, we rely on the types of comprehension questions included and proposed for the National Assessment of Educational Progress (NAEP) reading comprehension assessment (National Assessment Governing Board [NAGB], 2017). NAEP is the only national reading comprehension test that the U.S. government periodically administers to a sample of fourth graders, eighth graders, and twelfth graders. It is considered the gold standard for summative assessments:

- *"Locate and recall" questions.* These questions require students to locate key information in the text and recall it. The answers to the questions typically are right there in the text or in different parts of the text but adjacent to each other (NAGB, 2017, p. 37).

- *"Integrate and interpret" questions.* These questions require students to integrate and interpret key information in the text or across multiple texts. To answer them, students have to combine information in different parts of the text or across texts with what they already know about the topic or ideas in the text to make inferences for missing information in the text. The questions also ask students to utilize what they know about text structures and narrative or informational texts to interpret what the text means (NAGB, 2017, pp. 37–38).

- *"Critique and evaluate" questions.* These questions require students to critique and evaluate key information in the text. They ask students to critique the author's craft in composing the text or to determine whether the argument made was plausible. To answer these questions, students have to use what they know about "text, language, and the ways that authors manipulate language and ideas to achieve their goals" (NAGB, 2017, p. 38–39).

- *"Use and apply" questions.* These questions require students to use information from the text and apply it to something new, outside the text. They assess whether students can use information acquired in a text or a set of texts to create a product or project or to evaluate what is said in a different text. This is a proposed category for the 2026 NAEP reading comprehension test.

For more discussion about the role of questions in assessing students' comprehension, please see Chapter 7. Also, see Appendix C for generic question stems for narrative and informational texts.

Strategic Knowledge

Return to Figure 9.1, and look at Pathway 3, where there are three small boxes labeled General Purposes for Reading, Specific Purposes for Reading, and Knowledge of Strategies for Reading, and an arrow pointing to Strategic Knowledge. General purposes for reading include reading precisely and always reading for meaning, not reading as fast as possible. Readers also need to keep in mind how they will be using the text that they are reading. You read differently depending on whether you are reading *People's* magazine in the manicurist's massage chair, studying for a statistics exam, or trying to identify a bird in your field guide during a nature walk. Strategic knowledge includes how readers monitor their reading comprehension, the fix-up strategies that they use to repair any miscomprehension, and the strategies that they use to facilitate their comprehension (for more on strategies, see Chapter 6). A third question that needs to be asked is: How effectively does the student employ strategies to monitor, repair, and facilitate reading comprehension (Stahl et al., 2020)?

Strategy Checklist

You can assess students' use of strategies when they read by keeping a clipboard with a strategy checklist on it to record when you observed a student use a particular strategy. Form 9.3, at the end of the chapter, provides a strategy checklist that you may use or adapt for your class.

Periodically, you will want to meet with students in small groups or individually to evaluate how well they use strategies to comprehend the texts that they read. You particularly want to do this after you have explicitly taught a specific strategy during whole-group instruction and shared reading, as explained in Chapter 6. You also can employ think-alouds or strategy interviews to document students' use of strategies.

Think-Alouds

Think-alouds are a tool that you can use with students to help reveal how they approach and comprehend a text as they silently or orally read it. Before asking a student to participate in a think-aloud, you will need to model it, let the student practice doing it, and make sure the student understands how to participate in it. When you conduct the think-aloud, be sure to provide students with a text different from the one that they used to practice.

Although you can use unprompted and prompted think-alouds, when you want to know specific knowledge about a student's text comprehension, we recommend that you use a prompted think-aloud. In a prompted think-aloud, you preread the text and insert numbers in a copy of the text to target a student's knowledge of

Example of a Prompted Think-Aloud

THE DRIVE (1)

On Saturday, it was a beautiful day. My family decided to get ice cream and go for a drive. (2) After getting the ice cream, my dad happened (3) to turn into a dead-end street. He was behind a car that was going very slowly. There only was one drive-way where he could turn around. (4) When my mom saw that the car in front of us already had driven into the same driveway, (5) she voiced her embarrassment. (6) Then, we all gasped when the driver in front of us didn't stop to open the garage door, (7) but drove right through the garage and out the back of it! (8) My dad got out of our car to see if anyone was injured. (9) By then, the man in the other car was outside of it looking at the damage. (10) My dad said that he told the man, (11) "Don't worry, your home insurance should pay for your garage!" That's when my dad realized that a teenager, not the man, (12) was the driver. The man sadly told my dad, "It's not our house! Our son just got his driver's permit!" (13)

specific vocabulary, comprehension of information in dependent and/or independent clauses, strategy use, and comprehension of specific sections of the text. When students read the text, you ask them to stop at the number and to tell you everything that they are thinking. If students do not say anything, you may prompt them by reminding them to tell you what their minds are doing. The text box above shows what a text in a prompted think-aloud might look like.

Usually, the teacher audio-records the think-aloud and analyzes it later. To shorten the time it takes to analyze the think-aloud, you can create a checklist and use it while the student is doing the think-aloud, checking off the knowledge, skills, and strategies as the student displays them. After the think-aloud, you may want to ask your students to silently reread the text and to participate in a retelling to double-check their text comprehension. The think-aloud and follow-up activities are time-consuming but very informative when you work with students with comprehension difficulties.

Strategy Interviews

Another option is to conduct a strategy interview to find out what students know about their strategy use and metacognition. When you periodically ask students similar questions over the school year, and date their responses, you can keep track of their strategy awareness and metacognitive development. (See Stahl et al., 2020, for multiple assessment tools.) You can pose these questions to students during small-group instruction or during literacy conferences. When students have

comprehension difficulties, their answers to periodic strategy interviews are important for informing the comprehension interventions employed with them.

We suggest that you ask students some of the following questions:

- "When you don't understand everything in a story that you are reading, what do you do?"
- "When you are reading a text in science or social studies, and don't understand something, what do you do?"
- "What is easy for you to do when you read?"
- "What is difficult for you to do when you read?"
- "What do you think good readers do?"
- "Are you a good reader? If so, what makes you a good reader?"
- "How do you figure out unknown vocabulary when you read?"

The Importance of Using Multiple Comprehension Assessments

Lastly, the complex, hidden, and incremental nature of reading comprehension means that you should use multiple measures of reading comprehension across the school year. Because the mode (e.g., oral or written) that you choose for students to display their comprehension may limit what they show you, you should provide them with the opportunity to express their comprehension in varied ways: orally, through writing, by creating projects and products, and through student collaboration.

DIFFERENT TYPES OF ASSESSMENTS FOR SPECIFIC PURPOSES

At the beginning of this chapter, we introduced you to Table 9.1, which summarized the different purposes, types of information, and audiences addressed by summative assessments, interim assessments, and formative assessments. Below we discuss each type of assessment in some detail.

Summative Assessments

Summative assessments include end-of-unit basal reading tests and state-standards tests. When the test format, instructions, administration, and scoring procedures are the same, regardless of who takes the test, the tests are called standardized tests. Because student performance on state-standards tests are tied to funding decisions at the federal level, they are considered high-stakes tests. Here, we discuss large-scale summative assessments—that is, summative assessments that are piloted, field-tested, and administered to large numbers of students. Examples include NAEP, state-standards tests, and achievement tests, such as the Stanford Achievement Test 10 (Psychological Corporation, 2010).

Validity and Reliability

Validity and reliability are two types of statistical criteria that should be reported for large-scale summative assessments (Jhangiani et al., 2019). Validity refers to the extent that the test measures what it says it measures, or in our case, students' reading comprehension. A key validity question is: To what extent do the reading comprehension test scores that students obtain predict their scores on other comprehension indicators? Reliability indicates the consistency or stability of the test results. A key reliability question is: If students take the test more than once under the same testing conditions, to what extent will they get the same scores? When districts and schools choose large-scale summative assessments, they should select assessments with strong validity and reliability data.

Norm-Referenced and Standards-Based Summative Assessments

Summative assessments can be norm-referenced or standards-based. Norm-referenced assessments are designed so that students' scores fit on a bell curve, with most scores in the middle or at the mean, and smaller numbers of scores at the two ends. Students' scores are reported according to the percentile where they occur. If a student gets the score of 92nd percentile, then this means that they scored better than 92% of the other students who took the same test. Examples of norm-referenced summative assessments are the Gates–MacGinitie Reading Tests (MacGinitie et al., 2000), and the Stanford Achievement Test 10 (Psychological Corporation, 2010).

In contrast, standards-based assessments indicate what students can and cannot do according to performance criteria or standards. All students who meet the same standards get the same scores. Student scores typically are reported according to performance levels (e.g., needs improvement, basic, proficient, or advanced).

Currently, per the reauthorization of the Elementary and Secondary Education Act in 2015, or the Every Student Succeeds Act (ESSA, 2015), states that receive federal funds must assess their students' reading/ELA performance at least once each year in grades 3–8 and once in high school according to their state standards. Although states may ask for federal approval to substitute their own standards for the CCSS (NGA & CCSSO, 2010), many of them still use the CCSS for their state standards. In fact, more than half of the 50 states in the United States belong to two assessment consortia (Smarter Balanced and New Meridian), which develop tests tied to the CCSS standards for their state members to use (see *smarterbalanced.org* and *newmeridiancorp.org*).

Although the state-standards tests were supposed to inform teachers' instruction, Heritage (2007) observed that this really did not happen. State-standards tests sample students' performance on the standards, present summaries of students' performance, and rank students' performance so that state scores can be compared. They provide very little information on how teachers can improve their instruction or on how students can improve their comprehension. Also, as observed by Ms.

Winters in the opening vignette, schools usually receive the annual scores too late for teachers to use them to inform their current students' instruction.

Interim Assessments

Interim assessments measure students' reading comprehension performance at specific points in time during the school year. They need to be uniformly scored so that student performance can be tracked (Stahl et al., 2020). Examples of interim assessments include commercially produced kits such as the DRA (Beaver & Carter, 2019) and Fountas and Pinnell's Benchmark Assessment System (2010); IRIs such as the Qualitative Informal Reading Inventory (Lesley & Caldwell, 2010); and computer-adapted tests (CATs). CATs are computerized tests that employ technology to adjust the difficulty of questions and/or passages for each student based on the accuracy of the student's previous responses. Sometimes, teams of teachers create interim assessments. Some of the commercial interim assessments, such as the DRA and some of the CATs, provide validity and reliability data, while others, such as IRIs, do not.

Perie et al. (2009) explained that interim assessments serve instructional, predictive, and evaluation purposes (p. 5). For example, school personnel employ interim assessments to determine students' instructional and independent reading levels and/or to predict their performance on a summative assessment at the end of the school year. District personnel also aggregate student scores on interim assessments to evaluate the effectiveness of programs, curricula, or individual teachers.

Heritage (2007) argued that interim assessments had serious limitations. She reported that districts and schools initiated the use of interim assessments to supplement the limited information provided by summative assessments. She complained that interim assessments did not inform teachers' ongoing instruction because the amount of time between their administration was too long, and they did not provide the types of information that teachers needed. At their best, Heritage thought that interim assessments provided periodic snapshots of student performance.

Given the limitations and costs of interim assessments, we recommend that districts employ CATs to estimate third- to sixth-grade students' instructional and independent reading levels rather than other types of interim assessments. CATs take into account individual students' previous reading levels, so they may be more motivational for students who perform below grade level. A CAT will give a below-grade-level reader a much easier passage to read and questions to answer compared to the passage and questions given to a grade-level or above-grade-level reader. Also, CATs produce an instructional scoring range (e.g., Lexile between 670-820) for an individual student's reading level rather than a single score (e.g., fifth grade, Level T). Given that third- to sixth-grade students' reading comprehension performances are likely to vary according to their background knowledge, reading purposes, interest, and motivation for reading, the reading range probably is a "more accurate and instructionally useful metric" than a single score (Stahl et al., 2020, p. 208). In addition, CATs report students' reading scores in Lexiles, consistent with the CCSS (NGA & CCSSO, 2010) and reading resources such as ReadWorks, Newsela, and Lexile.com. Some of the CATs publish technical reports that provide validity and reliability information. Unlike benchmark kits, CATs do not take a lot of time to use. Kay reported that most CATs only take 30–45 minutes to estimate a student's reading level. Additionally, CATs provide much stronger psychometric data on their reliability and validity than benchmark kits do.

On the negative side, when CATs are used with students who read below third grade or far below their current grade level, it may be difficult for teachers to know what to emphasize in their instruction to help the students. In these cases, in addition to the CAT, we recommend that you administer a benchmark kit, a decoding measure, and a spelling inventory so that you obtain a more complete picture of the pressure points involved in the students' reading comprehension (Stahl et al., 2020).

Occasionally, students have scored well on the CAT, but have had poor reading comprehension performances in class. In these cases, a grade-level meeting between the student's content and reading teachers may be needed to review other data (e.g., formative assessment data).

Lastly, selecting and purchasing a CAT involves time and money. Before your district or school purchases a CAT, it should compare several of them by requesting and reviewing the technical guides and pilot-testing results. Also, we recommend that district personnel utilize Form 9.4, the CAT Shopping Guide (Stahl et al., 2020), at the end of this chapter, before deciding on which CAT to purchase.

Formative Assessments

Unlike summative and interim assessments, a major purpose of formative assessments is to inform the teacher's instruction so that the relationship between instruction and assessment is seamless (Osmundson, 2011; Shepard, 2009). When teachers design and implement formative assessment, they should monitor their students' progress in attaining specific state standards (Heritage, 2010), obtain diagnostic information for each student so that they can adjust students' instruction accordingly (Perie, et al., 2009), and provide explicit feedback to students, so that individual students become aware of their performance and improve it (Brookhart et al., 2010). Formative assessments should include student-self-evaluation, so that students set goals for their progress and self-evaluate it, and peer evaluation so that they collaborate with each other (Osmundson, 2011).

How to Initiate Formative Assessments

One way for teachers to initiate formative assessments is to review the reading comprehension assessment and instructional activities (tied to your state standards) that you already employ or plan to employ. We recommend that you consider the assessment activities described earlier in this chapter: running records/miscue analyses; oral/written retellings; oral/written comprehension questions; strategy checklists; strategy interviews; and/or think-alouds. Instructional activities that you may want to consider were presented in the preceding chapters in this book. Among others, they include written response logs; summary writing for expository texts; Discussion Webs; completion of graphic organizers; and participation in reciprocal teaching, collaborative strategic reading, or book clubs.

Next, we suggest that you identify the positive and negative factors that affect your students' comprehension (e.g., academic vocabulary, cognitive strategies, knowledge of text structures), and choose instructional activities that reveal your students' progress on these factors. Possible instructional activities from earlier chapters in this book include Word Wizard chart; Vocab-O-Gram; vocabulary note-books or student dictionaries; small-group participation in dialogic strategy instruction, student participation in integrated literacy and science/social studies instruction, and disciplinary writing.

One type of formative assessment that might be helpful with integrated disciplinary literacy instruction is the exit slip. At the end of a lesson or a unit of study, you provide each student with a quarter- to half-sheet of paper on which they write what they learned or did not learn or understand. In professional staff development work that Georgia conducted on formative assessment with bilingual elementary school teachers, the teachers liked the exit slip because it did not take very long and their students actually wrote what they understood or did not understand.

How to Operationalize Formative Assessments

To operationalize formative assessments, you should schedule a variety of daily, weekly, and monthly assessment and instructional activities. Most importantly, you will need to develop and implement a system of note-taking and record-keeping for each student so that you can keep track of your students' individual progress on the activities throughout the school year.

We also recommend that you schedule periodic literacy conferences (3–10 minutes) with each student. You should hold more conferences with poor readers and fewer conferences with strong readers. Keep in mind that individual literacy conferences should not compromise small group instructional time or in-depth assessments of high-level comprehension.

The conferences give you the time needed to do a running record/miscue analysis or for a student to do an oral retelling, answer comprehension questions, or participate in a think-aloud. Literacy conferences also provide time for you to share explicit feedback with individual students and for them to participate in self-evaluations by telling you what they do well when they read and what they need to improve. Form 9.5, at the end of the chapter, provides a sample literacy conference form that you could use. On this form, students write their own goals or next steps for improvement before you write your goals for them.

However, for self-evaluation and peer collaboration to work, you need to create a culture of respect in your classroom. Heritage (2007) recommended that you establish "classroom norms of students' listening respectfully to one another, responding positively and constructively, and of appreciating the different skill levels among peers" (p. 144).

Once you have created a safe and respectful environment, then you can ask students publicly to indicate those areas where they do well and are willing to help others, and those areas where they do not do well and could use help from others. A bilingual elementary school teacher with whom Georgia collaborated posted a magnetic poster on which she listed a topic that her class was working on and beneath the topic the following two categories (translation in brackets): ¿Puedes ayudarme? [Can you help me?] ¿Necesitas ayuda? [Do you need help?]. Students put colorful magnets with their names on them below the categories. When she held individual literacy conferences, she asked pairs of students to work together on the respective topic (García & Lang, 2018).

Common Formative Assessments

Given the amount of teacher time and effort that are involved in developing, implementing, and analyzing formative assessments, we recommend that you work with other teachers at your grade level to develop and implement common formative assessments. Many teachers in New York City take advantage of the New York State ELA Test released questions when constructing common formative assessments for instructional units (see Appendix C).

Frey and Fisher (2009) described how fifth-grade teachers in an urban school worked over 4 years to develop and implement common formative assessments that increased their students' literacy achievement. The teachers' goal was to use common assessment data to guide their standards-based instruction so that every student improved their literacy performance. The school principal supported their endeavor by organizing the school day so that 90 minutes each week were used for grade-level teacher meetings and 4 hours each month were used for professional staff development.

The school year was divided into 6-week assessment cycles, with three parts. In Part 1, the teachers agreed on their curricular foci tied to standards and how they would pace the work. They used a "backward design, in which" they planned their "curriculum and instruction based on the outcomes" they sought (Frey & Fischer, p. 675). In Part 2, they created 10–12 common assessment questions and a writing task, which every student had to answer and complete. For example, they asked students to read a paragraph entitled "Fire Fighters and Your Safety" and to choose answers to two multiple-choice questions: "What is the purpose of this paragraph?" "Which is the best topic sentence for this paragraph?" (Frey & Fischer, p. 678). During Parts 1 and 2 throughout the grade-level meetings, they reflected on what their students were doing well and on what they were not doing well and shared instructional strategies and materials. In Part 3, during the final grade-level meeting, they discussed their assessment results and explained "their hypotheses for [students'] incorrect responses and plan [for] future instruction and focused intervention plans" (Frey & Fischer, p. 675).

Stiggins and DuFour (2009) pointed out that when teachers effectively developed, implemented, and analyzed common formative assessments, the following benefits were possible:

1. Teachers identify the exact knowledge, strategies, skills, performance, and products that each student has "to master" for the current school year and what future teachers expect for the next year (p. 643).
2. Teachers work together to make instructional decisions based on their students' performance. "They decide where each student is in the learning progression . . . while the learning is happening . . . and where students are collectively across classrooms" (p. 643).
3. Teachers "identify curricular areas that need attention because many students are struggling" (p. 641).
4. Teachers "help each team member clarify strengths and weaknesses in his or her teaching and create a forum for teachers to learn from one another" (p. 641).
5. "Teachers . . . learn how to create high-quality assessments" because they "must agree on criteria for assessing student work and . . . practice applying those criteria until they can score the work consistently" (p. 644).

DEVELOPING A READING COMPREHENSION ASSESSMENT SYSTEM

Given the different purposes that summative, interim, and formative assessments serve, we recommend that schools and teachers utilize an assessment system that includes all three types of assessments. You need large-scale summative assessments to determine how well your students meet your state standards at the end of a school year and to gauge how your students' standards performance compares to those of other students in the state or assessment consortia. Interim assessments help you to establish independent and instructional reading levels and provide periodic progress indicators. Common formative assessments are the best levers for improving teachers' instruction and students' attainment of state standards. However, they take time and expertise to develop. So, until common formative assessments are developed and implemented, we recommend that individual teachers work together to develop and implement formative assessments with the students in their classes.

PLANNING COMPREHENSION INTERVENTIONS

Planning comprehension interventions for students in the intermediate grades is challenging due to the breadth of student differences and the difficulties involved in measuring growth in comprehension. When teachers plan interventions for constrained skills, the assessments clearly indicate the words and patterns that are mastered and the ones that need to be taught. However, the diagnostic and intervention relationship for reading comprehension is much more complex. Flanigan and Hayes (in press) thoroughly address the complexity of intervention in the intermediate grades.

Grouping Decisions

Although some states require that schools provide intervention for all students who score at or below a particular cut point on state tests, the cut point does not adequately indicate why the students obtained low scores. Students with the same numerical score may have very different needs. Grade-level teams should examine multiple sources of data from their school assessment system, including the data from Pathway 1 of the cognitive model (see Figure 9.1), to figure out the reading difficulties of individual students. At a minimum, student's reading fluency in context should be considered when planning how to group students for comprehension intervention.

Often students are placed in interventions not according to their specific reading needs, but according to classroom schedules, specifically when their classrooms have lunch or specials. To offset this, school personnel and grade-level teams should work together to create at least two intervention groups per intermediate grade level, so that the various needs of students are met and all students can make progress. If a student struggles with word recognition, then it is important for this need to be addressed, along with the standards for reading comprehension. In contrast, students who do not have word recognition challenges should be placed in a different group that explicitly focuses on reading comprehension and responding to texts in oral and written formats.

Comprehension Intervention Protocols

Classroom teachers and interventionists (including special educators) should view intervention as the place to develop students' reading comprehension and writing skills and strategies, not as a place for homework help. In earlier chapters, we described effective research-based instructional protocols that also demonstrated effectiveness when they were employed with students with comprehension difficulties. For instance, in Chapters 6 and 7, we described instructional protocols, such as reciprocal teaching, questioning the author, and collaborative strategic reading, that also work well in intervention settings. In addition, the Strategic Adolescent Reading Intervention (STARI) is effective for students in grades 6–9 who perform significantly below grade level (Kim et al., 2017). We refer you to Appendix B to access STARI materials. Self-regulated strategy development also has a long, robust history of effectiveness with all learners who need writing support (Graham & Harris, 1989; Harris et al., 2008; Santangelo et al., 2008).[2]

However, grade-level planning is essential so that the intervention can be aligned with the literacy instruction that occurs in the classroom. Many schools find it useful to share their grade-level curriculum calendar, which includes goals and standards, with all team members. For example, if the ELA classroom teacher instructs the students on how to structure an argument during an environmental unit, the interventionist should focus on the same standard, argument development. However, the interventionist may or may not use the same content.

ASSESSMENT CONSIDERATIONS FOR BILINGUAL STUDENTS

One of the biggest problems that affects the use of summative and interim English assessments with current and former emergent bilingual students is that it is difficult to know how much of their English reading test performance is due to their developing English proficiency or to their actual ability to comprehend English texts (García et al., 2008). Bilingual students often show increased reading comprehension of English texts when the assessment displays the questions in both languages and lets bilingual students use both languages along with translanguaging to answer the comprehension questions (García, 1991; García & Godina, 2017; Solano-Flores & Trumbull, 2003).

Even the assessment activities in interim and formative assessments, such as running records and oral miscue analyses, oral and written retellings, think-alouds, and comprehension questions, can be problematic. Teachers sometimes misinterpret bilingual students' varied pronunciation of English words in running records, miscue analyses, and decoding tests as a decoding problem rather than as an accent. During oral retellings and think-alouds, bilingual students, even those fairly proficient in English, often skip English syntactic features that do not exist in their L1, such as articles for Russian speakers and gender markers (e.g., *she* and *he*) for Chinese and Korean speakers. Successful bilingual readers utilize strategies unique to their bilingual status, which often are more predictive of their English reading comprehension than their utilization of monolingual strategies demonstrated by strong English readers (García & Godina, 2017; Jiménez et al., 1996). Cultural differences also may affect how bilingual students, compared to native English speakers, interpret and answer comprehension questions (García, 1991, 1998).

---

[2] For more information, see *https://iris.peabody.vanderbilt.edu/module/pow.*

To avoid the overclassification of bilingual students in special education, Public Law 94-12, the Education for All Handicapped Children Act, requires that bilingual students' academic performance, including their reading comprehension, be evaluated in their L1 and compared to their English performance before they can be identified as eligible for special education services. When bilingual students perform at grade level in their L1, then it is likely that their low English performance is due to their developing English proficiency and not to any cognitive or linguistic difficulties.

We agree with Hopewell and Escamilla's (2014) recommendation that school personnel employ a holistic bilingual perspective when evaluating bilingual students' reading comprehension by assessing their text comprehension in their L1 and English and comparing their reading performance to those of other bilingual students from the same language and cultural backgrounds. In a study with Latinx students who received simultaneous literacy instruction in Spanish and English, Hopewell and Escamilla (2014) found that the students performed at grade level in their L1, Spanish, but approximately one grade below grade level in their L2, English. Georgia reported similar findings in a study with Latinx fourth graders who learned to read in Spanish before English (García & Godina, 2017).

CONCLUSION

The hidden nature of reading comprehension makes it difficult to assess. To understand the reading comprehension of intermediate students, teachers need to employ a variety of classroom-based assessments and instructional activities that reveal different facets of their reading comprehension. To improve intermediate students' reading comprehension instruction and performance, we encourage schools to focus on their teachers' use of formative assessments with the ultimate goal of supporting their use of common formative assessments. Given the different features of summative, interim, and formative assessments, we also recommend that schools use them for different purposes as part of a comprehensive reading assessment system. When individual students demonstrate reading comprehension difficulties, then they should participate in interventions based on and organized according to the individual students' reading needs. Lastly, the best way to evaluate bilingual students' English reading comprehension is to let them use both their languages and translanguaging to demonstrate their comprehension of English texts.

FORM 9.1

Retelling Record (Narrative)

Oral _____ or Written _____

Date: _____ Pages: _____ Name and Author of Text: _____

Unprompted (U), Prompted (P), Response to Question (Q)	DOES THE RETELLING INCLUDE:	Yes/No and Comments
	Type of genre	
	Setting and its role	
	Main character	
	Other characters and their roles	
	A problem or goal	
	Initiating event	
	Episodes to resolve the problem or attain the goal	
	Problem resolution or goal attainment	
	Ending	
	Theme/Moral	

Note. Adapted with permission from Stahl and García (2015).

Retelling Record (Informational)

Oral _____ or Written _____

Date: _____ Pages: _____ Name and Author of Text: _____

Unprompted (U), Prompted (P), Response to Question (Q)	DOES THE RETELLING INCLUDE:	Yes/No and Comments
	Main ideas	
	Supporting details (subordinate ideas)	
	Organization according to text structure (identify)	
	Text structure clue words (list)	
	Appropriate inferences	
	Erroneous information	
	Understanding of key vocabulary (list)	

Note. Adapted with permission from Stahl and García (2015).

Strategy Checklist

Student Names	Prediction	Summarization	Questions and Answers	Clarification	Visualization	Comments

Note. Adapted with permission from Stahl and García (2015).

CAT Shopping Guide

	Test 1 (example)	Test 2
Cost	$12.00/student	
Grade levels/Subjects	ELA/Math	
Administration logistics (Time allocations, frequency, test window restraints)	45–60 minutes 3X/year 21-day window	
Test format	ELA–adaptive, multiple choice Math–multiple choice, object manipulation	
Technology information	IPad Chromebook Laptop Requires clicking, dragging and dropping	
Score reporting	Lexiles, percentiles Subgroup filters Class breakdown by goal report Excellent visuals	
Management system utility	Includes excellent school reports for this test. However, it requires manual entry of any other external data.	
Site design	Tabs provide clean design, easy access to levels of data	
Reliability and other technical information	Renormed every 3 years 10 million students in sample .70 correlation with our state ELA test .74 correlation with our state math test	

(continued)

Note. Worksheet and data adapted with permission from Queensbury Middle School, Queensbury, New York, in Stahl et al. (2020).

CAT Shopping Guide *(page 2 of 2)*

	Test 1 (example)	Test 2
Response to intervention (RTI) adaptability, cut scores	Goal-setting worksheet that includes projected growth	
Progress monitoring materials	Not available	
Accommodations for emergent bilinguals and special learners	Not available in Spanish, Text to speech available for a fee	
Professional development	Online training is included Fidelity checks available On-site training available for $3,000.00/day	
Freebies	Pilot video training accessibility	
Advantages	Data remain accessible for 3 years	
Other miscellaneous information	PPT provided at the end of each year to display trends in testing	
Next steps		

Literacy Conference Form

Name:	Date:

Points to Review:

Student Goal:

Teacher Goal:

Future Focus:

Note. Adapted with permission from García and Lang (2018).

English Language Arts College and Career Readiness Anchor Standards for Reading (NGA & CCSSO, 2010)

KEY IDEAS AND DETAILS

1. Read closely to determine what the text says explicitly and to make logical inferences from it; cite specific textual evidence when writing or speaking to support conclusions drawn from the text.

2. Determine central ideas or themes of a text and analyze their development; summarize the key supporting details and ideas.

3. Analyze how and why individuals, events, or ideas develop and interact over the course of a text.

CRAFT AND STRUCTURE

4. Interpret words and phrases as they are used in a text, including determining technical, connotative, and figurative meanings, and analyze how specific word choices shape meaning or tone.

5. Analyze the structure of texts, including how specific sentences, paragraphs, and larger portions of the text (e.g., a section, chapter, scene, or stanza) relate to each other and the whole.

6. Assess how point of view or purpose shapes the content and style of a text.

INTEGRATION OF KNOWLEDGE AND IDEAS

7. Integrate and evaluate content presented in diverse media and formats, including visually and quantitatively as well as in words.

8. Delineate and evaluate the argument and specific claims in a text, including the validity of the reasoning as well as the relevance and sufficiency of the evidence.

9. Analyze how two or more texts address similar themes or topics in order to build knowledge or to compare the approaches the authors take.

RANGE OF READING AND LEVEL OF COMPLEXITY

10. Read and comprehend complex literary and informational texts independently and proficiently.

Curriculum Resource Materials

ENGLISH LANGUAGE ARTS CURRICULUM MATERIALS

Bookworms Tier 1 curriculum materials: *https://openupresources.org/ela-curriculum/bookworms-k-5-reading-writing-curriculum*

Concept-oriented reading instruction (CORI) (integrated curriculum): *www.cori.umd.edu/research-projects/reading-engagement-project/materials*

Inclusion in Texas Network: *www.inclusionintexas.org*

New York State curriculum and assessment materials: *www.engageny.org*

Strategic Adolescent Reading Intervention (STARI): *www.serpinstitute.org/stari*

TextProject (a variety of resources for teachers and families): *http://textproject.org*

ELA Reading Material

Books from Epic!: *www.getepic.com/app/edu-dashboard*

Narrative and informational texts from Reading A–Z (paid subscription): *www.readinga-z.com*

Narrative and informational texts from ReadWorks: *www.readworks.org*

News articles from Newsela (five levels/text): *https://newsela.com*

News articles from Time for Kids (paid subscription): *www.timeforkids.com*

News and informational texts from Smithsonian Tween Tribune (four levels/text): *www.tweentribune.com*

Videos in every subject area from BrainPOP: *www.brainpop.com*

All are free unless indicated.

SCIENCE

Middle school science units from SERP: *www.serpinstitute.org/scigen*
Foss: The full option science program: *www.deltaeducation.com/foss/next-generation*
Science Unit from Islandwood: *https://communitywaters.org*
Smithsonian Science Education Center resources: *https://ssec.si.edu*

SOCIAL STUDIES

Social studies units from SERP: *www.serpinstitute.org/sogen*
Social studies units from Nell K. Duke: *www.nellkduke.org/project-place-units*

ALL CONTENT AREAS

Diagnostic materials for supporting core curriculum from IXL (paid subscription): *www.ixl.com*

NYS ELA Test Released Questions
Generic Questions for Discussions or Writing Prompts

LITERARY TEXTS

- What is the theme of the story? What lesson did the characters learn? Use two details from the story to support your answer.
- What key events develop the theme of the story? How?
- Why is the setting important to the story?
- How are the characters related?
- Write a summary of the story.
- What does (*action, quote*) tell you about the character?
- How does (*event, episode*) contribute to the development of the plot?
- Why is (*event, episode*) important to the story?
- How does (*character*) change throughout the story?
- How do paragraphs X to Y show a change in the story/character?
- How does (*character*) feel? Use two details from the passage to explain your response.
- How does paragraph X relate to paragraph Y?
- How did XXXX affect YYYY? Use two details from the story/text to support your answer.
- What does the writer mean by (*word or phrase*)?
- Define the meaning of (*word*) as it was used in sentence/story.
- Why does the author use the word (*word or phrase*) to describe XXXX? Use two details from the passage to explain your response.
- What other stories or movies teach this lesson? How does this lesson apply in your own life?

Adapted from New York State Education Department (2017).

INFORMATIONAL TEXTS

- Why did the author write this passage?
- What is this passage mostly about? What is the author teaching us about on this page?
- What is the main idea of this passage? Use two details from the article to support your response.
- Provide a main idea of the passage or a section of the passage. Ask students to provide the supporting details for that particular main idea.
- Write a summary.
- Create a sentence (or title) to summarize the main idea of the article.
- What information contributes to the organization of the passage?
- What text structure did the author use to explain XXXX? Why does the author use this text structure to explain this information? Use two details from the article to explain your response.
- Describe the structure of the passage and why it is important.
- Describe what (*word or phrase*) means in the passage.
- Why was (*specific event in passage*) an important event? Use two details from the article to support your answer.
- According to the texts/experiment, why did (*event/scientific outcome*) happen? Use evidence to support your answer.
- Based on the text/activity, what do *X* and *Y* have in common? What is the same or different about *X* and *Y*?
- How does paragraph *X* relate to paragraph *Y*?
- How did *XXXX* affect *YYYY*? Use two details from the article to support your answer.
- What is the author's position on (*issue*)? Identify the author's most valid claims for that argument OR create a passage with an alternative position and two claims to support your position.

References

Adger, C. T., Wolfram, W., & Christian, D. (2007). *Dialects in schools and communities* (2nd ed.). Routledge.

Alexander, P. A. (2018). Information management versus knowledge building: Implications for learning and assessment in higher education. In O. Zlatkin-Troitschanskaia, M. Toepper, H. A. Pant, C. Lautenbach, & C. Kuhn (Eds.), *Assessment of learning outcomes in higher education: Cross-national comparisons and perspectives* (pp. 43–56). Springer.

Almasi, J. F. (2003). *Teaching strategic processes in reading.* Guilford Press.

Alvermann, D. (1991). The Discussion Web: A graphic aid for learning across the curriculum. *The Reading Teacher, 45*(2), 92–99.

American Educational Research Association, American Psychological Association, & National Council on Measurement in Education. (1999). *Standards for educational and psychological testing 1999.* American Educational Research Association.

American Educational Research Association, American Psychological Association, & National Council on Measurement in Education. (2014). *Standards for educational and psychological testing 2014.* American Educational Research Association.

Anderson, R. C., & Freebody, P. (1983). Reading comprehension and the assessment and acquisition of word knowledge. *Advances in Reading/Language Research, 2,* 231–256.

Anderson, R. C., Reynolds, R, E., Schallert, D. L., & Goetz, E. T. (1977). Frameworks for comprehending discourse. *American Educational Research Journal, 14*(4), 367–381.

Annenberg Learner. (2021). *Writing: Big ideas.* Retrieved May 10, 2021, from *https://Learner. org/series/reading-writing-in-the-disciplines/writing-big-ideas.*

Arizona Department of Education. (2016). *Disciplinary literacy in grades 3–5 science.*

Armbruster, B. (1984). The problem of "inconsiderate text." In G. G. Duffy, L. R. Roehler, & J. Mason (Eds.), *Comprehension instruction* (pp. 202–217). Longman.

Armbruster, B. B., Anderson, T. H., & Ostertag, J. (1987). Does text structure/summarization instruction facilitate learning from expository text? *Reading Research Quarterly, 22*(3), 331–346.

Au, K. H. (1980). Participation structures in a reading lesson with Hawaiian children: Analysis of a culturally appropriate instructional event. *Anthropology & Education Quarterly, 11*(2), 91–115.

Au, K. H., & Jordan, C. (1981). Teaching reading to Hawaiian children: Finding a culturally appropriate solution. In H. Trueba, C. P. Guthrie, & K. H. Au (Eds.), *Culture and the bilingual classroom: Studies in classroom ethnography* (pp. 139–152). Newbury House.

Avi. (2012). *Sophia's war: A tale of the revolution.* Beach Lane Books.

Backer, D. (2018). The distortion of discussion. *Issues in Teacher Education, 25*(1), 3–16.

Baker, L., & Brown, A. L. (1984). Metacognitive skills and reading. In P. D Pearson, R. Barr, M. L. Kamil, & P. B. Mosenthal (Eds.), *Handbook of reading research* (Vol. I, pp. 353–394). Longman.

Banham, M. (1998). *The Cambridge guide to theater.* Cambridge University Press.

Baumann, J. F., & Bergeron, B. S. (1993). Story map instruction using children's literature: Effects on first graders' comprehension of central narrative elements. *Journal of Reading Behavior, 25*(4), 407–437.

Baumann, J. F., Seifert-Kessell, N., & Jones, L. A. (1992). Effect of think-aloud instruction on elementary students' comprehension monitoring abilities. *Journal of Reading Behavior, 24,* 143–172.

Bear, D. R., Invernizzi, M., Templeton, S., & Johnston, F. (2020). *Words their way: Word study for phonics, vocabulary, and spelling instruction* (7th ed.). Pearson.

Beaver, J. M., & Carter, M. (2019). *Developmental Reading Assessment,* (DRA, 3rd ed). Pearson Education.

Beck, I. L., & McKeown, M. G. (2001). Text talk: Capturing the benefits of read aloud experiences for young children. *The Reading Teacher, 55,* 10–35.

Beck, I. L., McKeown, M. G., & Blake, R. G. K. (2009). Rethinking reading comprehension instruction: A comparison of instructional strategies and content approaches. *Reading Research Quarterly, 44*(3), 218–253.

Beck, I. L., McKeown, M. G., Hamilton, R. L., & Kucan, L. (1997). *Questioning the Author: An approach for enhancing student engagement with text.* International Reading Association.

Beck, I. L., McKeown, M. G., & Kucan, L. (2002). *Bringing words to life.* Guilford Press.

Beck, I. L., McKeown, M. G., & McCaslin, E. S. (1983). Vocabulary development: All contexts are not created equal. *The Elementary School Journal, 83*(3), 177–181.

Beck, I. L., McKeown, M. G., Worthy, J., & Sandora, C. A. (1996). Questioning the Author: A year-long classroom implementation to engage students with text. *The Elementary School Journal, 96*(4), 385–414.

Beck, I. L., Perfetti, C., & McKeown, M. G. (1982). Effects of long-term vocabulary instruction on lexical access and reading comprehension. *Journal of Educational Psychology, 74*(4), 506–521.

Beck, S. (1997). The good, the bad & the ugly: Or, why it's a good idea to evaluate Web sources. Retrieved from *http://lib.nmsu.edu/instruction/eval.html.*

Beerer, K. (n.d.). Disciplinary literacy: Helping students develop insider knowledge. Retrieved from *www.discoveryeducation.com/details/disciplinary-literacy-helping-students-develop-insider-knowledge.*

Betts, E. A. (1946). *Foundations of reading instruction.* American Books.

Bezdicek, J., & García, G. E. (2012). Working with preschool English language learners: A sociocultural approach. In B. Yoon & H.-K. Kim (Eds.), *Teachers' roles in second language learning: Classroom applications of sociocultural theory* (pp. 171–188). Information Age.

Biancarosa, G., Afflerbach, P., & Pearson, P. D. (2020). Teaching reading for understanding: Summarizing the curriculum and instruction work of the five core Reading for Understanding. In P. D. Pearson, A. S. Palinscar, G. Biancarosa, & A. Berman (Eds.), *Reaping the rewards of the Reading for Understanding Initiative* (pp. 143–213). National Academy of Education.

Biskin, D. S., Hoskisson, K., & Modlin, M. (1976). Prediction, reflection, and comprehension. *Elementary School Journal, 77,* 131–139.

Blachowicz, C. L. Z. (1986). Making connections: Alternatives to the vocabulary notebook. *Journal of Reading, 29,* 643–649.

Blachowicz, C., & Fisher, P. J. (2014). *Teaching vocabulary in all classrooms* (5th ed.). Pearson.

Bloom, S. B., Engelhart, M. D., Furst, E. J., & Hill, W. H. (1956). *Taxonomy of educational objectives: The classification of educational goals. Handbook I: Cognitive domain.* David McKay.

Blything, L. P., Hardie, A., & Cain, K. (2019). Question asking during reading comprehension instruction: A corpus of how question type influences the linguistic complexity of primary school responses. *Reading Research Quarterly, 55*(3), 443–472.

Braillie, J. M. (2002). *Who was Albert Einstein?* Grosset & Dunlap.

Bravo, M., Hiebert, E. H., & Pearson, P. D. (2007). Tapping the linguistic resources of Spanish-English bilinguals: The role of cognates in science. In R. K. Wagner, A. Muse, & K. Tannenbaum (Eds.), *Vocabulary development and its implications for reading comprehension* (pp. 140–156). Guilford Press.

Bremer, C. D., Vaughn, S., Clapper, A. T., & Kim, A.-H. (2002). Collaborative strategic reading (CSR): Improving secondary students' reading comprehension skills. *Research to Practice Brief: Improving Secondary Education and Transition Services through Research, 1*(2), 1–8.

Brookhart, S. M., Moss, C. M., & Long, B. A. (2010). Teacher inquiry into formative assessment practices in remedial reading classrooms. *Assessment in Education: Principles, Policy, and Practice, 17*(1), 41–58.

Brown, L. T., Mohr, K. A. J., Wilcox, B. R., & Barrett, T. S. (2018). The effect of dyad reading and text difficulty on third graders' reading achievement. *Journal of Educational Research, 111*(5) 541–553.

Brown, R., & Coy-Ogan, L. (1993). The evolution of transactional strategies in one teacher's classroom. *Elementary School Journal, 94*(2), 221–233.

Brown, S., & Kappes, L. (2012). *Implementing the Common Core State Standards: A primer on "close reading of text."* Aspen Institute Education and Society Program.

Bryk, A. S., Gomez, L. M., Grunow, A., & LeMahieu, P. G. (2015). *Learning to improve: How America's schools can get better at getting better.* Harvard Education Press.

Bunch, M. B. (2012). *Aligning curriculum, instruction, and assessment.* Measurement Inc. Retrieved from *www.measurementinc.com.*

Buss, K. (2002). *Reading and writing nonfiction genres.* International Reading Association.

Buss, K., & Karnowski, L. (2000). *Reading and writing literary genres* (2nd ed.). International Reading Association.

California Department of Education. (2017). *History–social science framework for California public schools: K through grade 12.*

Calkins, L. (2015). *Units of study for teaching reading.* Heinemann.

Calkins, L. (2017). *A guide to reading workshop.* Heinemann.

Catalyzing Comprehension through Discussion and Debate. (CCDD). (2021a). What was learned . . . Retrieved May 10, 2021, from *https://ccdd.serpmedia.org/what-was-learned. html.*

Catalyzing Comprehension through Discussion and Debate (CCDD). (2021b). Educator resources. Retrieved May 10, 2021, from *https://ccdd.serpmedia.org/what-was-learned. html.*

Catalyzing Comprehension through Discussion and Debate (CCDD). (2021c). Elementary content-area literacy development. Retrieved May 10, 2021, from *www.serpinstitute.org/ educator-resources#Literacy.*

Cazden, C. (1988). *Classroom discourse: The language of teaching and learning.* Heinemann.

Center for Applied Linguistics. (2021). Sheltered Instructional Observation Protocol (SIOP). Retrieved from *https://cal.org/siop/about.*

Cervetti, G. N., Barber, J., Dorph, R., Pearson, P. D., & Goldschmidt, P. G. (2012). The impact of an integrated approach to science and literacy in elementary school classrooms. *Journal of Research in Science Teaching, 49,* 631–658.

Cervetti, G. N., Pearson, P. D., Barber, J., Hiebert, E. H., & Bravo, M. (2007). Integrating literacy and science. In M. Pressley, A. K. Billman, K. Perry, K. Refitt, & J. Reynolds (Eds.) *Shaping literacy achievement: The research we have, the research we need* (pp.157–174). Guilford Press.

Cervetti, G. N., Pearson, P. D., Bravo, M. A., & Barber, J. (2006). Reading and writing in the service of inquiry-based science. In R. Douglas, M. Klentschy, & K. Worth (Eds.), *Linking science and literacy in the K–8 classroom* (pp. 221–244). NSTA Press.

Cervetti, G. N., Wright, T. S., & Hwang, H. (2016). Conceptual coherence, comprehension, and vocabulary acquisition: A knowledge effect? *Reading and Writing, 29,* 761–779.

Chall, J. S. (1996). *Stages of reading development* (2nd ed.). Harcourt Brace.

Chen, Y.-C., Hand, B., & Park, S. (2016). Examining elementary students' oral and written argumentation practices through argument-based inquiry. *Science & Education, 25,* 277–320.

Chinn, C. A., Anderson, R. C., & Waggoner, M. A. (2001). Patterns of discourse in two kinds of literature discussion. *Reading Research Quarterly, 34*(4), 378–411.

Clay, M. M. (2013). *An observation survey of early literacy achievement* (3rd ed.). Heinemann.

Coiro, J. L. (2003). Rethinking comprehension strategies to better prepare students for critically evaluating content on the Internet. *NERA Journal, 39*(2), 29–34.

Coles, R. (2010). *The story of Ruby Bridges.* Scholastic.

Collier, V. P., & Thomas, W. P. (2017). Validating the power of bilingual schooling: Thirty-two years of large-scale, longitudinal research. *Annual Review of Applied Linguistics, 37,* 1–15.

Connor, C. M., Dombek, J., Crowe, E. C., Spencer, M., Tighe, E. L., Coffinger, S., et al. (2017). Acquiring science and social studies knowledge in kindergarten through fourth grade: Conceptualization, design, implementation, and efficacy testing of content-area literacy instruction (CALI). *Journal of Educational Psychology, 109*(3), 301–320.

Coxhead, A. (2000). A new academic word list. *TESOL Quarterly, 34*(2), 213–238.

Cummins, J. (1981). The role of primary language development in promoting educational success for language minority students. In California State Department of Education (Ed.), *Schooling and language minority students: A theoretical framework* (pp. 3–49). Evaluation, Dissemination and Assessment Center, California State University.

Cummins, J. (2000). *Language, power, and pedagogy.* Multilingual Matters.

Cummins, J. (2007). Pedagogies for the poor? Realigning reading instruction for low-income students with scientifically based research. *Educational Researcher, 36*(9), 564–572.

Cunningham, P. M., Hall, D. P., & Cunningham, J. W. (2000). *Guided reading the Four-Blocks™ way.* Carson-Dellosa.

Daniels, H. (2002). *Literature Circles: Voice and choice in book clubs and reading groups* (2nd ed.). Stenhouse.

De La Paz, S., Monte-Sano, C., Felton, M., Croninger, R., Jackson, C., & Piantedosi, K. W. (2016). A historical writing apprenticeship for adolescents: integrating disciplinary literacy with cognitive strategies. *Reading Research Quarterly, 52*(1), 31–52.

DeNicolo, C. P., Yu, M., Crowley, C. B., & Gable, S. L. (2017). Reimagining critical care and problematizing sense of school belonging as a response to inequality for immigrants and children of immigrants. *Review of Research in Education, 41,* 500–530.

Denner, P. R., & McGinley, W. J. (1992). Effects of prereading activities on junior high students' recall. *Journal of Educational Research, 86*(1), 11–19.

Denner, P. R., McGinley, W. J., & Brown, E. (1989). Effects of story impressions as a prereading/writing activity on story comprehension. *Journal of Educational Research, 82*(6), 320–326.

Dewitz, P., Jones, J., & Leahy, S. (2009). Comprehension strategy instruction in core reading programs. *Reading Research Quarterly, 44*(2), 102–126.

Donhan, J. (2013). Text sets, deep learning, and the Common Core. *School Library Monthly, 29*(6), 5–7.

Duhaylongsod, L., Snow, C. E., Selman, R., & Donovan, S. (2015). Toward disciplinary literacy: Design principles for curriculum to support both teachers and students in urban middle schools. *Harvard Educational Review, 85*(4), 587–608.

Durkin, D. (1978). What classroom observations reveal about reading comprehension instruction. *Reading Research Quarterly, 14,* 481–533.

Duschl, R. A., & Osborne, J. (2002). Supporting and promoting argumentation: Discourse in science education, *Studies in Science Education, 38*(1), 39–72.

Echevarría, J., & McDonough, R. (1993). *Instructional conversations in special education settings: Issues and accommodations* (Educational Practice Report No. 7). National Center for Research on Cultural Diversity and Second Language Learning,

Echevarría, J., Vogt, M. E., & Short, D. E. (2012). *Making content comprehensible for English learners: The SIOP model (SIOP series)* (4th ed.). Pearson.

Echevarría, J., Vogt, M. E., & Short, D. E. (2016). *Making content comprehensible for English learners: The SIOP model (SIOP series)* (5th ed.). Pearson.

Education for All Handicapped Children Act of 1975, Public Law No. 94–142.

Elleman, A. M., Lindo, E. J., Morphy, P., & Compton, D. L. (2009). The impact of vocabulary instruction on passage level comprehension of school-age children: A meta-analysis. *Journal of Research on Educational Effectiveness, 2*(1), 1–44.

Every Student Succeeds Act, 20 U.S.C. 6301. (2015). Retrieved from *www.congress. gov/114/plaws/publ95/PLAW-114pub95.pdf.*

Ferretti, R. P., MacArthur, C. D., & Okolo, C. M. (2001). Series of questions to examine historical evidence and writing strategies (compare-contrast). *Learning Disability Quarterly, 24*(1), 59–71.

Fisher, D., & Frey, N. (2014). Student and teacher perspectives on a close reading protocol. *Literacy Research and Instruction, 53*(1), 25–49.

Fisher, D., Frey, N., & Lapp, D. (2008). Shared readings: Modeling comprehension, vocabulary, text structures, and text features for older readers. *The Reading Teacher, 61,* 548–556.

Flanigan, K., & Hayes, L. (in press). *Literacy intervention in the middle grades 4–8.* Guilford Press.

Fordham, N. W., Wellman, D., & Sandmann, A. (2002) Taming the text: Engaging and supporting students in social studies readings. *The Social Studies, 93*(4), 149–158,

Fountas, I. C., & Pinnell, G. S. (2010). *Benchmark Assessment System* (2nd ed.). Heinemann.

Fountas, I., & Pinnell, G. S. (2016). *Guided reading: Responsive teaching across the grades* (2nd ed.). Heinemann.

Fox, T. (2004). Linking genre to standards and equity. *The Quarterly, 26*(4). Retrieved from *https://archive.nwp.org/cs/public/print/resource/2140.*

Francis, D. J., Lesaux, N. K., & August, D. (2006). Language of instruction. In D. August & T. Shanahan (Eds.), *Developing literacy in second-language learners: Report of the National Literacy Panel on Language Minority Children and Youth* (pp. 365–414). Erlbaum.

Frey, N., & Fischer, D. (2009). Using common formative assessments as a source of professional development in an urban American elementary school. *Teaching and Teacher Education, 25,* 674–680.

Gamse, B. C., Jacob, R. T., Horst, M., Boulay, B., & Unlu, F. (2008). *Reading First impact study: Final report* (NCEE 2009–4038). National Center for Education Evaluation and Regional Assistance, Institute of Education Sciences, U.S. Department of Education. Retrieved from *https://ies.ed.gov/ncee/pdf/20094038.pdf.*

Garas-York, K., Shanahan, L., & Almasi, J. F. (2013). Comprehension: High-level talk and writing about texts. In B. Taylor, & N. K Duke (Eds.), *Handbook of effective literacy instruction* (pp. 246–278). Guilford Press.

García, G. E. (1991). Factors influencing the English reading test performance of Spanish-speaking Hispanic children. *Reading Research Quarterly, 26*(4), 371–392.

García, G. E. (1998). Mexican-American bilingual students' metacognitive reading strategies: What's transferred, unique, problematic? *National Reading Conference Yearbook, 47,* 253–263.

García, G. E. (2003). The reading comprehension development and instruction of English Language Learners. In A. P. Sweet & C. E. Snow (Eds.), *Rethinking reading comprehension* (pp. 31–50). Guilford Press.

García, G. E., Bray, T. M., Mora, R. A., Primeaux, J., Ricklefs, M. A., Engel., L. C., et al. (2006). Working with teachers to change the literacy instruction of Latino students in urban schools. *National Reading Conference Yearbook, 55,* 155–170.

García, G. E., & DeNicolo, C. P. (2016). Improving the language and literacy assessment of emergent bilinguals. In L. Helman (Ed.), *Literacy development with English learners: Research based instruction in grades K–6* (2nd ed., pp. 78–108). Guilford Press.

García, G. E, & Godina, H. (2017). A window into bilingual reading: The bilingual reading practices of fourth-grade, Mexican-American children who are emergent bilinguals. *Journal of Literacy Research, 49*(2), 273–301.

García, G. E., & Lang, M. G. (2018). The link between standards and dual language teachers' Spanish literacy instruction and use of formative assessments. *Bilingual Research Journal, 41*(2), 167–186.

García, G. E., McKoon, G., & August, D. (2008). Language and literacy assessment. In D. August & T. Shanahan (Eds.), *Developing reading and writing in second-language learners: Lessons from the report of the National Literacy Panel on Language Minority Children and Youth* (pp. 251–274). Routledge, Center for Applied Linguistics, and the International Reading Association.

García, G. E., Sacco, L. J., & Guerrero-Aria, B. E. (2020). Cognate instruction and bilingual students' improved literacy performance. *The Reading Teacher, 73*(5), 617–625.

García, G. E., Taylor, B. M., Pearson, P. D., Bray, T. M., Primeaux, J., & Mora, R. (2021). Improvements in teachers' reading comprehension instruction and bilingual students' reading test performance in high-poverty schools. *Elementary School Journal, 121*(3), 357–384.

García, O. (2009). *Bilingual education in the 21st century: A global perspective.* Wiley-Blackwell.

García, O., & Wei, L. (2014). *Translanguaging: Language, bilingualism, and education.* Macmillan.

Gardner, D., & Davies, M. (2013). A new academic vocabulary list. *Applied Linguistics, 35*(3), 305–327.

Gaultney, J. F. (1995). The effect of prior knowledge and metacognition on the acquisition of a reading comprehension strategy. *Journal of Experimental Child Psychology, 59*(1), 142–153.

Gee, J. P. (1990). *Social linguistics and literacies: Ideology in discourses.* Falmer Press.

Genesee, F., Geva, E., Dressler, C., & Kamil, M. L. (2006). Synthesis: Cross-linguistic relationships. In D. August & T. Shanahan (Eds.), *Developing literacy in second-language learning: Report of the National Literacy Panel on Language Minority Children and Youth* (pp. 153–174). Erlbaum.

Godley, A. J., Sweetland, J., Wheeler, R. S., Minnici, A., & Carpenter, B. D. (2006). Preparing teachers for dialectally diverse classrooms. *Educational Researcher, 35*(8), 30–37.

Goldenberg, C. (1992/1993). Instructional conversations: Promoting comprehension through discussion. *The Reading Teacher, 46*(4), 316–326.

Goldman, S. R., Britt, M. A., Brown, W., Cribb, G., George, M., Greenleaf, C., et al. (2016). Disciplinary literacies and learning to read for understanding: A conceptual framework for disciplinary literacy. *Educational Psychologist, 51*(2), 219–246.

Goldman, S., R., Reyes, M., & Varnhagen, C. K. (1984). Understanding fables in first and second languages. *NABE Journal, 8*, 835–866.

Goldman, S. R., Snow, C., & Vaughn, S. (2016). Common themes in teaching reading for understanding: Lessons from three projects. *Journal of Adolescent & Adult Literacy, 60*(3), 255–264.

González, N., Moll, L. C., & Amanti, C. (Eds.). (2005). *Funds of knowledge: Theorizing practices in households, communities, and classrooms.* Erlbaum.

Goodman, Y. M., Watson, D. J., & Burke, C. L. (1987). *Reading miscue inventory: Alternative procedures.* Richard C. Owen.

Gough, P., & Tunmer, W. (1986). Decoding, reading, and reading disability. *Remedial and Special Education, 7*(1), 6–10.

Graesser, A. C., McNamara, D. S., & Kulikowich, J. M. (2011). Coh-metrix: Providing multilevel analyses of text characteristics. *Educational Researcher, 40*(5), 223–234.

Graham, S., & Harris, K. R. (1989). Improving learning disabled students' skills at composing essays: Self-instructional strategy training. *Exceptional Children, 56*(3), 201–214.

Guthrie, J. T., & Humenick, N. M. (2004). Motivating students to read: Evidence for classroom practices that increase motivation and achievement. In P. McCardle & V. Chabra (Eds.), *The voice of evidence in reading research (pp. 329–354).* Brookes.

Guthrie, J. T., Wigfield, A., Barbosa, P., Perencevich, K. C., Taboada, A., Davis, M. H., et al. (2004). Increasing reading comprehension and engagement through concept-oriented reading instruction. *Journal of Educational Psychology, 96,* 403–423.

Hacker, D., & Tenant, A. (2002). Implementing reciprocal teaching in the classroom: Overcoming obstacles and making modifications. *Journal of Educational Psychology, 94*(4), 699–718.

Hand, B., Norton-Meier, L., Gunel, M., & Akkus, R. (2016). Aligning teaching to learning: A 3-year study examining the embedding of language and argumentation into elementary science classrooms. *International Journal of Science and Math Education, 14,* 847–863.

Harcourt Brace. (2000). *Support for English language learners SDAIE: California edition* (Harcourt Science, Grade 3).

Harris, K. R., Graham, S., Mason, L., & Friedlander, B. (2008). *Powerful writing strategies for all students.* Brookes.

Hasbrouck, J., & Tindal, G. (2017). *An update to compiled ORF norms* (Technical Report No. 1702). Behavioral Research and Teaching, University of Oregon. *https://files.eric.ed.gov/fulltext/ED594994.pdf.*

Heath, S. B. (1982). Questioning at home and at school: A comparative study. In G. Spindler (Ed.), *Doing the ethnography of schooling: Educational anthropology in action* (pp. 102–131). Holt, Rinehart & Winston.

Heller, M. (1999). *Linguistic minorities and modernity: A sociolinguistic ethnography.* Longman.

Heritage, M. (2007). Formative assessment: What do teachers need to know and do? *Phi Delta Kappan, 89*(2), 140–145.

Heritage, M. (2010). *Formative assessment and next-generation assessment systems: Are we losing an opportunity?* Council of Chief State School Officers.

Hernández, H. (2000). *Multicultural education: A teacher's guide to linking context, process, and content* (2nd ed.). Pearson.

Herrenkohl, L. R., & Cornelius, L. (2013). Investigating students' scientific and historical argumentation. *Journal of the Learning Sciences, 22*(3), 413–461.

Hess, K. (2008). *Hess-TextStructures.KH08.pdf.* National Center for the Improvement of Educational Assessment.

Hill, D., & Fink, L. (2013). Three mentor texts that support code-switching pedagogies. *Voices from the Middle, 20*(4), 10–15.

Hinchman, K. A. & Moore, D. W. (2013). Close reading: A cautionary interpretation. *Journal of Adolescent and Adult Literacy, 56*(6) 441–450.

Hirsch, E. D., Jr. (2003). Reading comprehension requires knowledge—of words and the world. *American Educator, 27*(1), 10–29, 44–45.

Holdaway, D. (1982). Shared book experience: Teaching reading using favorite books. *Theory into Practice, 21,* 293–300.

Hoover, W. A., & Gough, P. B. (1990). The simple view of reading. *Reading and Writing: An Interdisciplinary Journal, 2*(2), 127–160.

Hoover, W. A., & Tunmer, W. E. (2018). The simple view of reading: Three assessments of its adequacy. *Remedial and Special Education, 39*(5), 304–312.

Hopewell, S., & Escamilla, K. (2014). Struggling reader or emerging biliterate student? Reevaluating the criteria for labeling emerging bilingual students as low achieving. *Journal of Literacy Research, 46*(1), 68–89.

Hussar, B., Zhang, J., Hein, S., Wang, K., Roberts, A., Cui, J., et al. (2020). *The condition of education (2020)*. National Center for Education Statistics.

Jadallah, M., Miller, B. W., Anderson, R. C., Nguyen-Jahiel, K., Zhang, J., Archodidou, A., et al. (2009). Collaborative reasoning about a science and public policy issue. In M. McKeown & L. Kucan (Eds.), *Bringing reading research to life* (pp. 170–193). Guilford Press.

Jhangiani, R. S., Chiang, I-C. A., Cuttler, C., & Leighton, D. C. (2019). *Research methods in psychology* (4th ed.). Retrieved June 6, 2001, from *https://www.kpu.pressbooks.pub/psychmethods4e/buy/*.

Jiménez, R. T., David, S., Pacheco, M., Risko, V. J., Pray, L., Fagan, K., et al. (2015). Supporting teachers of English learners by leveraging students' linguistic strengths. *The Reading Teacher, 68*(6), 406–412.

Jiménez, R. T., García, G. E., & Pearson, P. D. (1995). Three children, two languages, and strategic reading: Case studies in bilingual/monolingual reading. *American Educational Research Journal, 32*, 31–61.

Jiménez, R. T., García, G. E., & Pearson, P. D. (1996). The reading strategies of bilingual Latina/o students who are successful English readers: Opportunities and obstacles. *Reading Research Quarterly, 31*(1), 90–112.

Jones, S. M., LaRusso, M., Kim, J., Kim, H. Y., Selman, R., Uccelli, P., et al. (2019). Experimental effects of word generation on vocabulary, academic language, perspective taking, and reading comprehension in high-poverty schools. *Journal of Research on Educational Effectiveness, 12*(3), 448–483.

Kamil, M. L., Borman, G. D., Dole, J., Kral, C. C., Salinger, T., & Torgesen, J. (2008). *Improving adolescent literacy: Effective classroom and intervention practices: A Practice Guide* (NCEE No. 2008–4027). National Center for Education Evaluation and Regional Assistance, Institute of Education Sciences, U.S. Department of Education. *https://ies.ed.gov/ncee/wwc/docs/practiceguide/adlit_pg_082608.pdf*.

Keehne, C. N. K., Wai'ale'ale Sarsona, M. W., Kawakami, A. J., & Au, K. H. (2018). Culturally responsive literacy instruction and learning. *Journal of Literacy Research, 50*(2), 141–166.

Kieffer, M. J., & Box, C. D. (2013). Derivational morphological awareness, academic vocabulary, and reading comprehension in linguistically diverse sixth graders. *Learning and Individual Differences, 24*, 168–175.

Kim, J. S., Hemphill, L., Troyer, M. T., Thomson, J. M., Jones, S. J., LaRusso, M., et al. (2017). Engaging struggling adolescent readers to improve reading skills. *Reading Research Quarterly, 52*(3), 357–382.

Kim, S., & Hand, B. (2015). An analysis of argumentation discourse patterns in elementary teachers' science classroom discussions. *Journal of Science Teacher Education, 26*, 221–236.

Kintsch, W. (1988). The role of knowledge in discourse comprehension: A construction–integration model. *Psychological Review, 95,* 163–182.

Kintsch, W. (1998). *Comprehension: A paradigm for cognition.* Cambridge University Press.

Klingner, J. K., & Vaughn, S. (1996). Reciprocal teaching of reading comprehension strategies for students with learning disabilities who use English as a second language. *The Elementary School Journal, 96*(3), 275–293.

Klingner, J. K., & Vaughn, S. (1999). Promoting reading comprehension, content learning and English acquisition through collaborative strategic reading. *The Reading Teacher, 52,* 738–747.

Klingner, J., Vaughn, S., Boardman, A., & Swanson, E. (2012). *Now we get it: Boosting comprehension with collaborative strategic reading.* Wiley.

Klingner, J. K., Vaughn, S., & Schumm, J. S. (1998). Collaborative strategic reading during social studies in heterogeneous fourth-grade classrooms. *The Elementary School Journal, 99*(1), 3–22.

LaBerge, D., & Samuels, S. J. (1974). Toward a theory of automatic information processing in reading. *Cognitive Psychology, 6,* 293–323.

Ladson-Billings, G. (1995). Toward a theory of culturally relevant pedagogy. *American Educational Research Journal, 32*(3), 465–491.

Lee, C., & García, G. E. (2021). Understanding Korean-American first-graders' written translanguaging practices. *Linguistics and Education, 66,* 100998.

LeMahieu, P. G., Grunow, A., Baker, L., Nordstrom, L. E., & Gomex, L. M. (2017). Networked improvement communities: The discipline of improvement science meets the power of networks. *Quality Assurance in Education, 25*(1), 5–25.

Lesaux, N., & Geva, E. (2006). Synthesis: Development of literacy in language minority students. In D. August & T. Shanahan (Eds.), *Developing literacy in second-language learners: Report of the National Literacy Panel on Language Minority Children and Youth* (pp. 53–74). Erlbaum.

Leslie, L., & Caldwell, J. S. (2016). *Qualitative Reading Inventory–6.* Pearson.

Levesque, K. C., Kieffer, M. J., & Deacon, S. H. (2018). Inferring meaning from meaningful parts: The contributions of morphological skills to the development of children's reading comprehension. *Reading Research Quarterly, 54*(1), 63–80.

Lindfors, J. W. (1987). *Children's language and learning* (2nd ed.). Prentice-Hall.

Lonigan, C., J., & Burgess, S. R. (2017). Dimensionality of reading skills with elementary-school-age children, *Scientific Studies of Reading, 21*(3), 239–253.

Lowry, L. (1989) *Number the stars.* Houghton Mifflin Harcourt.

Lubliner, S. (2001). *A practical guide to reciprocal teaching.* Wright Group/Mc-Graw Hill.

Lubliner, S., & Hiebert, E. H. (2011). An analysis of English-Spanish cognates as a source of general academic language. *Bilingual Research Journal, 34*(1), 76–93.

Lupo, S. M., Berry, A., Thacker, E., Sawyer, A., & Merritt, J. (2019). Rethinking text sets to support knowledge building and interdisciplinary learning. *The Reading Teacher, 73*(4), 513–524.

Lupo, S. M., Strong, J. Z., Lewis, W., Walpole, S., & McKenna, M. C. (2018). Building background knowledge through reading: Rethinking text sets. *Journal of Adult Literacy 61*(4), 433–444.

MacGinitie, W. H., MacGinitie, R. K., Maria, K., Dreyer, L. G. (2000). *Gates MacGinitie Reading Tests*. Riverside Publishing.

Malloy, J. A., Tracy, K. N., Scales, R. Q., Menickelli, K., & Scales, W. D. (2020). It's not about being right: Developing argument through debate. *Journal of Literacy Research, 52*(1), 79–100.

Maloch, B. (2004). One teacher's journey: Transitioning into literature discussion groups. *Language Arts, 81*(4), 312–322.

Maloch, B. (2005) Moments by which change is made: A cross-case exploration of teacher mediation and student participation in literacy events. *Journal of Literacy Research, 37* (1), 95–142.

Marzano, R. J. (2009, September 1). Six steps to better vocabulary instruction. *Educational Leadership*, pp. 83–84.

McGinley, W. J., & Denner, P. R. (1987). Story impressions: A pre-reading/writing activity. *Journal of Reading, 31*(3), 248–253.

McTigue, J., & Lyman, F. T. (1988). Cueing thinking in the classroom: The promise of theory-embedded tools. *Educational Leadership, 45*, 18–24.

Meyer, B., Wijekumar, K., & Lei, P. (2018). Comparative signaling generated for expository texts by 4th–8th graders: variations by text structure, strategy instruction, comprehension skill, and signal word. *Reading and Writing, 31*, 1937–1968.

Miller, A. C., & Keenan, J. M. (2009). How word reading skill impacts text memory: The centrality deficit and how domain knowledge can compensate. *Annuals of Dyslexia, 59*(2), 99–113.

Morpurgo, M. (2010). *An elephant in the garden*. Fiewel and Friends.

Murphy, P. K., Wilkinson, I. A. G., Soter, A. O., Hennessy, M. N., & Alexander, J. F. (2009). Examining the effects of classroom discussion on students' comprehension of text: A meta-analysis. *Journal of Educational Psychology, 101*(9), 740–764.

Nagy, W. E., & Anderson, R. C. (1984). How many words are there in printed school English? *Reading Research Quarterly, 19*, 304–330.

Nagy, W. E., García, G. E., Durgunoğlu, A. Y., & Hancin-Bhatt, B. (1993). Spanish–English bilingual students' use of cognates in English reading. *Journal of Reading Behavior, 25*(3), 241–259.

Nagy, W. E., & Townsend, D. (2012). Words as tools: Learning academic vocabulary as language acquisition. *Reading Research Quarterly, 47*(1), 91–108.

National Academies of Sciences, Engineering, and Medicine (2018). *How people learn II: Learners, contexts, and cultures*. National Academies Press.

National Assessment Governing Board (NAGB, 2017). *Reading framework for the 2017 National Assessment of Educational Progress*. U.S. Department of Education.

National Council for the Social Studies. (2013). *College, career, and civic life: framework for social studies state standards: Guidance for enhancing the rigor of K–12 civics, economics, geography, and history (C3SSSS)*.

National Governors Association Center for Best Practices & Council of Chief State School Officers. (2010). *Common core state standards for English language arts & literacy in history/ social studies, science, and technical subjects*.

National Institute of Child Health and Human Development. (2000). *Teaching children to read:*

An evidence-based assessment of the scientific research literature on reading and its implications for reading instruction.

National Reading Panel. (2000). *Report of the subgroups: National Reading Panel.* National Institute of Child Health and Human Development.

National Research Council. (2012). *Education for life and work: Developing transferable knowledge and skills in the 21st century.* National Academies Press.

Next Generation Science Standards Lead States. (2013). *Next generation science standards for states, by states.* National Academies Press.

New York State Education Department. (2017). 2017 Grades 3–6 English Language Arts Test Released Questions. Retrieved from *www.engageny.org/resource/released-2017-3-8-ela-and-mathematics-state-test-questions.*

Nystrand, M., Gamoran, A., Kachur, R., & Prendergrast, C. (1997). *Opening dialogue: Understanding the dynamics of language learning in the English classroom.* Teachers College Press.

O'Brien, D., Stewart, R., & Moje, E. (1995). Why content literacy is difficult to infuse into the secondary school: Complexities of curriculum, pedagogy, and school culture. *Reading Research Quarterly, 30*(3), 442–463.

O'Connor, R. E., Bell, K. M., Harty, K. R., & Larkin, L. R. (2002). Teaching reading to poor readers in the intermediate grades: A comparison of text difficulty. *Journal of Educational Psychology, 94*(3), 474–485.

Osmundson, E. (2011, February). *Effective use of classroom formative assessments for the CCSS.* Paper presented at CCSS: Planning for Effective Implementation—Symposium, Portland, OR. Retrieved from *http://ode.state.or.us.*

Padrón, Y. N. (1992). The effect of strategy instruction on bilingual students' cognitive strategy use in reading. *Bilingual Research Journal, 16*(3–4), 35–51.

Palincsar, A. S., & Brown, A. L. (1984). Reciprocal teaching of comprehension-fostering and comprehension-monitoring activities. *Cognition and Instruction, 2,* 117–175.

Palincsar, A. S., David, Y., & Brown, A. L. (1989). *Using reciprocal teaching in the classroom: A guide for teachers.* Unpublished manual, University of Michigan, Ann Arbor.

Paris, S. G. (2005). Reinterpreting the development of reading skills. *Reading Research Quarterly, 40*(2), 184–202.

Paris, S. G., & Hamilton, E. E. (2009). The development of children's reading comprehension. In S. E. Israel & G. G. Duffy (Eds.), *Handbook of research on reading comprehension* (pp. 32–53). Routledge.

Paris, S. G., Lipson, M. Y., & Wixson, K. K. (1983). Becoming a strategic reader. *Contemporary Educational Psychology, 8,* 293–316.

Pearson, P. D., & Gallagher, M. C. (1983). The instruction of reading comprehension. *Contemporary Educational Psychology, 8*(3), 317–344.

Pearson P. D., Hansen, J., & Gordon, C. (1979). The effect of background knowledge on young children's comprehension of explicit and implicit information. *Journal of Reading Behavior, 11*(3), 201–209.

Pearson, P. D., McVee, M. B., & Shanahan, L. E. (2019). In the beginning: The historical and conceptual genesis of the gradual release of responsibility. In M. B. McVee, E. Ortlieb, J. S. Reichenberg, & P. D. Pearson (Eds.), *The gradual release of responsibility in literacy research and practice* (pp. 1–22). Emerald Publishing.

Pearson, P. D., Palincsar, A. S., Biancarosa, G., & Berman, A. I. (Eds). (2020). *Reaping the rewards of the Reading for Understanding Initiative.* National Academy of Education.

Perfetti, C., & Adlof, S. (2012). Reading comprehension: A conceptual framework from word meaning to text meaning. In J. P. Sabatini, E. R. Albro, & T. Reilly (Eds.), *Measuring up: Advances in how to assess reading ability* (pp. 3–20). Rowman & Littlefield Education.

Perie, M., Marion, S., & Gong, B. (2009). Moving toward a comprehensive assessment system: A framework for considering interim assessments. *Educational Measurement: Issues and Practice, 28*(3), 5–13.

Perry, D., & Delpit, L. (Eds.). (1998). *The real Ebonics debate: Power, language, and the education of African-American children.* Beacon Press.

Piloneata, P. (2010). Instruction of research-based comprehension strategies in basal reading programs. *Reading Psychology, 31*(2), 150–175.

Pressley, M., Almasi, J., Schuder, T., Bergman, J., Hite, S., El-Dinary, P. B., et al. (1994). Transactional instruction of comprehension strategies: The Montgomery County, Maryland, SAIL program. *Reading & Writing Quarterly, 10*(1), 5–19.

Pressley, M., El-Dinary, P. B., Gaskins, I., Schuder, T., Bergman, J. L., Almasi, J., et al. (1992). Beyond direct explanation: Transactional instruction of reading comprehension strategies. *Elementary School Journal, 92,* 513–555.

Psychological Corporation. (2010). *Stanford Achievement Test 10.* Harcourt Brace.

Public Broadcasting Service. (2005). *Do you speak American?* [TV program]. Specifically, "DYSA African American English (or Ebonics) in the classroom" [YouTube video excerpt]. *www.youtube.com/watch?v=xX1-FgkfWo8.*

RAND Reading Study Group. (2002). *Reading for understanding: Toward an R&D program in reading comprehension.* RAND Corporation.

Raum, E. (2020). *The scoop on clothes, homes, and daily life in Colonial America.* Capstone Press.

Reading Rockets. (2021). The DR-TA. Retrieved April 16, 2021, from *www.readingrockets.org/strategies/drta.*

Recht, D. R., & Leslie, L. (1988). Effects of prior knowledge on good and poor readers' memory of text. *Journal of Educational Psychology, 80,* 16–20.

Reznitskaya, A., Kuo, L. J., Clark, A. M., Miller, B., Jadallah, M., Anderson, R. C., et al. (2009). Collaborative reasoning: A dialogic approach to group discussions. *Cambridge Journal of Education, 39*(1), 29–48.

Rickford, J. R. (1999). *African American vernacular English: Features, evolution, educational implications.* Wiley-Blackwell.

Robinson, A. (2019). SAT/ACT prep online guides & tips: The 9 literary elements you'll find in every story. *https://blog.prepscholar.com/literary-elements-list-examples.*

Rolstad, K., Mahoney, K., & Glass, G. V. (2005). The big picture: A meta-analysis of program effectiveness research on English language learners. *Educational Policy, 19*(4), 572–594.

Romance, N. R., & Vitale, M. (1992). A curriculum strategy that expands time for in-depth elementary science instruction by using science-based reading strategies: Effects of a year-long study in grade four. *Journal of Research in Science Teaching, 29*(6), 545–554.

Romance, N. R., & Vitale, M. (2017). Implications of a cognitive science model integrating literacy in science on achievement in science and reading: Direct effects in grades 3–5 with transfer to grades 6–7. *International Journal of Science and Math Education, 15,* 979–995.

Rosenblatt, L. M. (1978). *The reader, the text, the poem. The transactional theory of the literary work.* Southern Illinois University Press.

Rosenshine, B., & Meister, C. (1994). Reciprocal teaching: A review of the research. *Review of Educational Research, 64,* 479–530.

Ryan, P. M. (2012) *Esperanza rising.* Scholastic.

Santangelo, T., Harris, K. R., & Graham, S. (2008). Using self-regulated strategy development to support students who have "trubol giting thangs into werds." *Remedial and Special Education, 29*(2), 78–89.

Saunders, W. M., & Goldenberg, C. (1999). Effects of instructional conversations and literature logs on limited and fluent-English proficient students' story comprehension and thematic understanding. *The Elementary School Journal, 99*(4), 277–301.

Schwanenflugel, P. J., Kuhn, M. R., Morris, R. D., Morrow, L. M., Meisinger, E. B., Woo, D. G., et al. (2009). Insights into fluency instruction: Short- and long-term effects of two reading programs. *Literacy Research and Instruction, 48*(4), 318–336.

Scieszka, J. (1989). *The true story of the 3 little pigs/by A. Wolf.* Viking Kestrel.

Seibert, P. (2001). *The three little pigs.* School Specialty Publishing.

Shanahan, C., & Shanahan, T. (2014). Does disciplinary literacy have a place in elementary school? *The Reading Teacher, 67*(8), 636–639.

Shanahan, T. (2014). This is not close reading (but we'll tell you what is). *Instructor, 123*(4), 28–30.

Shanahan, T., & Beck, I. L. (2006). Effective literacy teaching for English-language learners. In D. August & T. Shanahan (Eds.), *Developing literacy in second-language learners: Report of the National Literacy Panel on Language-Minority Children and Youth* (pp. 415–488). Erlbaum.

Shanahan, T., Callison, K., Carriere, C., Duke, N. K., Pearson, P. D., Schatschneider, C., et al. (2010). *Improving reading comprehension in kindergarten through 3rd grade: A practice guide* (NCEE 2010–4038). National Center for Education Evaluation and Regional Assistance, Institute of Education Sciences, U.S. Department of Education.

Shanahan, T., Fisher, D., & Frey, N. (2012). The challenge of challenging text. *Reading: The Core Skill, 69*(6), 58–62.

Shanahan, T., & Shanahan, C. (2008). Teaching disciplinary literacy to adolescents: Rethinking content area literacy. *Harvard Educational Review, 78*(1), 40–59.

Shepard, L. (2009). Commentary: Evaluating the validity of formative and interim assessment. *Educational Measurement: Issues and Practice, 28*(3), 32–37.

Sidek, C. S. (n.d.). SDAIE teaching strategies. *www.csus.edu/indiv/l/limb/314/pdf/sdaie.pdf.*

Siegelson, K. L., & Pinkney, B. (1999). *In the time of the drums.* Lee & Low Books.

Slavin, R. E., & Cheung, A. (2005). A synthesis of research on language of reading instruction for English language learners. *Review of Educational Research, 75*(2), 247–284.

Smith, P. (2016). A distinctly American opportunity: Exploring non-standardized English(es) in literacy practice and policy. *Policy Insights from the Behavioral and Brain Sciences, 3*(2), 194–202.

Smitherman, G. (1999). *Talkin that talk: African American language and culture.* Routledge.

Snow, C. (2006). Cross-cutting themes and future research directions. In D. August & T. Shanahan (Eds.), *Developing literacy in second-language learners: Report of the National Literacy Panel on Language Minority Children and Youth* (pp. 631–651). Erlbaum.

Snow, C. E. (2018). Simple and not-so-simple views of reading. *Remedial and Special Education, 39*(5), 313–316.

Solano-Flores, G., & Trumbull, E. (2003). Examining language in context: The need for new research and practice paradigms in the testing of English-language-learners. *Educational Researcher, 32*(2), 3–13.

Soter, A. O., Wilkinson, I. A., Murphy, P. K., Rudge, L., Reninger, K., & Edwards, M. (2008). What the discourse tells us: Talk and indicators of high-level comprehension. *International Journal of Educational Research, 47*(6), 372–391.

Stahl, K. A. D. (2008). The effects of three instructional methods on the reading comprehension and content acquisition of novice readers. *Journal of Literacy Research, 40*, 359–393.

Stahl, K. A. D. (2009). Comprehensive synthesized comprehension instruction in primary classrooms: A story of successes and challenges. *Reading and Writing Quarterly, 25*(4), 334–355.

Stahl, K. A. D. (2012). Complex text or frustration level text: Using shared reading to bridge the difference. *The Reading Teacher, 66*, 47–51.

Stahl, K. A. D. (2014). What counts as evidence? *The Reading Teacher, 68*(2), 103–106.

Stahl, K. A. D., & Bravo, M. (2010). Contemporary classroom vocabulary assessment for content areas. *The Reading Teacher, 63*, 566–578.

Stahl, K. A. D., Flanigan, K., & McKenna, M. C. (2020). *Assessment for reading instruction* (4th ed.). Guilford Press.

Stahl, K. A. D., & García, G. E. (2015). *Developing reading comprehension: Effective instruction for all students in PreK–2.* Guilford Press.

Stahl, S. A., & Fairbanks, M. M. (1986). The effects of vocabulary instruction: A model-based meta-analysis. *Review of Educational Research, 56*, 72–110.

Stahl, S. A., & Heubach, K. M. (2005). Fluency-oriented reading instruction. *Journal of Literacy Research, 37*, 25–60.

Stahl, S. A., & Jacobson, M. G. (1986). Vocabulary difficulty, prior knowledge, and text comprehension. *Journal of Reading Behavior, 18*, 309–324,

Stahl S. A., Jacobson, M. G., Davis, C. E., & Davis, R. L. (1989). Prior knowledge and difficult vocabulary in the comprehension of unfamiliar text. *Reading Research Quarterly, 24*, 27–43.

Stahl, S. A., & Kapinus, B. A. (1991). Possible sentences: Predicting word meanings to teach content area vocabulary. *The Reading Teacher, 45*, 36–43.

Stahl, S. A., & Nagy, W. E. (2006). *Teaching word meanings.* Erlbaum.

Stanovich, K. E. (1986). Matthew effects in reading: Some consequences of individual differences in the acquisition of literacy. *Reading Research Quarterly, 21*, 360–407.

Stauffer, R. G. (1969). *Directing reading maturity as a cognitive process.* Harper & Row.

Steffensen, M. S., Joag-Dev, C., & Anderson, R. C. (1979). A cross-cultural perspective on reading comprehension. *Reading Research Quarterly, 15*(1), 10–29.

Stiggins R., & DuFour, R. (2009, May). Maximizing the power of formative assessments. *Phi Delta Kappan*, pp. 640–644.

Swanborn, M. S. L., & de Glopper, K. (1999). Incidental word learning while reading: A meta-analysis. *Review of Educational Research, 69*(3), 261–285.

Tamki, J. (2019, July 11). What does the author of *Where the Crawdads Sing* think you should read? *The New York Times.*

Taylor, B. M., Pearson, P. D., Clark, K., & Walpole, S. (2000). Effective schools and accomplished teachers: Lessons about primary grade reading instruction in low-income schools. *Elementary School Journal, 101,* 121–166.

Taylor, B. M., Pearson, P. D., Peterson, D. S., & Rodriguez, M. C. (2002). Looking inside classrooms: Reflecting on the "how" as well as the "what" in effective reading instruction. *The Reading Teacher, 56,* 70–79.

Taylor, B. M., Pearson, P. D., García, G. E., Stahl, K. A. D., & Bauer, E. B. (2006). Improving students' reading comprehension. In K. A. D. Stahl & M. C. McKenna (Eds.), *Reading research at work: Foundations of effective practice* (pp. 303–315). Guilford Press.

Teale, W. H., Paciga, K. A., & Hoffman, J. L. (2007). Beginning reading instruction in urban schools: The curriculum gap ensures a continuing achievement gap. *The Reading Teacher, 61*(4), 344–348.

Templeton, S., Bear, D. B., Invernizzi, M., Johnston, F., Flanigan, K., Townsend, D., et al. (2015). *Vocabulary their way: Word study with middle and secondary students* (2nd ed.). Pearson.

TESOL Trainers. (2016). SIOP component: Lesson preparation. Retrieved from *www.tesoltrainers.com/siop-lesson-preparation.html.*

Tolkien, J. R. R. (2013). *The Hobbit.* Houghton Mifflin Harcourt.

Trosclair. (2000). *Cajun night before Christmas.* Pelican.

Turner, J. D., & Mitchell, C. D. (2019). Sustaining culture, expanding literacies: Culturally relevant literacy pedagogy and gradual release of responsibility. In M. B. McVee, E. Ortlieb, J. Reichenberg, & P. D. Pearson (Eds.), *The gradual release of responsibility in literacy research and practice* (pp. 229–244). Emerald Publishing.

Twenge, J. M., Martin, G. N., & Spitzburg, B. H. (2019). Trends in U.S. adolescents' media use, 1976–2016: The rise of digital media, the decline of TV, and the (near) demise of print. *Psychology of Popular Media Culture, 8*(4), 329–345.

U.S. Department of Education, Office of Elementary and Secondary Education. (2002). *Guidance for the Reading First program.*

University of Oregon. (2020). *Dynamic Indicators of Basic Literacy Skills* (8th ed.). University of Oregon Center on Teaching and Learning.

Vacca, J. C., & Vacca, R. T. (2004). *Content area reading: Literacy and learning across the curriculum* (8th ed.). Allyn & Bacon.

Van Allsburg, C. (1979). *The garden of Abdul Gasazi.* HMH Books for Young Readers.

VanSledright, B., & Kelly, C. (1998). Reading American history: The influence of multiple sources on six fifth graders. *Elementary School Journal, 98,* 239–265.

Velasco, P., & García, O. (2014). Translanguaging and the writing of bilingual learners. *Bilingual Research Journal, 37*(1), 6–23.

Vygotsky, L. (1978). *Mind in society.* Harvard University Press.

Wade, S., Thompson, A., & Watkins, W. (1994). The role of belief systems in authors' and readers' construction of texts. In R. Garner & P. A. Alexander (Eds.), *Beliefs about text and instruction with text* (pp. 265–293). Erlbaum.

Wang, J., & Herman, J. (2006). Evaluation of Seeds of Science/Roots of Reading Project: Shoreline Science and Terrarium Investigations. CSE Technical Report 676. CRESST/University of California, Los Angeles. *https://cresst.org/wp-content/uploads/R676.pdf.*

Wang, Z., Sabatini, J., O'Reilly, T., & Weeks, J. (2019). Decoding and reading comprehension:

A test of the decoding threshold hypothesis. *Journal of Educational Psychology, 11*(3), 387–401.

Wei, L. (2018). Translanguaging as a practical theory of language. *Applied Linguistics, 39*(1), 9–30.

Wheeler, R., Cartwright, K. B., & Swords, R. (2012). Factoring AAVE into reading assessment and instruction. *The Reading Teacher, 65*(5), 616–425.

Wheeler, R., & Swords, R. (2006). *Codeswitching: Teaching Standard English in urban class-rooms.* National Council of Teachers of English.

Wheeler, R., & Swords, R. (2010). *Codeswitching lessons: Grammar strategies for linguistically diverse writers.* Heinemann.

WiDA. (2020). *Can do descriptors. Key uses edition. Grades 4 & 5. https://wida.wisc.edu/sites/ default/files/resource/CanDo-KeyUses-Gr-4-5.pdf.*

Wilkinson, I. A. G., & Son, E. H. (2011). A dialogic turn in research on learning and teaching to comprehend. In M. Kamil, P. D. Pearson, E. B. Moje, & P. Afflerbach (Eds.), *The handbook of reading research* (Vol. IV, pp. 359–387). Routledge.

Williams, J. P. (2005). Instruction in reading comprehension for primary grade students: A focus on text structure. *The Journal of Special Education, 39*(1), 6–18.

Williams, J. P., Stafford, K. B., Lauer, K. D., Hall, K. M., & Pollini, S. (2009). Embedding reading comprehension training in content-area instruction. *Journal of Educational Psychology, 101*(1), 1–20.

Wineburg, S. (1991). On the reading of historical texts: Notes on the breach between school and academy. *American Education Research Journal, 28*(3), 495–519.

Wolsey, T. D., & Lapp, D. (2017). *Literacy in the disciplines: A teachers' guide for grades 5–12.* Guilford Press.

Woodson, J. (2013). *This is the rope: A story from the Great Migration.* Penguin Group.

WordGen Elementary. (2021). WordGen Elementary and English learners. Retrieved May 13, 2021, from *www.serpinstitute.org/wordgen-weekly/wge-with-english-learners.*

Wright, T. S., & Cervetti, G. N. (2016). A systematic review of the research on vocabulary instruction that impacts comprehension. *Reading Research Quarterly, 52*(2), 203–226.

Zhang, J., Anderson, R. C., & Nguyen-Jahiel, K. (2013). Language rich discussions for English learners. *International Journal of Educational Research, 58*, 44–60.

Zhang, J., & Stahl, K. A. D. (2011/2012). Collaborative Reasoning: Language-rich discussions for English language learners. *The Reading Teacher, 65*, 257–260.

Index

Note. *f* or *t* following a page number indicates a figure or a table.